# CRE▲TIVE
## HOMEOWNER®

# HER Plans
## HOME®

### HOUSE PLANS SELECTED BY
### WOMEN FOR WOMEN

CREATIVE HOMEOWNER®, Upper Saddle River, New Jersey

Vice President and Publisher: Timothy O. Bakke
Production Director: Kimberly H. Vivas

Home Plans Editor: Kenneth D. Stuts
Home Plans Consultant: James McNair
Home Plans Designer Liaison: Sara Markowitz

Design and Layout: Arrowhead Direct (David Kroha, Cindy DiPierdomenico, Judith Kroha); Maureen Mulligan

Cover Design: Kathy Wityk, David Geer

Current Printing (last digit)
10 9 8 7 6 5 4 3 2 1

Her Home Plans
Library of Congress Control Number: 2007932959
ISBN-10: 1-58011-386-9
ISBN-13: 978-1-58011-386-1

CREATIVE HOMEOWNER®
A Division of Federal Marketing Corp.
24 Park Way
Upper Saddle River, NJ 07458
**www.creativehomeowner.com**

*Note: The homes as shown in the photographs and renderings in this book may differ from the actual blueprints. When studying the house of your choice, please check the floor plans carefully.*

# Contents

# WELCOME TO *HER HOME PLANS*

*A totally new "woman-centric" approach to selecting and buying home plans*

C hoosing a dream home plan is one of the most intimidating parts of building a new home because it's often difficult for prospective homeowners to visualize their finished house and how it will "live." Add this to the fact that, according to the National Association of Home Builders, women are the sole or primary decision makers in 91 percent of all home purchases, and you have the reasons why we present the *Her Home Plans* collection the way we do.

*Her Home Plans* has created a unique new way to help you narrow the search for a design that fits your personal style and needs. The home plans were designed around the four key areas that research shows most women look for in a home design:

- Entertaining
- De-stressing
- Flexible Living
- Storing

How did this new approach come about? In January 2003, Linda Reimer recognized a need to reach out to women in the dreaming or planning stage of building or remodeling a home. It didn't take long for Reimer's vision to become reality. She founded *Her Home* magazine and began offering home plans with her "woman-centric" approach. From the start, the goal was to provide practical information to help women make the major decisions they would have to make in the process.

"Building a home is a major investment. Today, women are much more involved in the entire home construction process," says Reimer. "In fact, research shows that women make 91 percent of the home building and buying decisions."

*Her Home Plans* takes the process of selecting a new home and easily translates the information into a color-coded floor plan system. This revolutionary concept allows

**91% of all new home purchases** are either made by women or primarily influenced by women (Smith-Dahmer, 2006)

**Women make 83%** of all consumer purchases. (*Business Week*)

the prospective home buyer to look at the plans in a completely new way.

According to Reimer: "Women want knowledge in advance of construction and all throughout the building process. They need this information in order to make intelligent decisions."

Taking a woman-centric approach means designing everything from "her" perspective. Women intuitively look at home design through the filter of "how the home lives." She imagines how she would entertain in the home. She looks for ways the home will be a refuge from her busy

lifestyle and help her de-stress. She picks up on the home's storage—or lack of it. Her natural, nurturing instinct and tendency to anticipate future events also means her home must be flexible enough to accommodate today's needs as well as tomorrow's.

Reimer explains, "In our research, we discovered there are four primary aspects that are important to women when selecting a

# Her Plans
## at a Glance™

Storing
Entertaining
Flexible Living
De-Stressing

The homes in *Her Home Plans* were designed around the four key areas that research shows most women look for in a home design. A unique "Her Plans at a Glance" color-coding system highlights **Entertaining** (yellow), **De-Stressing** (blue), **Flexible Living** (green), and **Storing** Areas (orange).

## entertaining

**Yellow:** Yellow areas encompass formal rooms for entertaining as well as informal, open living spaces, outdoor rooms, kitchens that encourage quests to gather around a snack bar, rooms for media related get-togethers (watching movies or sports events), and areas ideal for groups playing cards or board games.

For more on entertaining areas, see pages 192–195.

## de-stressing

**Blue:** Buyers looking for ways to de-stress their lives will appreciate homes with lots of blue spaces. Some blue areas offer relaxation, such as personal get-aways, a privately located master suite, a walk-in shower or whirlpool, a porch, or a craft area. Others provide unusual organizational features such as split vanities, mud rooms, and drop zones that keep keys, briefcases, and other items where they're easy to locate.

For more on de-stressing areas, see pages 140–141.

## flexible living

**Green:** Green areas designate rooms that offer flexible living space that can adapt to unique situations. Rooms that can be combined to create in-law suites, home offices (occasionally even his and her offices), bedroom/bath arrangements that work well for the blended families, music rooms, homeschool rooms, offices that can become dining rooms, or dens that become guest rooms.

For more on flexible living areas, see pages 134–137.

## storing

**Orange:** Those who never have enough storage will be drawn to homes with more orange areas, which highlight extra storage capacity in the garage or laundry room, rear foyer storage, generous kitchen pantries, and linen closets and additional unfinished areas in the basement or on the upper level.

For more on storing areas, see pages 188–191.

home plan: flexible living spaces and entertaining, storage, and de-stressing areas. From a design perspective you have to look at a floor plan through the lens of 'how does the home live?' because that's the way women view a home."

## How the Home Lives

### Entertaining
Whether formal or casual, entertaining often involves food, so the kitchen oftentimes becomes the hub of activity with many guests and visitors gathering there. Women feel that a kitchen entertains well if it is open to other entertaining areas, including dining spaces, the great room, and outdoor living spaces. An open floor plan also eases the stresses of transporting food around the house while entertaining guests. It

should also eliminate clutter by providing plenty of organized storage where it is needed.

With a growing emphasis on casual entertaining, outside entertaining should be a natural extension of your home's flow. Covered porches are especially appreciated if inclement weather threatens your outdoor plans. For some, adding screens around the porch to control bugs means being able to truly enjoy being outside. Still others will opt for windows all around, turning their outdoor living space into a true four-season room. These porches not only provide a wonderful place for entertaining guests but will possibly become your favorite area in the house to relax and enjoy a sunrise or watch the children catch fireflies in the backyard.

When it comes to media-related entertaining, the first issue to settle is where the big-screen TV goes. Wall-mounted plasma and LCD monitors are eliminating the need for deep built-in entertainment centers, while surround-sound systems are being discreetly installed within walls and ceilings. This approach ensures that one no longer has to decorate their home around the entertainment electronics or have their decorations and furniture covered with wires.

### De-Stressing
Research suggests that stress is the most compelling theme for women. They want their home to be their sanctuary, their personal haven. When women were asked to identify how they like to relax at home, the most frequent response was soaking in a tub. Yet women were fairly evenly split over where they wanted the tub (not nec-

essarily in the master bath) because many acknowledged that they rarely had time to actually enjoy a bath. But when asked to choose between a master bath offering a standard (4-foot) shower plus a tub or a bathroom with an oversized shower and no tub, most women admitted they would get more use out of the shower, especially one with a spa showering system or at least two showerheads.

An outdoor living space was the second most common response to the question of where women de-stress, which includes porches, decks, and other areas that one can unwind and enjoy a breath of fresh air after a stressful day.

Research also revealed nothing is more stressful for moms than getting the entire family out the door on time in the morning with everything they need. This discovery led to designing rear foyers offering solutions such as drop zones, a bench for removing shoes, and even lockers for the children. Kids know how to use lockers to quickly grab their lunch money, backpacks, gym clothes, and jackets as they dash out the door. Lockers also add the benefit of minimizing the potential of people's things getting mixed together, which creates more unnecessary stress and confusion.

As we've become increasingly comfortable with family and friends coming into our homes through the garage, women are becoming adamant that the rear foyer entrance not double as the laundry room. Having people traipse past dirty laundry increases stress levels!

When it came to de-stressing activities, other frequently mentioned responses included reading or privately watching a little TV (accompanied by requests for a sitting area in the master bedroom or a cozy hearth room), working out

**92% of women** use the Internet to shop for homes, making them the most powerful online audience of home buyers (*"Multitasking Women,"* Building Women, *Summer 2005*)

(answered by an exercise room), or pursuing hobbies (ideally an "out of public view" spot, not the dining room table).

## Flexible Living

Women are more likely than men to consider how a home will meet their family's needs in the future. This is especially true for Baby Boomers, the so-called "sandwich generation," who often find themselves caring for aging parents or welcoming adult children back home for a time. Home plans with a pair of adjacent secondary bedrooms shown as an optional guest suite are very appealing to Baby Boomers because they provide both private sleeping and living spaces.

A significant number of today's buyers are blended families. These buyers are especially interested in home plans that provide suitable bathroom arrangements for boys and girls coming from different families. When it comes to sharing a bathroom, at a minimum, women in these families are looking for a bath with the toilet/shower area separate from the main area. Private vanities are even better. An emerging trend may well be private half baths with only the tub/shower space shared.

With more and more couples working from home, women are trying to share an office with their husbands. Whether adapting a spare bedroom, converting the dining room, or carving out enough space for a pocket office, his and her offices are in demand. These offices require the design elements that provide a balance of privacy and professionalism with the ability to enjoy each other's company.

Women worry about their family literally outgrowing their home. The solution is to offer unfinished areas, especially on a second level or over a garage or in a basement. Families can configure these spaces as the need arises, turning them into whatever type of room the growing family desires,

such as an additional bedroom or home office, without adding the cost of finishing them into the mortgage up front.

## Storing

As a nation, we're cooking less but not eating less. That means an increasing need for storage of prepared foods and take-out containers. When we do cook, we have many more small appliances to make it easier—which, in turn, requires extra space for the bread maker, indoor grill, food processor, and crock pot. No wonder women are asking for larger, better organized pantries.

Eliminate unsightly clutter from keys, newspapers, mail, change, and cell phones dropped on the kitchen table or island by including a drop zone near the entry from the garage. Drop zones can also incorpo-

rate a recharging center for cell phones and the video camera, a tall space for hanging umbrellas, and a cork board for write-on board for messages.

Efficient use of all the available space means allowing for storage in the garage too. Thinking in terms of zones—gardening zone, tool zone, holiday-storage zone, camping equipment zone, etc.—keeps clutter from entering the house and ensures that everything will stay organized.

"It really boils down to two basic points," says Reimer, "Women want their needs met, and they want thoughtful options—now and as their lifestyles change." *Her Home Plans* is the result of thoughtful, careful design with her perspective in mind. It's all about giving her the home she wants—her home, her way.

# Ten Steps You Should Do Before Submitting Your Plans For a Permit

### 1. Check Your Plans To Make Sure That You Received What You Ordered

You should immediately check your plans to make sure that you received exactly what you ordered. All plans are checked for content prior to shipping, but mistakes can happen. If you find an error in your plans call 1-800-523-6789, all plans are drawn on a particular type of foundation and all details of the plan will illustrate that particular foundation. If you ordered an alternate foundation type. It should be included immediately after the original foundation. Tell your builder which foundation you wish to use and disregard the other foundation.

### 2. Check To Make Sure You Have Purchased the Proper Plan License

If you purchased prints, your plan will have a round red stamp stating, "If this stamp is not red it is an illegal set of plans." This license grants the purchaser the right to build one home using these construction drawings. It is illegal to make copies, doing so is punishable up to $150,000 per offense plus attorney fees. If you need more prints, call 1-800-523-6789. The House Plans Market Association monitors the home building industry for illegal prints.

It is also illegal to modify or redraw the plan if you purchased a print. If you purchased prints and need to modify the plan, you can upgrade to the reproducible master or CAD file - call 1-800-523-6789. If you purchased a reproducible master or CAD file you have the right to modify the plan and make up to 10 copies. A reproducible master or CAD files comes with a license that you must surrender to the printer or architect making your changes.

### 3. Complete the "Owner Selection" Portion of the Building Process

The working drawings are very complete, but there are items that you must decide upon. For example, the plans show a toilet in the bathroom, but there are hundreds of models to choose from. Your individual selection should be made based upon the color, style, and price you wish to pay. This same thing is true for all of the plumbing fixtures, light fixtures, appliances, and interior finishes (for the floors. walls and ceilings) and the exterior finishes. The selection of these items are required in order to obtain accurate competitive bids for the construction of your home

### 4. Complete Your Permit Package by Adding Other Documents That May Be Required

Your permit department, lender, and builder will need other drawings or documents that must be obtained locally. These items are explained in the next three items.

### 5. Obtain a Heating & Cooling Calculation and Layout

The heating and cooling system must be calculated and designed for your exact home and your location. Even the orientation of your home can affect the system size. This service is normally provided free of charge by the mechanical company that is supplying the equipment and installation. However, to get an unbiased calculation and equipment recommendation, we suggest employing the services of a mechanical engineer.

### 6. Obtain a Site Plan

A site plan is a document that shows the relationship of your home to your property. It may be as simple as the document your surveyor provides, or it can be a complex collection of drawings such as those prepared by a landscape architect. Typically, the document prepared by a surveyor will only show the property boundaries and the footprint of the home. Landscape architects can provide planning and drawings for all site amenities, such as driveways and walkways, outdoor structures such as pools, planting plans, irrigation plans, and outdoor lighting.

### 7. Obtain Earthquake or Hurricane Engineering if You Are Planning To Build in an Earthquake or Hurricane Zone

If you are building in an earthquake or hurricane zone, your permit department will most likely require you to submit calculations and drawings to illustrate the ability of your home to withstand those forces. This information is never included with pre-drawn plans because it would penalize the vast majority of plan purchasers who do not build in those zones. A structural engineer licensed by the state where you are building usually provides this information.

### 8. Review Your Plan To See Whether Modifications Are Needed

These plans have been designed to assumed conditions and do not address the individual site where you are building. Conditions can vary greatly including soil conditions, wind and snow loads, and temperature any one of these conditions may require some modifications of your plan. For example, if you live in an area that receives snow, structural changes may be necessary. We suggest:

(i) Have your soil tested by a soil-testing laboratory so that subsurface conditions can be determined at your specific building site. The findings of the soil-testing laboratory should be reviewed by a structural engineer to determine if the existing plan foundation is suitable or if modifications are needed.

(ii) Have your entire plan reviewed by your builder or a structural engineer to determine if other design elements, such as load bearing beams, are sized appropriately for the conditions that exist at your site.

Now that you have the complete plan, you may discover items that you wish to modify to suit your own personal taste or decor. To change the drawings, you must have the reproducible masters or CAD files (see item 2). We can make the changes for you. For complete information regarding modifications, including our fees, go to www.creativehomeowner.com and click the "resources" button on the home page; then click on "our custom services."

### 9. Record Your Blueprint License Number

Record your blueprint license number for easy reference. If you or your builder should need technical support, the license number is required.

### 10. Keep One Set of Plans as Long as You Own the Home

Be sure to file one copy of your home plan away for safe keeping. You may need a copy in the future if you remodel or sell the home. By fling a copy away for safe keeping, you can avoid the cost of having to purchase plans later on.

## Plan #701067

**Dimensions:** 44' W x 26' D
**Levels:** 1
**Square Footage:** 1,125
**Bedrooms:** 3
**Bathrooms:** 2
**Foundation:** Basement; crawl space for fee
**Material List Available:** Yes
**Price Category:** B

This traditional, economical split-level ranch home is the ideal beginning for the growing family.

*Images provided by designer/architect.*

**Features:**

• Entry: Through the covered stoop is this small entryway, which gives you two options for entertaining. A few short steps lead to the great room, providing a charming introduction to the home, while the basement, finished to your taste, awaits beneath the descending stairs.

• Great Room: Cathedral ceilings and their connection to both kitchen and dining room make this space open and inviting for family and guests alike.

• Kitchen: This efficiently designed L-shaped kitchen features a snack bar and flows into

the dining room, providing an easy transition between preparing and serving.

• Master Suite: A cozy, romantic area, this master suite includes a walk-in closet and private master bath. The area is self-contained for privacy but close enough to the other bedrooms to comfort young families.

• Basement: This spacious area is yours for the designing. A small space is reserved for the laundry, while the remaining area is full of possibility. Finish the basement for an extra bedroom or even a fun entertainment and game room.

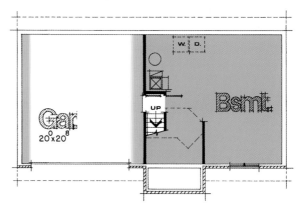

**Basement Level Floor Plan**

*Copyright by designer/architect.*

## Plan #701314

**Dimensions:** 40' W x 48'8" D

**Levels:** 1

**Square Footage:** 1,195

**Bedrooms:** 3

**Bathrooms:** 2

**Foundation:** Basement; crawl space or slab for fee

**Materials List Available:** Yes

**Price Category:** B

*This home, as shown in the photograph, may differ from the actual blueprints. For more detailed information, please check the floor plans carefully.*

*Images provided by designer/architect.*

This compact one-level home uses an open plan to make the most of its square footage.

**Features:**

• Ceiling Height: 8 ft.

• Covered Porch: This delightful area, located off the kitchen, provides a private spot to enjoy some fresh air.

• Open Plan: The family room, dining area and kitchen share a big open a sense of spaciousness.

Moving so easily between these interrelated areas provides the convenience demanded by a busy lifestyle.

• Master Suite: An open plan is convenient, but it is still important for everyone to have their private space. The master suite enjoys its own bath and walk-in closet. The secondary bedrooms share a nearby bath.

• Garage: Here you will find parking for two cars and plenty of extra storage space as well.

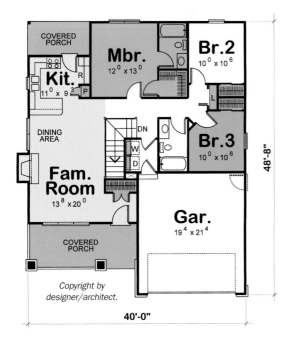

*Copyright by designer/architect.*

*Rendering reflects floor plan.*

## Plan #701142

**Dimensions:** 40' W x 47'8" D
**Levels:** 1
**Square Footage:** 1,205
**Bedrooms:** 2
**Bathrooms:** 2
**Foundation:** Basement; crawl space or slab for fee
**Material List Available:** Yes
**Price Category:** B

This home boasts a beautiful arched entry.

**Features:**

- **Great Room:** Enter this large gathering area from the foyer; the warmth of the fireplace welcomes you home. The 10-ft.-high ceiling gives the area an open feeling.

- **Kitchen:** Family and friends will enjoy gathering in this cozy kitchen, with its attached breakfast room. The area provides access to a future rear patio. The garage and laundry area are just a few steps away.

- **Master Suite:** This private area features a stepped ceiling in the sleeping area and a large window for backyard views. The master bath boasts a whirlpool bathtub, a separate shower, and dual vanities.

- **Secondary Bedroom:** A large front window brings light into this comfortable bedroom. A full bathroom is located nearby.

*Images provided by designer/architect.*

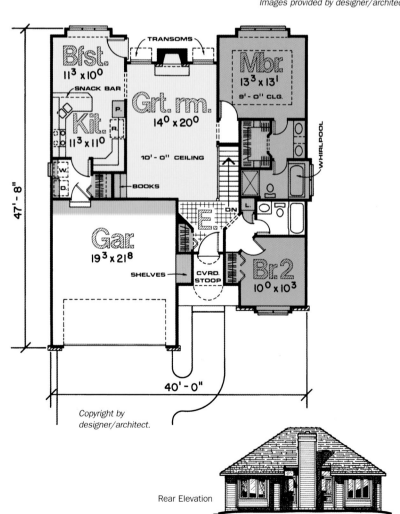

Rear Elevation

## Plan #701143

**Dimensions:** 40' W x 47'8" D

**Levels:** 1

**Square Footage:** 1,212

**Bedrooms:** 2

**Bathrooms:** 2

**Foundation:** Basement; crawl space or slab for fee

**Material List Available:** Yes

**Price Category:** B

*Images provided by designer/architect.*

With its roomy interior and basic layout, this plan is a perfect starter or retirement home.

**Features:**

- **Great Room:** This room boasts a 10-ft.-high ceiling, which can be enjoyed while reading a book in front of your fireplace.

- **Kitchen:** The pantries and cabinets in this kitchen will hold all of your groceries, even when you stock up on items. The snack bar is a great place to grab a bite to eat or to chat and unwind.

- **Master Suite:** Tucked away next to the great room, this master suite provides privacy and luxury with his and her sinks and a large closet.

- **Garage:** This two-car garage is accessible from both inside and outside, avoiding the need to dodge raindrops when unloading the car

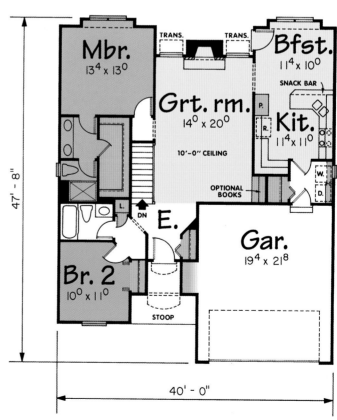

*Copyright by designer/architect.*

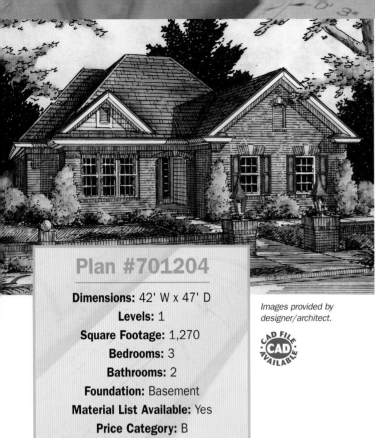

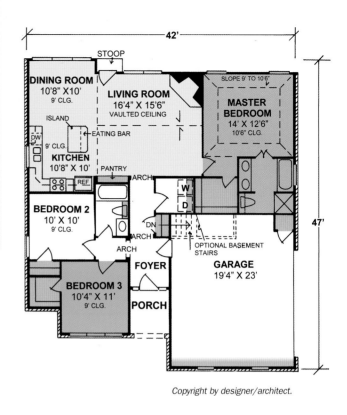

Images provided by designer/architect.

## Plan #701204

**Dimensions:** 42' W x 47' D

**Levels:** 1

**Square Footage:** 1,270

**Bedrooms:** 3

**Bathrooms:** 2

**Foundation:** Basement

**Material List Available:** Yes

**Price Category:** B

Copyright by designer/architect.

Images provided by designer/architect.

## Plan #701141

**Dimensions:** 50' W x 46' D

**Levels:** 1

**Square Footage:** 1,271

**Bedrooms:** 3

**Bathrooms:** 2

**Foundation:** Basement; crawl space or slab for fee

**Material List Available:** Yes

**Price Category:** B

Copyright by designer/architect.

Rear Elevation

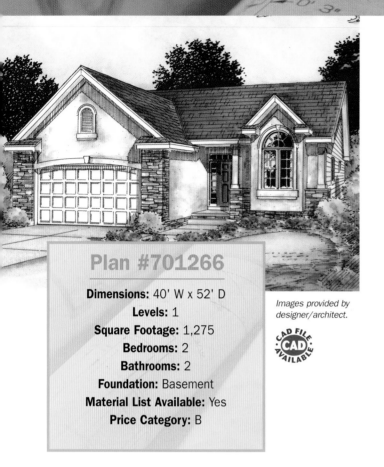

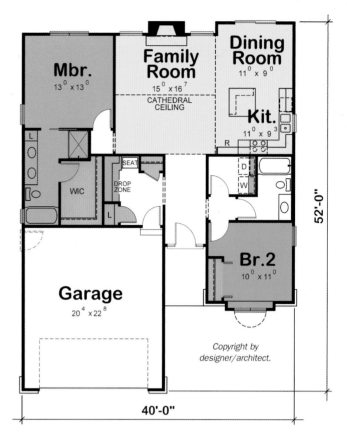

*Images provided by designer/architect.*

**CAD FILE CAD AVAILABLE**

*Copyright by designer/architect.*

## Plan #701266

**Dimensions:** 40' W x 52' D

**Levels:** 1

**Square Footage:** 1,275

**Bedrooms:** 2

**Bathrooms:** 2

**Foundation:** Basement

**Material List Available:** Yes

**Price Category:** B

---

*Images provided by designer/architect.*

**CAD FILE CAD AVAILABLE**

*Copyright by designer/architect.*

## Plan #701235

**Dimensions:** 42' W x 37'4" D

**Levels:** 2

**Square Footage:** 1,297

**Main Level Sq. Ft.:** 658

**Upper Level Sq. Ft.:** 639

**Bedrooms:** 3

**Bathrooms:** 2½

**Foundation:** Basement

**Material List Available:** Yes

**Price Category:** B

## Plan #701093

**Dimensions:** 47' W x 47' D

**Levels:** 1

**Square Footage:** 1,333

**Bedrooms:** 3

**Bathrooms:** 2

**Foundation:** Basement; crawl space or slab for fee

**Material List Available:** Yes

**Price Category:** B

*Images provided by designer/architect.*

This one-story home boasts multiple places that are ideal for relaxing.

**Features:**

- Covered Porches: This house features two porches, one at the front, and one at the rear. These spaces are perfect for relaxing with guests or loved ones after a long day.

- Great Room: Be a part of all the action while relaxing in front of the fireplace in this airy and spacious great room.

- Kitchen: Perfect for entertaining, this kitchen is open to both the dining room and the great room. The island can be used in many ways, such as holding trays of food or as a station for beverages.

- Master Suite: Function meets design in this bedroom, with 10-ft.-high ceilings, a private bath, and walk-in closet.

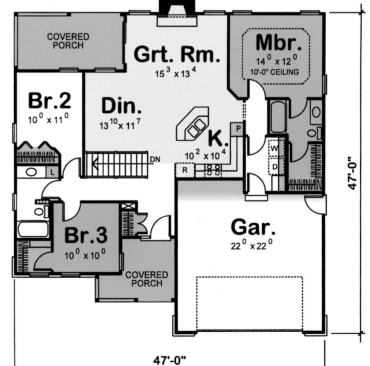

*Copyright by designer/architect.*

## Plan #701092

**Dimensions:** 49'4" W x 44' D

**Levels:** 1

**Square Footage:** 1,335

**Bedrooms:** 3

**Bathrooms:** 2

**Foundation:** Basement; crawl space or slab for fee

**Material List Available:** Yes

**Price Category:** B

The classic European design of this home will be a pleasure to come home to everyday.

*Images provided by designer/architect.*

**Features:**

- Covered Porches: Relax on one of two porches. You have your choice between one located in the front and the other in the back of the house

- Great Room: Located in the center of the home, this great room is roomy and relaxing, with enough space to fit everyone around the fireplace.

- Dining Room: A few steps up from the great room, this dining room is connected to the kitchen, making entertaining easy. The dining room also opens out to a covered porch, which is perfect for meals outside or watching the children play in the yard after dinner.

- Master Suite: This room is perfect for unwinding. It features 10-ft.-high ceilings and a luxurious bathtub.

- Storage Space: This upstairs storage area is great for those extra items that don't get a lot of use.

### Bonus Area Floor Plan

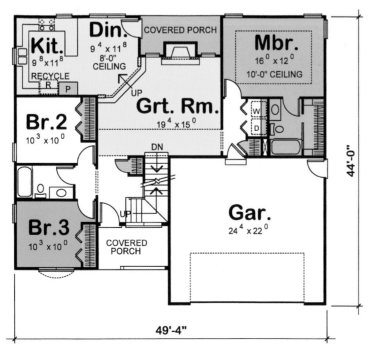

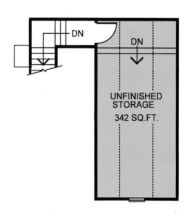

*Copyright by designer/architect.*

## Plan #701038

**Dimensions:** 50' W x 46' D
**Levels:** 1
**Square Footage:** 1,339
**Bedrooms:** 3
**Full Bathrooms:** 2
**Foundation:** Basement
**Materials List Available:** Yes
**Price Category:** B

You'll love this compact design if you're looking for either a starter home or a luxurious place to spend your retirement years.

**Features:**

• Foyer: A covered stoop and arched entry open to this gracious foyer, where you'll love to greet guests.

• Great Room: From the foyer, you'll walk into this large area with its 10-ft. ceilings. A fireplace gives you a cozy spot on chilly days and cool evenings.

• Kitchen: This kitchen is truly step-saving and convenient. In addition to plenty of counter and storage space, it features a snack bar and an adjoining breakfast area.

• Master Suite: A 9-ft. ceiling gives a touch of elegance to the bedroom, and the walk-in closet adds practicality. In the bath, you'll find two vanities and a whirlpool tub.

• Garage: There's room for storage, a work bench, and three cars in this huge garage.

## Plan #701002

**Dimensions:** 42' W x 54' D

**Levels:** 1

**Square Footage:** 1,347

**Bedrooms:** 3

**Bathrooms:** 2

**Foundation:** Basement; crawl space or slab for fee

**Materials List Available:** Yes

**Price Category:** B

This home's convenient single level and luxury amenities are a recipe for gracious living.

**Features:**

- Ceiling Height: 8 ft. except as noted.

- Great Room: The entry enjoys a long view into this great room where a pair of transom-topped windows flanks the fireplace and a 10-ft. ceiling visually expands the space.

- Snack Bar: This special feature adjoins the great room, making it a real plus for informal entertaining, as well as the perfect spot for family get-togethers.

- Kitchen: This well-designed convenient kitchen features a door to the backyard, a pantry, and convenient access to the laundry room.

- Master Suite: Located at the back of the home for extra privacy, the master suite feels like its own world. It features a tiered ceiling and sunlit corner whirlpool.

*Images provided by designer/architect.*

*This home, as shown in the photograph, may differ from the actual blueprints. For more detailed information, please check the floor plans carefully.*

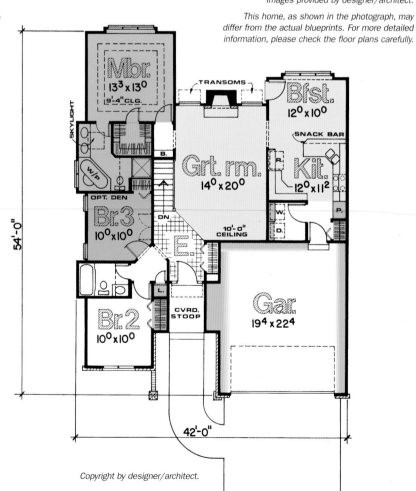

*Copyright by designer/architect.*

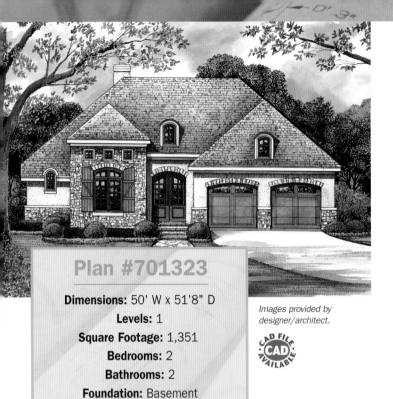

## Plan #701323

**Dimensions:** 50' W x 51'8" D

**Levels:** 1

**Square Footage:** 1,351

**Bedrooms:** 2

**Bathrooms:** 2

**Foundation:** Basement

**Material List Available:** Yes

**Price Category:** B

*Images provided by designer/architect.*

CAD FILE AVAILABLE

*Copyright by designer/architect.*

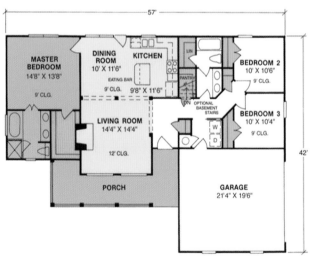

## Plan #701203

**Dimensions:** 57' W x 42' D

**Levels:** 1

**Square Footage:** 1,359

**Bedrooms:** 3

**Bathrooms:** 2

**Foundation:** Basement

**Material List Available:** Yes

**Price Category:** B

*Images provided by designer/architect.*

CAD FILE AVAILABLE

*Copyright by designer/architect.*

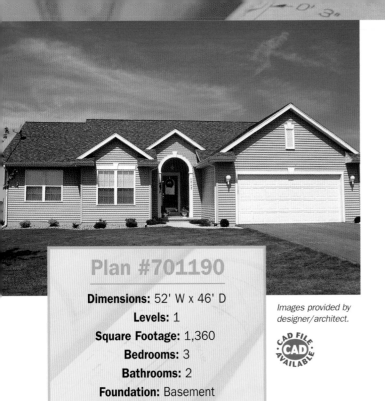

## Plan #701190

**Dimensions:** 52' W x 46' D
**Levels:** 1
**Square Footage:** 1,360
**Bedrooms:** 3
**Bathrooms:** 2
**Foundation:** Basement
**Material List Available:** Yes
**Price Category:** B

*Images provided by designer/architect.*

*Copyright by designer/architect.*

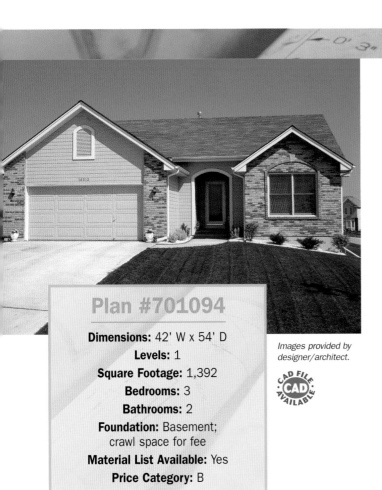

## Plan #701094

**Dimensions:** 42' W x 54' D
**Levels:** 1
**Square Footage:** 1,392
**Bedrooms:** 3
**Bathrooms:** 2
**Foundation:** Basement; crawl space for fee
**Material List Available:** Yes
**Price Category:** B

*Images provided by designer/architect.*

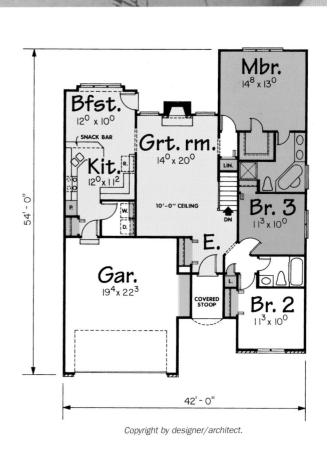

*Copyright by designer/architect.*

## Plan #701129

**Dimensions:** 49' W x 58' D
**Levels:** 1
**Square Footage:** 1,416
**Bedrooms:** 3
**Bathrooms:** 2
**Foundation:** Slab;
basement for fee
**Material List Available:** Yes
**Price Category:** B

*Images provided by designer/architect.*

• Kitchen: Thanks to a strategically located snack bar, this functional kitchen is open to both the dining and living rooms. The eating area is great for quick snacks or putting away the groceries.

• Bedrooms: All three bedrooms feature 9-ft.-high ceilings. The master suite has access to a private bath, while the other two bedrooms share a bathroom.

• Shop: Located off of the two-car garage, the shop provides a place to work on a project or just get away and unwind.

Multiple porches, a shop, and a snack bar set this one-story plan apart from the rest.

**Features:**

• Porches: At the front of the house, an ample 9-ft.-high ceiling covers this large open porch. At the rear, the screened-in porch connects to the dining room, making it the perfect spot for meals outside.

Living Room

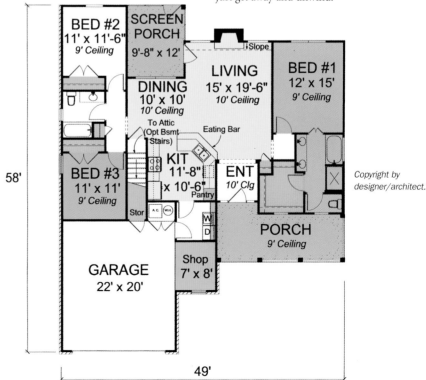

*Copyright by designer/architect.*

Images provided by designer/architect.

## Plan #701009

**Dimensions:** 50' W x 58' D
**Levels:** 1
**Square Footage:** 1,422
**Bedrooms:** 3
**Bathrooms:** 2
**Foundation:** Basement; crawl space or slab for fee
**Materials List Available:** Yes
**Price Category:** B

This amenity-filled home is perfect for the growing family or as a retirement retreat.

**Features:**

- Ceiling Height: 8 ft. unless otherwise noted.
- Great Room: This inviting space is the perfect place for gatherings of all sizes. It shares 12-ft. ceilings with the dining room and kitchen.

- Dining Room: In addition to the 12-ft. ceiling, arched openings, and built-in book cases make this an elegant place to dine.
- Private Porch: After dinner, step through a door in the dining room to enjoy a summer breeze in this inviting porch.
- Master Suite: The boxed ceiling lends drama to this suite and a walk-in closet adds convenience. Luxury comes from the whirlpool bath.
- Garage: You won't be short of parking and storage space in this two-bay garage. As a bonus there is space for a workbench.

## SMARTtip
### Window Cornices

You can transform plain rooms by making jogs in cornice molding that will hold shades, blinds, and other window treatments. You can create individual pockets over each window or continue the molding past narrow wall sections between windows to form a more expansive detail. Housings below the cornice can be painted or papered.

## Plan #701147

**Dimensions:** 48' W x 32' D
**Levels:** 1
**Square Footage:** 1,429
**Bedrooms:** 3
**Bathrooms:** 2
**Foundation:** Basement
**Materials List Available:** Yes
**Price Category:** B

This home is perfect for raising a family and would be a welcome addition to any neighborhood.

*Images provided by designer/architect.*

**Features:**

- Great Room: Walk into this home and you will be greeted by this spacious and inviting great room, complete with a fireplace for pretend campfires or for relaxing after the kids have gone to bed.

- Kitchen: This kitchen is connected to a sunny breakfast room. It surrounds the family cook with workspace and storage.

- Bedrooms: The bedrooms and bathroom in this house are all easily accessed by a hallway, perfect for checking up on the children.

- Basement: A large basement provides ample space for storage, play, or work.

## Main Level Floor Plan

## Basement Level Floor Plan

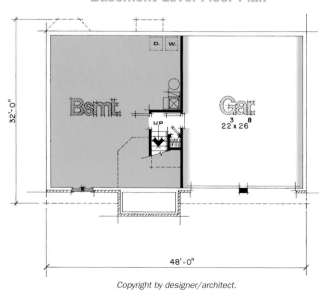

*Copyright by designer/architect.*

## Plan #701189

**Dimensions:** 50' W x 58' D

**Levels:** 1

**Square Footage:** 1,433

**Bedrooms:** 3

**Bathrooms:** 2

**Foundation:** Basement

**Material List Available:** Yes

**Price Category:** B

*Images provided by designer/architect.*

This home would look great in any neighborhood.

**Features:**

- **Covered Porch:** A wonderful place to relax with friends and family, this porch welcomes you into the beautiful home.

- **Great Room:** This large great room, featuring a high ceiling and fireplace, will be a favorite place to gather. Large windows flank the fireplace, which will flood the space with natural light.

- **Kitchen:** Conveniently located near the garage to aid in unloading groceries, this kitchen has plenty of cabinets. The snack bar will add extra seating to the adjacent breakfast room.

- **Master Suite:** Featuring a large sleeping area and a walk-in closet, this master suite has plenty of room for two. The master bath boasts dual vanities, a stall shower, and a large tub.

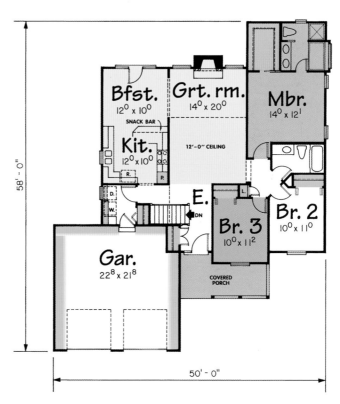

*Copyright by designer/architect.*

## Plan #701327

**Dimensions:** 45'4" W x 38' D

**Levels:** 2

**Square Footage:** 1,463

**Main Level Sq. Ft.:** 716

**Upper Level Sq. Ft.:** 747

**Bedrooms:** 3

**Bathrooms:** 2½

**Foundation:** Basement

**Materials List Available:** Yes

**Price Category:** B

*Images provided by designer/architect.*

This convenient and elegant home is designed to expand as the family does.

**Features:**

• Ceiling Height: 8 ft. unless otherwise noted.

• Family Room: An open staircase to the second level visually expands this room where a built-in entertainment center maximizes the floor space. The whole family will be drawn to the warmth from the handsome fireplace.

• Kitchen: Cooking will be a pleasure in this

bright and efficient kitchen that features a corner pantry. A snack bar offers a convenient spot for informal family meals.

• Dining Area: This lovely bayed area adjoins the kitchen.

• Room to Expand: Upstairs is 258 sq. ft. of unfinished area offering plenty of space for expansion as the family grows.

• Garage: This two-bay garage offers plenty of storage space in addition to parking for cars.

**CAD FILE AVAILABLE**

### Main Level Floor Plan

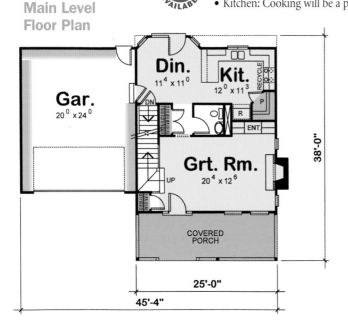

### Upper Level Floor Plan

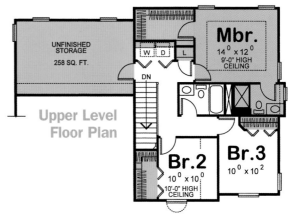

*Copyright by designer/architect.*

## Plan #701034

**Dimensions:** 48' W x 50' D

**Levels:** 1

**Square Footage:** 1,479

**Bedrooms:** 2

**Bathrooms:** 2

**Foundation:** Basement

**Materials List Available:** Yes

**Price Category:** B

*Images provided by designer/architect.*

This home is ideal if the size of your live-in family is increasing with the addition of a baby, or if it's decreasing as children leave the nest.

**Features:**

- **Entry:** This entry gives you a long view into the great room that it opens into.

- **Great Room:** An 11-ft. ceiling and a fireplace framed by transom-topped windows make this room comfortable in every season and any time of day or night.

- **Den:** French doors open to this den, with its picturesque window. This room would also make a lovely third bedroom.

- **Kitchen:** This kitchen has an island that can double as a snack bar, a pantry, and a door into the backyard.

- **Master Suite:** A large walk-in closet gives a practical touch; you'll find a sunlit whirlpool tub, dual lavatories, and a separate shower in the bath.

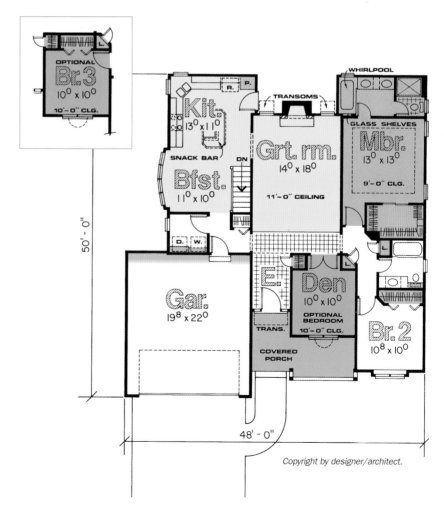

*Copyright by designer/architect.*

## Plan #701287

**Dimensions:** 45' W x 56' D

**Levels:** 1

**Square Footage:** 1,482

**Bedrooms:** 3

**Bathrooms:** 2

**Foundation:** Basement

**Material List Available:** Yes

**Price Category:** B

*Images provided by designer/architect.*

This flexible floor plan provides a host of lifestyle options.

**Features:**

- Family Room: You'll find it easy to entertain in this spacious family room, which features a soaring cathedral ceiling and fireplace.

- Kitchen: This spacious kitchen is open to the dining room, making serving between the oven and the table easy. The island is perfect for a cooktop, or it can be used as a snack bar for a casual meal.

- Bedrooms: Siblings can share the nearby bathroom and enjoy having ample closet space for storage. One of the bedrooms can easily be transformed into a workspace.

- Garage: This two-car garage opens up to both the outside and the inside of the house, making those trips to unload the car much easier.

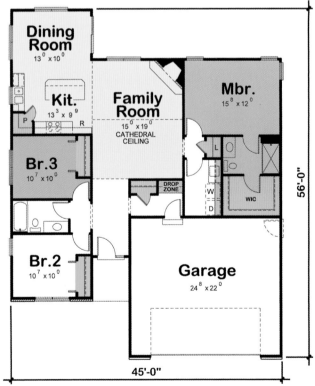

*Copyright by designer/architect.*

## Plan #701005

**Dimensions:** 48' W x 52' D

**Levels:** 1

**Square Footage:** 1,496

**Bedrooms:** 3

**Bathrooms:** 2

**Foundation:** Basement

**Materials List Available:** Yes

**Price Category:** B

A beautiful starter or retirement home with all the amenities you'd expect in a much bigger house.

**Features:**

- Ceiling Height: 8 ft.

- Great Room: A cathedral ceiling visually expands the great room making it the perfect place for family gatherings or formal entertaining.

- Formal Dining Room: This elegant room is ideal for entertaining dinner guests. It conveniently shares a wet bar and service counter with a bayed breakfast area next door.

- Breakfast Area: In addition to the service area shared with the dining room, this cozy area features a snack bar, pantry, and desk that's perfect for household paperwork.

- Master Suite: The master bedroom features special ceiling details. It's joined by a private bath with a whirlpool, shower, and spacious walk-in closet.

- Garage: The two-bay garage offers plenty of storage space.

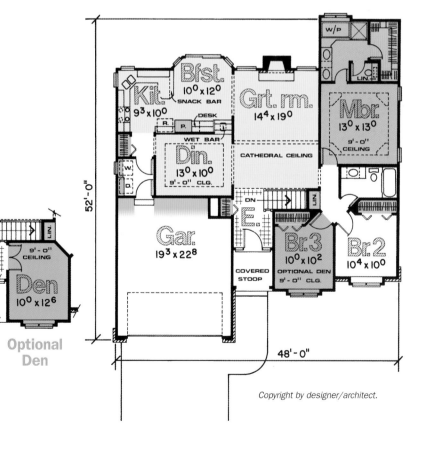

**Optional Den**

## Plan #701163

**Dimensions:** 42' W x 54' D
**Levels:** 1
**Square Footage:** 1,499
**Bedrooms:** 2
**Bathrooms:** 2
**Foundation:** Basement
**Material List Available:** Yes
**Price Category:** B

*Images provided by designer/architect.*

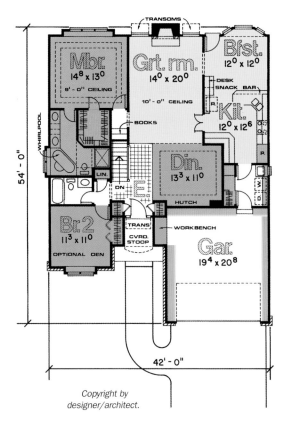

*Copyright by designer/architect.*

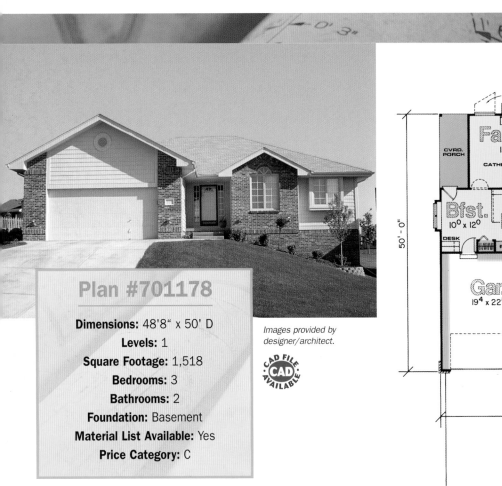

## Plan #701178

**Dimensions:** 48'8" x 50' D
**Levels:** 1
**Square Footage:** 1,518
**Bedrooms:** 3
**Bathrooms:** 2
**Foundation:** Basement
**Material List Available:** Yes
**Price Category:** C

*Images provided by designer/architect.*

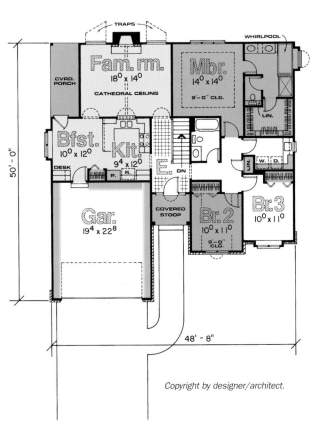

*Copyright by designer/architect.*

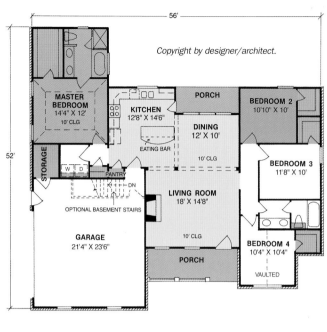

*Images provided by designer/architect.*

## Plan #701114

**Dimensions:** 56' W x 52' D

**Levels:** 1

**Square Footage:** 1,539

**Bedrooms:** 4

**Bathrooms:** 2

**Foundation:** Slab; basement for fee

**Material List Available:** Yes

**Price Category:** C

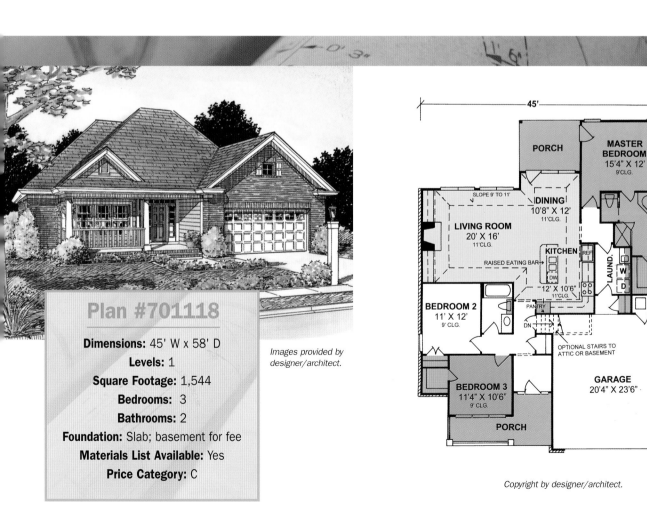

*Images provided by designer/architect.*

## Plan #701118

**Dimensions:** 45' W x 58' D

**Levels:** 1

**Square Footage:** 1,544

**Bedrooms:** 3

**Bathrooms:** 2

**Foundation:** Slab; basement for fee

**Materials List Available:** Yes

**Price Category:** C

## Plan #701138

**Dimensions:** 27' W x 50' D
**Levels:** 2
**Square Footage:** 1,550
**Main Level Sq. Ft.:** 733
**Upper Level Sq. Ft.:** 817
**Bedrooms:** 3
**Bathrooms:** 2½
**Foundation:** Basement;
crawl space for fee
**Material List Available:** Yes
**Price Category:** C

*Images provided by designer/architect.*

Impress your guests with the airy spaciousness of this home.

**Features:**

- **Family Room:** Complete with a fireplace and an entertainment center, this family room will make your house the most popular one in the neighborhood.

- **Kitchen:** This kitchen is perfect for hosting parties because of its openness to the family room and dining room.

- **Master Suite:** A large master bedroom with 9-ft. ceiling invites you in after a long day. Need more space? An optional second walk-in closet can be added so you'll always have plenty of room for storage.

*Copyright by designer/architect.*

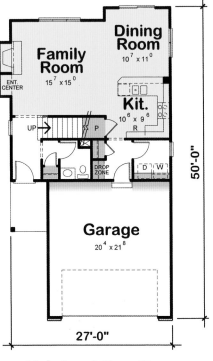

**Family Room**
15⁷ x 15⁰

**Dining Room**
10⁷ x 11⁰

**Kit.**
10⁶ x 9⁶

ENT. CENTER

UP

DROP ZONE

**Garage**
20⁴ x 21⁸

27'-0"

50'-0"

**Main Level Floor Plan**

**Mbr.**
15⁴ x 15⁰

9'-0" CEILING

WIC

OPEN TO BELOW

DN

**Br.2**
10⁰ x 12⁰

**Br.3**
10⁰ x 12⁰

**Upper Level Floor Plan**

## Plan #701036

**Dimensions:** 50' W x 52'8" D
**Levels:** 1
**Square Footage:** 1,554
**Bedrooms:** 3
**Bathrooms:** 2
**Foundation:** Basement
**Materials List Available:** Yes
**Price Category:** C

The high ceilings and well-placed windows make this home bright and airy.

**Features:**

- **Great Room:** A soaring cathedral ceiling sets the tone for this gracious room. Enjoy the fireplace that's framed by views to the outside.

- **Dining Room:** A 10-ft. ceiling highlights formality, while a built-in display cabinet and picturesque window give it even more character.

- **Kitchen:** This well-designed kitchen shares a snack bar with the breakfast area.

- **Breakfast Area:** Natural light streams into this room, and the door to the backyard lets everyone move outside for a meal or drink in fine weather.

- **Master Suite:** A tray ceiling gives elegance to the bedroom, with its practical walk-in closet. The bath features a sunlit whirlpool tub, double vanity, and separate shower.

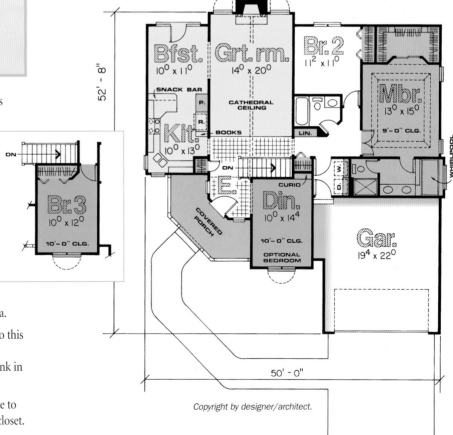

Copyright by designer/architect.

## Plan #701152

**Dimensions:** 50' W x 50' D

**Levels:** 1

**Square Footage:** 1,561

**Bedrooms:** 2

**Bathrooms:** 2

**Foundation:** Basement

**Material List Available:** Yes

**Price Category:** C

*Images provided by designer/architect.*

Beauty, comfort, and convenience are all yours in this wonderful traditional home.

**Features:**

- **Living Room:** This room works around your family's needs. Use it as a traditional living room for entertaining guests or as an extra bedroom.

- **Great Room:** Your home will be the most popular place for a party with this great room's open floor plan.

- **Breakfast Room:** The children will never again lose papers or assignments around the house thanks to this room's convenient desk. Open shelves provide extra space for book bags and other necessities.

- **Master Suite:** You'll have enough closet space for your year-round wardrobe in this suite's large walk-in closet. After a long day, relax in your whirlpool tub while you watch the stars through the skylight.

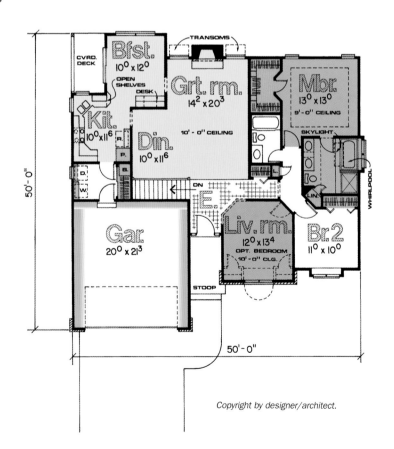

*Copyright by designer/architect.*

## Plan #701234

**Dimensions:** 52' W x 48' D

**Levels:** 2

**Square Footage:** 1,562

**Main Level Sq. Ft.:** 676

**Upper Level Sq. Ft.:** 886

**Bedrooms:** 3

**Bathrooms:** 2½

**Foundation:** Basement

**Material List Available:** Yes

**Price Category:** C

This two-story design is both functional and compact. It is the perfect starter home.

**Features:**

- Family Room: This large family room is connected to both the dining room and the kitchen. The open design allows you to decide how the space works best for you and your lifestyle.

- Kitchen: Both stylish and convenient, this kitchen features good traffic flow and an island that can be utilized in a variety of ways.

- Master Suite: This master suite becomes more than just a place to sleep thanks to the sitting area and double doors opening to the bath, which features his and her sinks.

- Secondary Bedrooms: Two additional bedrooms are located across the hall from the master suite, along with a bathroom the kids can share.

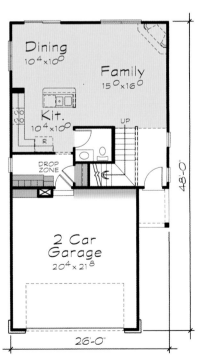

**Main Level Floor Plan**

**Upper Level Floor Plan**
*Copyright by designer/architect.*

## Plan #701324

**Dimensions:** 50' W x 65' D
**Levels:** 1
**Square Footage:** 1,574
**Bedrooms:** 3
**Bathrooms:** 2
**Foundation:** Basement
**Material List Available:** Yes
**Price Category:** C

This home's beautiful exterior and interesting architecture make it a standout in the neighborhood.

**Features:**

- **Family Room:** This octagonal family room with 12-ft. tray ceiling is perfect for entertaining guests or just relaxing. Windows line part of the room, making for beautiful and interesting views.

- **Kitchen:** The U-shape of this kitchen makes it easy for the chef in the family to find what they need.

- **Eating Area:** This eating area connects the kitchen to the screened-in porch in the rear of the home, offering the opportunity to enjoy outdoor dining.

- **Master Suite:** Feel luxurious and pampered every day in this master suite. It features 11-ft. ceiling and his and her sinks.

*Images provided by designer/architect.*

*This home, as shown in the photograph, may differ from the actual blueprints. For more detailed information, please check the floor plans carefully.*

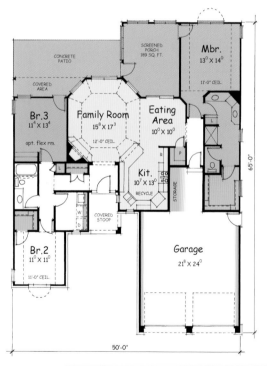

**Optional Floor Plan**

*Copyright by designer/architect.*

Rear View

## Plan #701162

**Dimensions:** 48' W x 60' D

**Levels:** 1

**Square Footage:** 1,580

**Bedrooms:** 3

**Bathrooms:** 2

**Foundation:** Basement

**Material List Available:** Yes

**Price Category:** C

*Images provided by designer/architect.*

The inviting exterior design of this home will welcome friends and neighbors.

**Features:**

- Covered Stoop: Enter through this covered stoop, where you can greet guests, hang plants, or simply sit back and enjoy the view.

- Great Room: Cozy up by the fire under the cathedral ceiling in this spacious great room.

- Kitchen: Everything is at your fingertips with the functionality and convenience of this kitchen design.

- Master Suite: This master suite is filled with luxuries that you'll adore, such as his and hers sinks and a whirlpool tub.

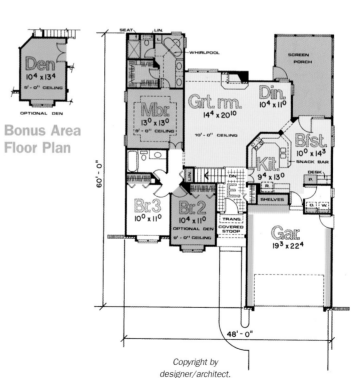

**Bonus Area Floor Plan**

*Copyright by designer/architect.*

## Plan #701280

**Dimensions:** 41' W x 60' D
**Levels:** 1
**Square Footage:** 1,592
**Bedrooms:** 2
**Bathrooms:** 2
**Foundation:** Basement
**Material List Available:** Yes
**Price Category:** C

*Images provided by designer/architect.*

Relax with this home's simple, but elegant, design and flexible layout.

**Features:**

- Covered Porch: Enter your oasis through this large covered porch, where you can greet guests, hang plants, or simply sit back and enjoy the view.

- Family Room: Cozy up by the fire under the cathedral ceiling in this spacious family room.

- Kitchen: Everything is at your fingertips with the functionality and convenience of this kitchen design.

- Flex Room: Your wish is this room's command. This flex room could be a home office, an extra bedroom, or whatever you choose.

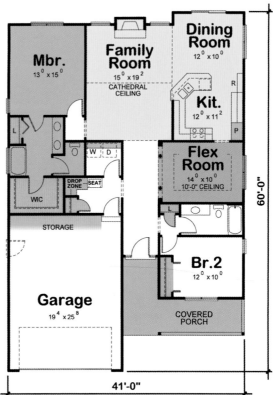

*Copyright by designer/architect.*

## Plan #701164

**Dimensions:** 38' W x 44'4" D
**Levels:** 2
**Square Footage:** 1,594
**Main Level Sq. Ft.:** 869
**Upper Level Sq. Ft.:** 725
**Bedrooms:** 3
**Bathrooms:** 2½
**Foundation:** Basement
**Material List Available:** Yes
**Price Category:** C

*Images provided by designer/architect.*

This charming home is the perfect place for you and your family.

**Features:**

- **Living Room:** This living room, boasting a cathedral ceiling and fireplace, is the perfect place for entertaining guests. This room is open to the dining room, which makes gathering guests for dinner even easier.

- **Kitchen:** The open-air design of this kitchen and breakfast area leaves plenty of options for creating a space to suit your family's needs. The snack bar is perfect for grabbing lunches, eating casual meals, or just chatting.

- **Master Suite:** The large bedroom is perfect for relaxing after a long day. Unwind in the luxurious whirlpool tub. The large walk-in closet allows for easy organization-never sort through piles of clothes again, everything you own is all right in front of you.

- **Secondary Bedrooms:** Two additional bedrooms are located down the hallway. Siblings can share the bathroom that is directly between the two rooms.

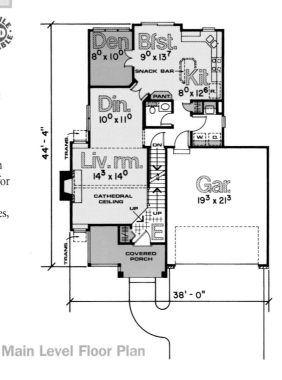

**Main Level Floor Plan**

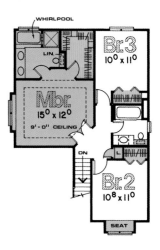

**Upper Level Floor Plan**

*Copyright by designer/architect.*

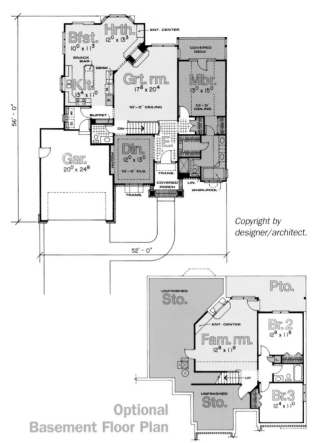

Copyright by
designer/architect.

Images provided by
designer/architect.

**CAD FILE AVAILABLE**

## Plan #701179

**Dimensions:** 52' W x 56' D

**Levels:** 1

**Square Footage:** 1,595

**Bedrooms:** 1

**Bathrooms:** 2½

**Foundation:** Basement

**Material List Available:** Yes

**Price Category:** C

**Optional
Basement Floor Plan**

## Plan #701128

**Dimensions:** 49' W x 60' D

**Levels:** 1

**Square Footage:** 1,595

**Bedrooms:** 3

**Bathrooms:** 2

**Foundation:** Slab; basement for fee

**Material List Available:** Yes

**Price Category:** C

Images provided by
designer/architect.

**Optional Gameroom**

Copyright by designer/architect.

## Plan #701066

**Dimensions:** 50' W x 48' D
**Levels:** 1.5
**Square Footage:** 1,596
**Main Level Sq. Ft.:** 1,191
**Upper Level Sq. Ft.:** 405
**Bedrooms:** 3
**Bathrooms:** 2½
**Foundation:** Basement;
crawl space or slab for fee
**Material List Available:** Yes
**Price Category:** C

*Images provided by designer/architect.*

**Main Level Floor Plan**

Mbr.
15⁰ x 12⁰
9'-0" CEILING
WHIRLPOOL
LIN.

Kit.
10⁰ x 12⁰
SNACK BAR
P. R.

Bfst.
10⁰ x 11²
TRANSOMS

Grt. rm.
13⁸ x 19⁴
10'-0" CEILING
TRANS.

Gar.
20⁸ x 21⁰

COVERED PORCH

48' - 0"
50' - 0"

**Upper Level Floor Plan**

Br. 2
10¹ x 11⁰

Br. 3
10¹ x 11⁰

DN

OPEN TO BELOW

LIN.

*Copyright by designer/architect.*

---

## Plan #701300

**Dimensions:** 45' W x 60' D
**Levels:** 1
**Square Footage:** 1,596
**Bedrooms:** 2
**Bathrooms:** 2
**Foundation:** Basement
**Material List Available:** Yes
**Price Category:** C

*Images provided by designer/architect.*

CAD FILE AVAILABLE

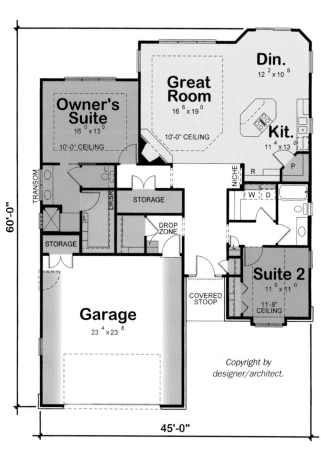

Owner's Suite
16⁰ x 13⁰
10'-0" CEILING

TRANSOM
DRSR.
L
STORAGE

Great Room
16⁶ x 19⁰
10'-0" CEILING

DROP ZONE

Din.
12² x 10⁸

Kit.
11⁴ x 13⁰

NICHE
R
P
W   D

STORAGE

Garage
23⁴ x 23⁸

COVERED STOOP

Suite 2
11⁰ x 11⁰
11'-8" CEILING

60'-0"
45'-0"

*Copyright by designer/architect.*

## Plan #701069

**Dimensions:** 48'8" W x 48' D

**Levels:** 1

**Square Footage:** 1,604

**Bedrooms:** 3

**Bathrooms:** 2

**Foundation:** Basement; crawl space for fee

**Material List Available:** Yes

**Price Category:** C

This sweet traditional home is beautifully designed with practicality in mind.

**Features:**

- Great Room: With plenty of room for entertaining, this space creates an inviting atmosphere and features a cathedral ceiling and a fireplace.

- Breakfast Room: Transitioning between the kitchen and the great room, this room brings an abundance of light into the home through an entire boundary of bay windows. Equipped with a wet bar, a desk, and the pantry, the space keeps convenience in mind.

- Dining Room: The great room opens into this elegant dining room, complete with a built-in hutch, for stylish dinner parties. The space also shares the wet bar with the breakfast room.

- Master Suite: Privacy, romance, relaxation, and comfort are a few things that come to mind in this bedroom. A skylight lends natural light to the master bath, which features dual vanities, a shower, and a whirlpool bathtub. The walk-in closet acts as one vast storage space or, with a bit of separation, can be shared by two.

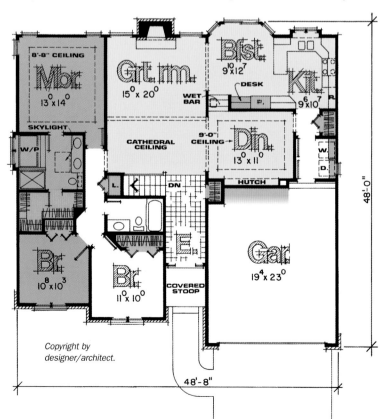

Copyright by designer/architect.

## Plan #701122

**Dimensions:** 57' W x 59' D

**Levels:** 1

**Square Footage:** 1,604

**Bedrooms:** 3

**Bathrooms:** 2

**Foundation:** Slab; basement for fee

**Material List Available:** Yes

**Price Category:** C

*Images provided by designer/architect.*

Second floor dormers accent the design of this home, which features multiple porches.

**Features:**

- Porches: A large porch graces the front of the home, while three porches are located around back. Escape the rain, and the bugs, when entertaining in the screened-in porch, which features a wet bar.

- Kitchen: This kitchen is wide and open, allowing for multiple cooks to make dishes at the same time. An eating bar provides space to eat casually or keep food for guests.

- Master Suite: Directly attached to the screened-in porch, the master suite has his and her sinks, and a large closet.

- Attic: Upstairs, this large attic can be used for storage or converted into an optional game room for the kids and kids-at-heart.

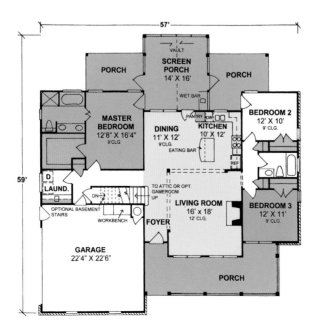

**Bonus Area Floor Plan**

*Copyright by designer/architect.*

## Plan #701161

**Dimensions:** 40' W x 42' D
**Levels:** 2
**Square Footage:** 1,605
**Main Level Sq. Ft.:** 845
**Upper Level Sq. Ft.:** 760
**Bedrooms:** 3
**Bathrooms:** 2½
**Foundation:** Basement
**Material List Available:** Yes
**Price Category:** C

*Images provided by designer/architect.*

**Features:**

- **Great Room:** This room truly has a grand feeling, thanks to the soaring ceiling and its openness to the second floor. Guests will love sitting by the fireplace enjoying the beauty of the room.

- **Kitchen:** This kitchen features enough storage space to fit every last one of your spoons, pans, and cutting boards and still has a window to allow in the sunshine.

- **Master Suite:** A 10-ft.-high ceiling, a whirlpool bathtub, and a large walk-in closet make this master suite a luxurious retreat.

A classic and traditional design makes this home charming and distinctive.

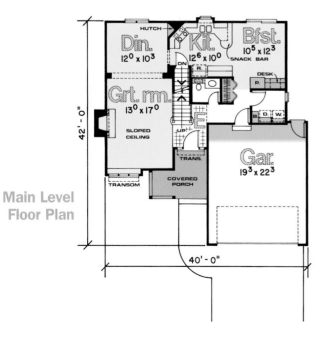

**Main Level Floor Plan**

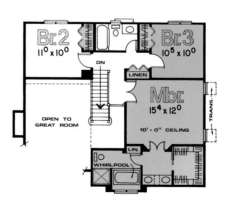

**Upper Level Floor Plan**

*Copyright by designer/architect.*

## Plan #701236

**Dimensions:** 50' W x 52' D
**Levels:** 1
**Square Footage:** 1,620
**Bedrooms:** 2
**Bathrooms:** 2
**Foundation:** Basement
**Material List Available:** Yes
**Price Category:** C

If you love traditional homes with a twist, this could be your dream house.

**Features:**

- Great Room: The octagon shape and 11-ft.-high tray ceiling make this breathtaking space the natural center for gathering with family.

- Kitchen: The convenience of this kitchen can be found in the expansive workspace, large pantry, and direct access to the dining room.

- Master Suite: A large window, a 10-ft.-high ceiling, and a dual vanity make this room enjoyable and relaxing.

- Garage: The three-car garage has room for your cars as well as extra storage space.

## Plan #701033

**Dimensions:** 51' W x 52' D

**Levels:** 1

**Square Footage:** 1,622

**Bedrooms:** 3

**Bathrooms:** 2

**Foundation:** Basement

**Materials List Available:** Yes

**Price Category:** C

*Images provided by designer/architect.*

**Optional Third Bedroom Floor Plan**

## Plan #701299

**Dimensions:** 47' W x 56' D

**Levels:** 1

**Square Footage:** 1,626

**Bedrooms:** 2

**Bathrooms:** 2

**Foundation:** Slab

**Material List Available:** Yes

**Price Category:** C

*Images provided by designer/architect.*

CAD FILE AVAILABLE

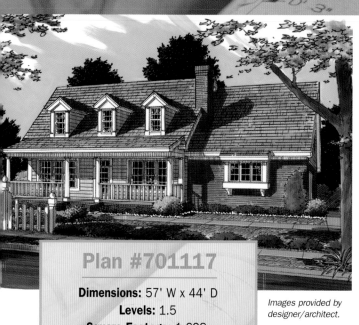

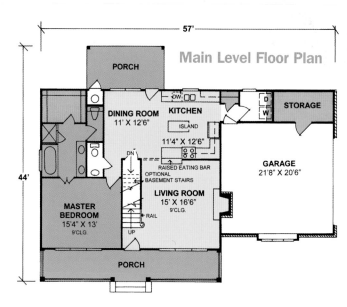

57'

44'

PORCH

DINING ROOM
11' X 12'6"

KITCHEN
ISLAND
11'4" X 12'6"

DW

D W

STORAGE

GARAGE
21'8" X 20'6"

RAISED EATING BAR
OPTIONAL
BASEMENT STAIRS

DN

LIVING ROOM
15' X 16'6"
9'CLG.

RAIL

UP

MASTER
BEDROOM
15'4" X 13'
9'CLG.

PORCH

*Images provided by
designer/architect.*

## Plan #701117

**Dimensions:** 57' W x 44' D
**Levels:** 1.5
**Square Footage:** 1,628
**Main Level Sq. Ft.:** 1,101
**Upper Level Sq. Ft.:** 527
**Bedrooms:** 3
**Bathrooms:** 2½
**Foundation:** Slab; basement for fee
**Material List Available:** Yes
**Price Category:** C

**Upper Level
Floor Plan**

*Copyright by
designer/architect.*

RAIL
DN

BEDROOM 2
13' X 11'

BEDROOM 3
13' X 11'

FUTURE
BONUS ROOM
21'8" X 16'

DORMER
OPEN
TO
BELOW

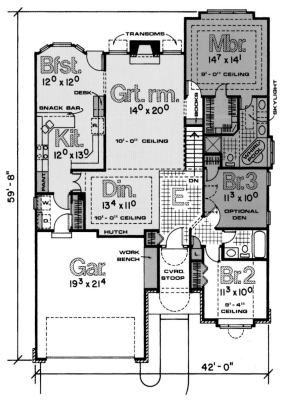

## Plan #701079

**Dimensions:** 42' W x 59'8" D
**Levels:** 1
**Square Footage:** 1,636
**Bedrooms:** 3
**Bathrooms:** 2
**Foundation:** Basement;
crawl space for fee
**Material List Available:** Yes
**Price Category:** C

*Images provided by
designer/architect.*

59'-8"

TRANSOMS

Bfst.
12⁰ x 12⁰

DESK

SNACK BAR

Kit.
12⁰ x 13⁰

PANT.

W
D

Grt. rm.
14⁰ x 20⁰
10'-0" CEILING

BOOKS

Mbr.
14⁷ x 14¹
9'-0" CEILING

SKYLIGHT

WHIRL
POOL

Din.
13⁴ x 11⁰
10'-0" CEILING

DN

E

Br.3
11³ x 10⁰
OPTIONAL
DEN

HUTCH

Gar.
19³ x 21⁴

WORK
BENCH

CVRD.
STOOP

L

Br.2
11³ x 10⁰
9'-4"
CEILING

42'-0"

*Copyright by designer/architect.*

## Plan #701282

**Dimensions:** 42' W x 48' D
**Levels:** 1.5
**Square Footage:** 1,638
**Main Level Sq. Ft.:** 1,173
**Upper Level Sq. Ft.:** 465
**Bedrooms:** 3
**Bathrooms:** 2½
**Foundation:** Basement
**Material List Available:** Yes
**Price Category:** C

*Images provided by designer/architect.*

**Main Level Floor Plan**

**Upper Level Floor Plan**

*Copyright by designer/architect.*

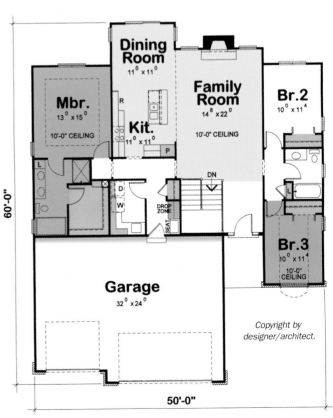

## Plan #701219

**Dimensions:** 50' W x 60' D
**Levels:** 1
**Square Footage:** 1,642
**Bedrooms:** 3
**Bathrooms:** 2
**Foundation:** Basement
**Material List Available:** Yes
**Price Category:** C

*Images provided by designer/architect.*

*Copyright by designer/architect.*

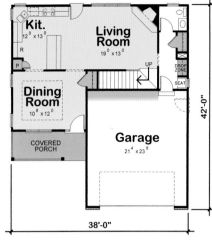

## Main Level Floor Plan

Kit.
12⁰ x 13⁰

Living Room
19⁰ x 13⁰

UP

DROP ZONE

SEAT

Dining Room
10⁸ x 12⁰

Garage
21⁴ x 23⁸

COVERED PORCH

42'-0"

38'-0"

Br.2
11⁰ x 10¹⁰

Mbr.
14⁰ x 13⁰

WIC

DN

Br.3
11⁰ x 10¹⁰

UNFINISHED STORAGE 85 SQ. FT.

D W

WIC

OPTIONAL UNFINISHED STORAGE 130 SQ. FT.

Mbr.
16⁰ x 13⁰

WIC

### Upper Level Floor Plan
*Copyright by designer/architect.*

### Optional Upper Level Floor Plan

*Images provided by designer/architect.*

CAD FILE AVAILABLE

## Plan #701276

**Dimensions:** 38' W x 42' D

**Levels:** 2

**Square Footage:** 1,649

**Main Level Sq. Ft.:** 807

**Upper Level Sq. Ft.:** 842

**Bedrooms:** 3

**Bathrooms:** 2½

**Foundation:** Basement

**Material List Available:** Yes

**Price Category:** C

---

### Upper Level Floor Plan

Br.2
10⁰ x 11⁶

W/P

LIN

Mbr.
12⁰ x 16⁰

9'-0" CLG.

DN

10'-0" CLG.

OPEN TO BELOW

Br.3
10⁰ x 11⁰

PLANTS

Grt. rm.
18¹ x 14⁰

Bfst.
10⁰ x 12⁵

Kit.
8¹⁰ x 11³

DESK

Din.
10⁰ x 12⁴

Gar.
21³ x 21⁸

COVERED PORCH

40'-0"

44'-0"

### Main Level Floor Plan
*Copyright by designer/architect.*

*Images provided by designer/architect.*

## Plan #701073

**Dimensions:** 44' W x 40' D

**Levels:** 2

**Square Footage:** 1,650

**Main Level Sq. Ft.:** 891

**Upper Level Sq. Ft.:** 759

**Bedrooms:** 3

**Bathrooms:** 2½

**Foundation:** Basement; crawl space for fee

**Material List Available:** Yes

**Price Category:** C

## Plan #701008

**Dimensions:** 62' W x 56' D
**Levels:** 1
**Square Footage:** 1,651
**Bedrooms:** 2
**Bathrooms:** 2
**Foundation:** Basement;
crawl space or slab for fee
**Materials List Available:** Yes
**Price Category:** C

This elegant home is packed with amenities that belie its compact size.

**Features:**

- Ceiling Height: 8 ft.

- Dining Room: The foyer opens into a view of the dining room, with its distinctive boxed ceiling.

- Great Room: The whole family will want to gather around the fireplace and enjoy the views and sunlight streaming through the transom-topped window.

- Breakfast Area: Next to the great room and sharing the transom-topped windows, this cozy area invites you to linger over morning coffee.

- Covered Porch: When the weather is nice, take your coffee through the door in the breakfast area and enjoy this large covered porch.

- Master Suite: French doors lead to this comfortable suite featuring a walk-in closet. Enjoy long, luxurious soaks in the corner whirlpool accented with boxed windows.

*Images provided by designer/architect.*

**Optional Bedroom**

*Copyright by designer/architect.*

SMARTtip

## Finishing Your Fireplace with Tile

An excellent finishing material for a fireplace is tile. Luckily, there are reproductions of art tiles today. Most showrooms carry examples of Arts and Crafts, Art Nouveau, California, Delft, and other European tiles. Granite, limestone, and marble tiles are affordable alternatives to custom stone slabs.

## Plan #701022

**Dimensions:** 46' W x 48' D
**Levels:** 2
**Square Footage:** 1,660
**Main Level Sq. Ft.:** 1,265
**Upper Level Sq. Ft.:** 395
**Bedrooms:** 3
**Bathrooms:** 2½
**Foundation:** Basement
**Materials List Available:** Yes
**Price Category:** C

*Images provided by designer/architect.*

This elegant home is designed for architectural interest and gracious living.

**Features:**

• Ceiling Height: 8 ft. unless otherwise noted.

• Great Room: Family and guests will be drawn to this inviting, sun-filled room with its 13-ft. ceiling and raised-hearth fireplace.

• Formal Dining Room: An angled ceiling lends architectural interest to this elegant room. Alternately, this room can be used as a parlor.

• Master Suite: Corner windows are designed to ease furniture placement. The sun lit whirlpool bath invites you to take time to luxuriate and rejuvenate. There's a double vanity, separate shower, and a walk-in closet.

• Garage: This two bay garage offers plenty of space for storage in addition to parking.

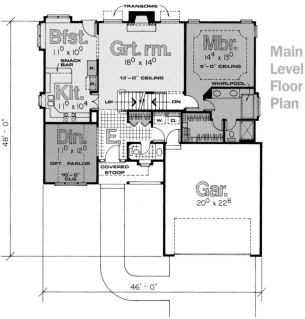

**Main Level Floor Plan**

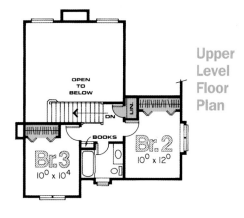

**Upper Level Floor Plan**

*Copyright by designer/architect.*

## Plan #701277

**Dimensions:** 38' W x 42' D
**Levels:** 2
**Square Footage:** 1,660
**Main Level Sq. Ft.:** 807
**Upper Level Sq. Ft.:** 853
**Bedrooms:** 3
**Bathrooms:** 2½
**Foundation:** Basement
**Material List Available:** Yes
**Price Category:** C

*Images provided by designer/architect.*

You'll fall in love with the spacious feeling of this home— perfect for a growing family.

**CAD FILE AVAILABLE**

**Features:**

• Living Room: This expansive living room, complete with a fireplace, is great for entertaining guests or for down time with the family.

• Kitchen: Connected to the living room, this kitchen is perfect for the home cook to get work done while still keeping an eye on the kids.

• Dining Room: This large and conveniently located dining room is perfect for holiday dinners. The room opens out to a covered porch, ideal for great meals outside or after-dinner chats.

• Master Suite: This large master suite is located close to the secondary bedrooms, so it is easy to check up on little ones. The private bath boasts dual sinks and a large tub for relaxing.

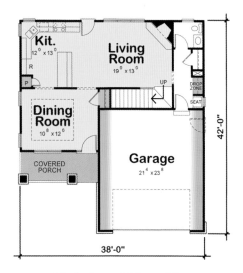

**Main Level Floor Plan**

**Upper Level Floor Plan**

*Copyright by designer/architect.*

## Plan #701004

**Dimensions:** 55'4" W x 48' D
**Levels:** 1
**Square Footage:** 1,666
**Bedrooms:** 3
**Bathrooms:** 2
**Foundation:** Basement; crawl space or slab for fee
**Materials List Available:** Yes
**Price Category:** C

An efficient floor plan and plenty of amenities create a luxurious lifestyle.

**Features:**

• Ceiling Height: 8 ft. except as noted.

• Entry: Enjoy summer breezes on the porch; then step inside the entry where sidelights and an arched transom create a bright, cheery welcome.

• Great Room: The 10-ft. ceiling and the transom-topped windows flooding the room with light provide a sense of spaciousness. The fireplace adds warmth and style.

• Dining Room: You'll usher your guests into this room located just off the great room.

• Breakfast Area: Also located off the great room, the breakfast area offers another dining option.

• Master Suite: The master bedroom is highlighted by a tray ceiling and a large walk-in closet. Luxuriate in the private bath with its sunlit whirlpool, separate shower, and double vanity.

*Images provided by designer/architect.*

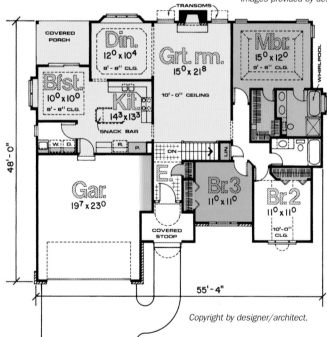

*Copyright by designer/architect.*

SMARTtip

## Carpeting

Install the best underlayment padding available, as well as the highest grade of carpeting you can afford. This will guarantee a feeling of softness beneath your feet and protect your investment for years to come by reducing wear and tear on the carpet.

## Plan #701232

**Dimensions:** 56' W x 48' D

**Levels:** 1

**Square Footage:** 1,672

**Bedrooms:** 3

**Bathrooms:** 2

**Foundation:** Basement

**Material List Available:** Yes

**Price Category:** C

*Images provided by designer/architect.*

*This home, as shown in the photograph, may differ from the actual blueprints. For more detailed information, please check the floor plans carefully.*

*Copyright by designer/architect.*

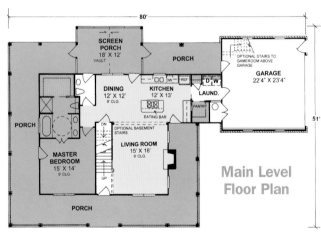

## Plan #701125

**Dimensions:** 80' W x 51' D

**Levels:** 1.5

**Square Footage:** 1,675

**Main Level Sq. Ft.:** 1,241

**Upper Level Sq. Ft.:** 434

**Bedrooms:** 3

**Bathrooms:** 2½

**Foundation:** Slab; basement for fee

**Material List Available:** Yes

**Price Category:** C

*Images provided by designer/architect.*

**Main Level Floor Plan**

**Upper Level Floor Plan**

*Copyright by designer/architect.*

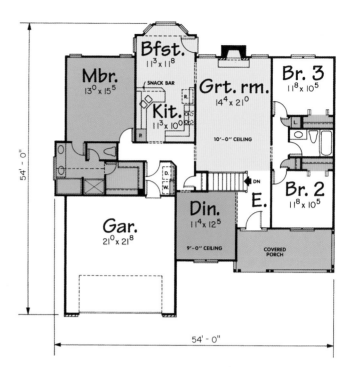

## Plan #701095

**Dimensions:** 54' W x 54' D

**Levels:** 1

**Square Footage:** 1,691

**Bedrooms:** 3

**Bathrooms:** 2

**Foundation:** Basement; crawl space for fee

**Material List Available:** Yes

**Price Category:** C

Bfst. $11^3 \times 11^8$

Mbr. $13^0 \times 15^5$

SNACK BAR

Kit. $11^3 \times 10^0$

Grt. rm. $14^4 \times 21^0$

10'-0" CEILING

Br. 3 $11^8 \times 10^5$

Br. 2 $11^8 \times 10^5$

Din. $11^4 \times 12^5$

9'-0" CEILING

E.

Gar. $21^0 \times 21^8$

COVERED PORCH

DN

54' - 0"

54' - 0"

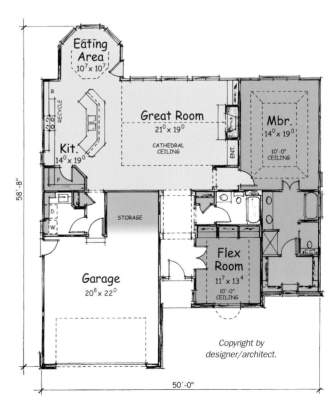

## Plan #701213

**Dimensions:** 50' W x 58'8" D

**Levels:** 1

**Square Footage:** 1,692

**Bedrooms:** 2

**Bathrooms:** 2

**Foundation:** Basement

**Material List Available:** Yes

**Price Category:** C

Eating Area $10^7 \times 10^7$

Great Room $21^0 \times 19^0$

CATHEDRAL CEILING

Mbr. $14^0 \times 19^0$

10'-0" CEILING

RECYCLE

Kit. $14^0 \times 19^0$

STORAGE

Garage $20^8 \times 22^0$

Flex Room $11^7 \times 13^4$

10'-0" CEILING

58' - 8"

50'-0"

## Plan #701191

**Dimensions:** 54' W x 45'4" D
**Levels:** 1.5
**Square Footage:** 1,694
**Main Level Sq. Ft.:** 1,298
**Upper Level Sq. Ft.:** 396
**Bedrooms:** 3
**Bathrooms:** 2½
**Foundation:** Basement
**Material List Available:** Yes
**Price Category:** C

This traditional home is complete with special touches that make it a wonderful place to live.

**Features:**

- Great Room: This centrally located great room with a 10-ft.-high ceiling and a fireplace is the perfect place to gather with guests.

- Kitchen: A wood-framed kitchen adds beauty and grace to any meal. The connecting breakfast room creates a great place to sit and enjoy the sunshine.

- Master Suite: Located on the first floor, this master suite features a large shower, dual sinks, and a large space to relax.

- Secondary Bedrooms: Upstairs, the two secondary bedrooms are wonderful for older children. Siblings can share the bathroom located between the rooms.

**Main Level Floor Plan**

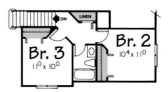

**Upper Level Floor Plan**

## Plan #701146

**Dimensions:** 54' W x 54' D

**Levels:** 1

**Square Footage:** 1,697

**Bedrooms:** 3

**Bathrooms:** 2

**Foundation:** Basement

**Material List Available:** Yes

**Price Category:** C

*This home, as shown in the photograph, may differ from the actual blueprints. For more detailed information, please check the floor plans carefully.*

Enter through the covered stoop into a home that has everything you need on one level; even the bedrooms are easy to reach.

### Features:

- **Great Room:** Your guests and your family will love to be in this room sitting by the fireplace under the 10-ft. ceiling.

- **Kitchen:** This centrally located kitchen is great for entertaining or for late-night snacks.

- **Breakfast Room:** With its cathedral ceiling and large windows, this room is great for drinking your morning coffee and watching the sunrise.

- **Master Suite:** The luxurious amenities, including a 10-ft.-high ceiling, a skylight, and a whirlpool bath, will make you feel like you're at a spa every time you go to your room.

*Images provided by designer/architect.*

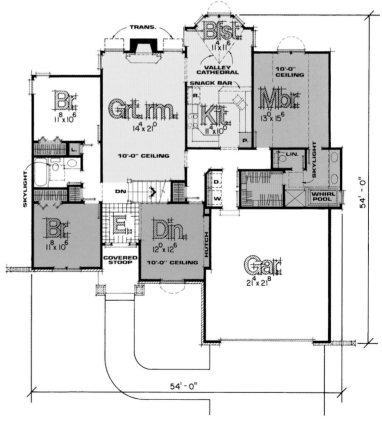

*Copyright by designer/architect.*

## Plan #701315

**Dimensions:** 40' W x 47'8" D
**Levels:** 2
**Square Footage:** 1,699
**Main Level Sq. Ft.:** 1,268
**Upper Level Sq. Ft.:** 431
**Bedrooms:** 3
**Bathrooms:** 2½
**Foundation:** Basement; crawl space or slab for fee
**Material List Available:** Yes
**Price Category:** C

This design is great for lovers of open space and roomy entertaining areas.

CAD FILE AVAILABLE

**Features:**

- Family Room: Guests can relax by the fireplace while enjoying the wonderful aromas drifting from the kitchen.

- Kitchen: This kitchen is open to the family room and breakfast room, creating the perfect space for when guests come over. An island provides space for food or drinks.

- Master Suite: A 10-ft.-high step ceiling and massive walk-in closet make this room enjoyable and relaxing.

- Secondary Bedrooms: Upstairs, two additional bedrooms share a bathroom and a large computer area for homework.

*This home, as shown in the photograph, may differ from the actual blueprints. For more detailed information, please check the floor plans carefully.*

*Images provided by designer/architect.*

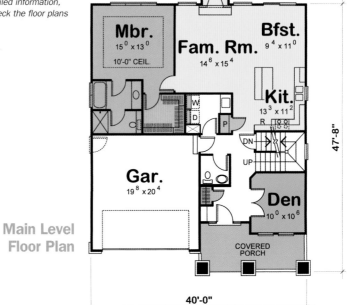

**Main Level Floor Plan**

**Upper Level Floor Plan**

*Copyright by designer/architect.*

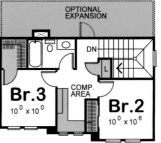

## Plan #701173

**Dimensions:** 46' W x 41'4" D
**Levels:** 2
**Square Footage:** 1,700
**Main Level Sq. Ft.:** 904
**Upper Level Sq. Ft.:** 796
**Bedrooms:** 3
**Bathrooms:** 2½
**Foundation:** Basement
**Material List Available:** Yes
**Price Category:** C

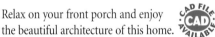

Relax on your front porch and enjoy the beautiful architecture of this home.

### Features:

- **Porch:** A large covered porch welcomes visitors to the home and provides a wonderful space for relaxing on a warm summer day.

- **Great Room:** This great room invites guests into the house and provides space for relaxing in front of the fireplace before going to the attached dining room.

- **Kitchen:** This U-shaped kitchen provides ample counter space for the family chef to create everyone's favorite dish. The snack bar is a great place to put appetizers or park little helpers in the kitchen.

- **Master Suite:** This master suite features a whirlpool bath, dual sinks, a large walk-in closet, and a 9-ft.-high ceiling.

*Images provided by designer/architect.*

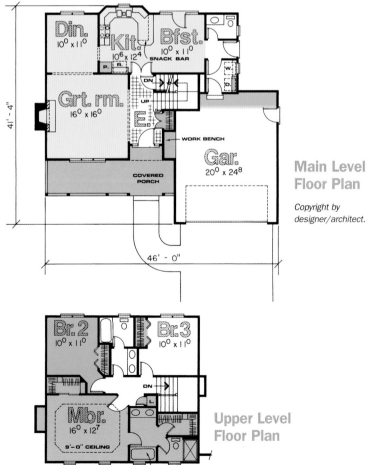

**Main Level Floor Plan**

*Copyright by designer/architect.*

**Upper Level Floor Plan**

# Plan #701159

**Dimensions:** 53'4" W x 54'10" D
**Levels:** 1
**Square Footage:** 1,710
**Bedrooms:** 3
**Bathrooms:** 2
**Foundation:** Basement
**Material List Available:** Yes
**Price Category:** C

This one-story plan features many luxurious amenities usually reserved for larger homes.

**Features:**

- **Dining Room:** With its 10-ft. ceilings and ample floor plan, this dining room offers spacious elegance.

- **Breakfast Room:** Sunlight floods through the windows of this breakfast room, a perfect spot for a leisurely cup of coffee or a quick bite at the snack bar.

- **Master Suite:** You'll never want to leave this roomy oasis, complete with huge walk-in closet, whirlpool bath, skylight, and 9-ft. step ceiling.

- **Optional Room:** This third bedroom can be transformed into your choice of den, home office, or sunroom.

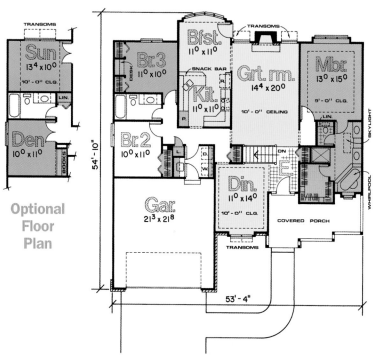

## Plan #701264

**Dimensions:** 52' W x 50' D
**Levels:** 1
**Square Footage:** 1,719
**Bedrooms:** 3
**Bathrooms:** 2
**Foundation:** Basement
**Material List Available:** Yes
**Price Category:** C

If you need a three-bedroom home without the extra frills or expense, this efficient plan may be your solution.

*Images provided by designer/architect.*

### Features:

- **Family Room:** The whole family can gather in front of the angled fireplace in this warm and inviting family room.

- **Kitchen:** Open to both the family room and dining room, this kitchen allows the resident chef to cook and serve with ease. The island is perfect for entertaining and everyday meals.

- **Master Suite:** This large master suite has a full bath complete with his and her sinks and a private commode.

- **Secondary Bedrooms:** Located across the hall from the master suite, two secondary bedrooms are perfect for siblings.

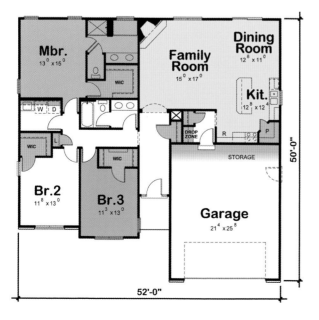

### Optional Floor Plan

BSMT. STAIR OPTION ADDS 87 SQ.FT.

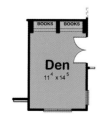

Den
11⁴ x 14⁵

*Copyright by designer/architect.*

## Plan #701071

**Dimensions:** 60' W x 50' D
**Levels:** 1
**Square Footage:** 1,735
**Bedrooms:** 3
**Bathrooms:** 2
**Foundation:** Basement;
crawl space for fee
**Material List Available:** Yes
**Price Category:** C

*Images provided by designer/architect.*

A handsome brick facade and welcoming covered entry with arched trim give this home an elegant modernity. The compact design is misleading, as this home contains the amenities of a larger space.

### Features:

- **Great Room:** With large windows, light from the dining room windows, and a door that opens to the backyard, you are never too removed from cool breezes and singing birds in warm weather. The fireplace and the smell of a holiday meal from the dining room combine to make this space a cozy retreat in winter.

- **Kitchen:** This efficiently designed L-shaped kitchen includes an island and a desk for organizing grocery lists, the family calendar, and mail. Opening into the bright and cheerful breakfast room, the kitchen gleans light from the trio of windows and free space in this adjoining room.

- **Master Suite:** This area features bay windows and a uniquely efficient design. The walk-in closet is placed just within the master bath, and a door separates the toilet and shower from the whirlpool tub and dual sinks.

- **Garage:** An entry to the house from this two-car garage feeds into the laundry room, a clean transition from adventuring outdoors to coming home.

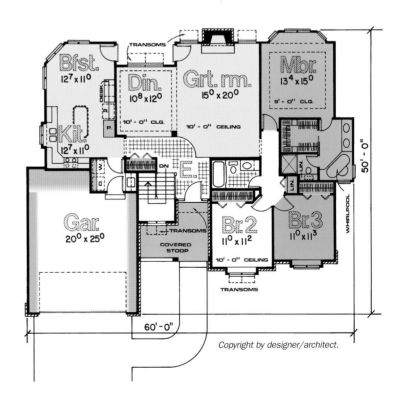

*Copyright by designer/architect.*

## Plan #701269

**Dimensions:** 56' W x 64' D
**Levels:** 1
**Square Footage:** 1,755
**Bedrooms:** 3
**Bathrooms:** 2
**Foundation:** Slab; crawl space or basement for fee
**Material List Available:** Yes
**Price Category:** C

*Images provided by designer/architect.*

This traditional home is great for a young family or for those seeking to scale down.

**Features:**

• Family Room: This spacious family room features a cathedral ceiling and a fireplace nestled between bookshelves and an entertainment center.

• Kitchen: Two kitchen options include an open design with an angled kitchen island or a more private plan offering additional wall space and a straight-angled island.

• Master Suite: This master suite opens up to a private bath with his and her sinks, angled tub, and a roomy closet for all of your needs.

• Secondary Bedrooms: Two secondary bedrooms share a bathroom, perfect for children or guests.

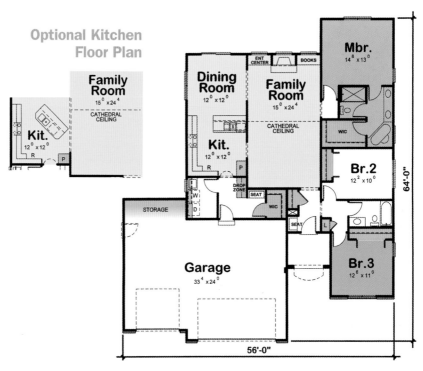

*Copyright by designer/architect.*

## Plan #701183

**Dimensions:** 55'4" W x 49'8" D

**Levels:** 1

**Square Footage:** 1,758

**Bedrooms:** 3

**Bathrooms:** 2

**Foundation:** Basement

**Material List Available:** Yes

**Price Category:** C

*Images provided by designer/architect.*

Enjoy the country feel and flow of this home built for today's family.

**Features:**

- Great Room: This centrally located great room features an 11-ft. ceiling and fireplace to enjoy with family and friends.

- Kitchen: This kitchen plan provides a large workspace, snack bar, and direct access to the breakfast room and great room.

- Breakfast room: This cozy spot for morning coffee features convenient access to the backyard.

- Master Suite: This wonderfully sized master suite has a private bath with a private commode, his and hers sink, and whirlpool bath.

*Copyright by designer/architect.*

## Plan #701006

**Dimensions:** 46' W x 58' D

**Levels:** 1

**Square Footage:** 1,762

**Bedrooms:** 3

**Bathrooms:** 2

**Foundation:** Slab;
crawl space or basement for fee

**Materials List Available:** Yes

**Price Category:** C

*Images provided by designer/architect.*

The entry has a trio of arched openings that leads you to other areas of this amenity-packed home.

**Features:**

- Ceiling Height: 8 ft. except as noted.

- Eating Bar: Conveniently located between the kitchen and family room, this is sure to be a favorite spot for informal entertaining and family gatherings.

- Family room: A wall of windows, a fireplace, and a vaulted ceiling stretching to 11 ft. work together to make this a bright and warm room.

- Kitchen: There's no shortage of counter space in this well-planned kitchen that features a center island in addition to the eating bar.

- Master Suite: Luxuriate at the end of the day in this large bedroom with its decorative tray ceiling and walk-in closet. Enjoy the pampering bath with its sunlit corner whirlpool flanked by vanities.

- Garage: Two bays provide room for cars and plenty of storage as well.

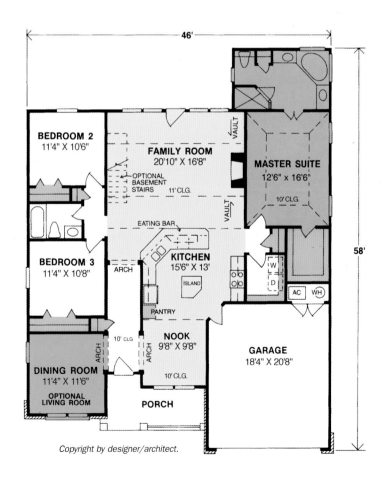

*Copyright by designer/architect.*

# Plan #701248

**Dimensions:** 62' W x 48' D

**Levels:** 1

**Square Footage:** 1,763

**Bedrooms:** 3

**Bathrooms:** 2½

**Foundation:** Basement

**Material List Available:** Yes

**Price Category:** C

*Images provided by designer/architect.*

This lovely home, accented by exterior stonework, is a great combination of traditional details and modern comforts.

**Features:**

- Family Room: After dinner, relax in front of the fireplace in this family room, which features a dramatic cathedral ceiling.

- Kitchen: With its expansive work surfaces, large island, and walk-in pantry, this generous kitchen makes cooking and entertaining a delight.

- Master Suite: Retreat from the cares of the day in this master suite, featuring a 10-ft. step ceiling and capacious corner tub.

- Garage: This three-car garage is large enough for multiple cars and storage.

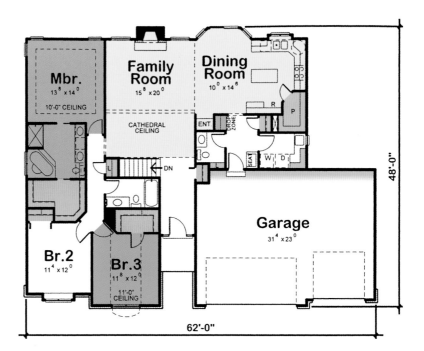

*Copyright by designer/architect.*

## Plan #701301

**Dimensions:** 54' W x 60' D
**Levels:** 1
**Square Footage:** 1,765
**Bedrooms:** 1
**Bathrooms:** 2
**Foundation:** Slab
**Material List Available:** Yes
**Price Category:** C

*Images provided by designer/architect.*

Step into this inviting house, and you'll instantly feel like you've arrived home.

**Features:**

• Dining Room: This uniquely shaped dining room features multiple windows that will delight your guests. The dining room also leads to the covered patio, a perfect spot for alfresco cocktails or dessert.

• Kitchen: This kitchen plan features a large workspace and a square snack bar, perfect for a casual meal with the family.

• Master Suite: This spacious master suite feels even larger, thanks to its 10-ft. ceilings.

• Flex Room: Depending on your family's needs, this room can function as a home office, den, or guest bedroom.

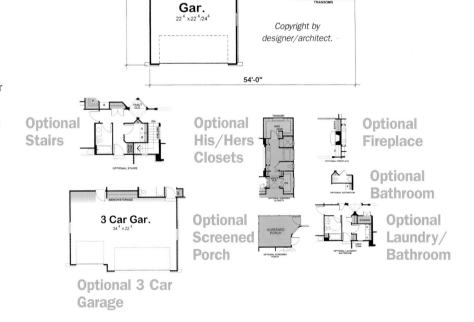

**Optional Stairs**

**Optional His/Hers Closets**

**Optional Fireplace**

**Optional Bathroom**

**Optional Screened Porch**

**Optional Laundry/ Bathroom**

**Optional 3 Car Garage**

## Plan #701062

**Dimensions:** 40'8" W x 46' D
**Levels:** 2
**Square Footage:** 1,768
**Main Level Sq. Ft.:** 905
**Upper Level Sq. Ft.:** 863
**Bedrooms:** 3
**Bathrooms:** 2½
**Foundation:** Basement
**Materials List Available:** Yes
**Price Category:** C

*Images provided by designer/architect.*

You'll love this design if you're looking for a home to complement a site with a lovely rear view.

**Features:**

- Great Room: A trio of lovely windows looks out to the back of this home. The French doors in this room open to the breakfast area for everyone's convenience.

- Kitchen: Designed to suit a gourmet cook, this kitchen includes a roomy pantry and an island with a snack bar.

- Breakfast Area: The boxed window here is perfect for houseplants or a collection of culinary herbs. A door leads to the rear porch, where you'll love to dine in good weather.

- Master Suite: On the upper level, the bedroom features a cathedral ceiling, two walk-in closets, and a window seat. The bath also has a cathedral ceiling and includes dual lavatories, a large dressing area, and a sunlit whirlpool tub.

### Main Level Floor Plan

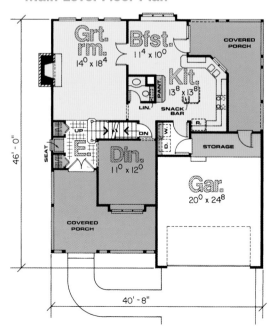

### Upper Level Floor Plan

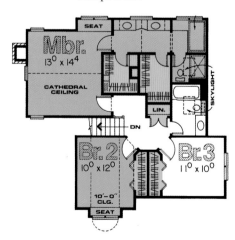

*Copyright by designer/architect.*

## Plan #701088

**Dimensions:** 39'4" W x 46' D

**Levels:** 2

**Square Footage:** 1,771

**Main Level Sq. Ft.:** 866

**Upper Level Sq. Ft.:** 905

**Bedrooms:** 4

**Bathrooms:** 2½

**Foundation:** Basement;
crawl space for fee

**Material List Available:** Yes

**Price Category:** C

*Images provided by designer/architect.*

This beautiful home will be a proud addition to any neighborhood.

**Features:**

• Covered Porch: This outdoor room is the perfect place to share a cold drink with friends and family.

• Family Room: With its multiple windows and cozy fireplace, this expansive family room will be a favorite spot for get-togethers.

• Kitchen: The family chef will enjoy preparing and serving meals in this modern kitchen, which features a snack bar and direct access to the breakfast room.

• Master Suite: Generous closet space, a whirlpool bath, and his and her sinks make this master bedroom a welcoming place to begin and end the day.

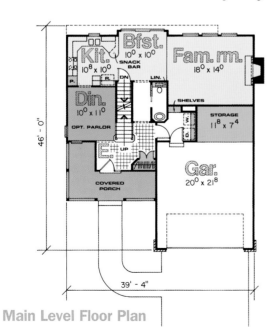

**Main Level Floor Plan**

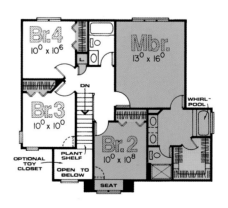

**Upper Level Floor Plan**

*Copyright by designer/architect.*

## Plan #701026

**Dimensions:** 52' W x 51'4" D

**Levels:** 2

**Square Footage:** 1,772

**Main Level Sq. Ft.:** 1,314

**Upper Level Sq. Ft.:** 458

**Bedrooms:** 3

**Bathrooms:** 2½

**Foundation:** Basement

**Materials List Available:** Yes

**Price Category:** C

*Images provided by designer/architect.*

This home features architectural details reminiscence of earlier fine homes.

**Features:**

- Ceiling Height: 8 ft. unless otherwise noted.

- Foyer: This grand entry soars two-stories high. The U-shaped staircase with window leads to a second-story balcony.

- Great Room: You'll be drawn to the impressive views through the triple-arch windows at the front and rear of this room.

- Kitchen: Designed for maximum efficiency, this kitchen is a pleasure to be in. It features a center island, a full pantry, and a desk for added convenience.

- Breakfast Area: This area adjoins the kitchen. Both rooms are flooded with sunlight streaming from a shared bay window.

- Master Suite: The stylish bedroom includes a walk-in closet. Luxuriate in the whirlpool tub at the end of a long day .

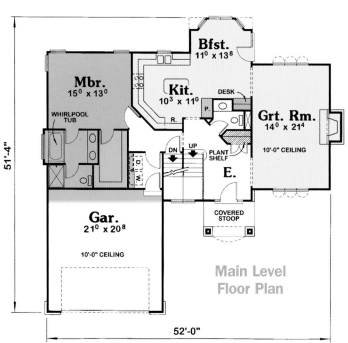

**Main Level Floor Plan**

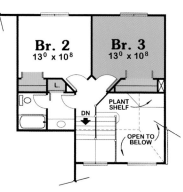

*Copyright by designer/architect.*

**Upper Level Floor Plan**

## Plan #701158

**Dimensions:** 54' W x 48'8" D
**Levels:** 1.5
**Square Footage:** 1,778
**Main Level Sq. Ft.:** 1,348
**Upper Level Sq. Ft.:** 430
**Bedrooms:** 3
**Bathrooms:** 2½
**Foundation:** Basement
**Material List Available:** Yes
**Price Category:** C

*Images provided by designer/architect.*

Walk up the path to this well-designed home, and you'll enter a residence that's just right for you and your family.

**Features:**

- **Great Room:** With its dramatic sloped ceiling and cozy fireplace, this great room is the ideal place to gather with family and guests.

- **Kitchen:** This well-designed kitchen features open access to both the breakfast room and dining room. The snack bar is a wonderful option for meals and entertaining.

- **Master Suite:** The ultimate in luxury, this expansive suite features a bedroom with 10-ft. step ceiling that leads to a bathroom with whirlpool tub, separate toilet room, his and her sinks, and two roomy closets.

- **Additional Bedrooms:** On the second floor, two bedrooms with a shared bath are perfect for children or overnight guests.

**Main Level Floor Plan**

Bfst. 12⁴x10⁸
Grt. rm. 18⁰x16⁰
Mbr. 15⁰x13⁰ 10'-0"CLG.
SNACK BAR
Kit. 12⁴x10⁸
SLOPED CEILING
SHELVES
HUTCH
Din. 12⁰x13⁰
W/P
Gar. 20'x24⁷
COVERED PORCH
48'-8"
54'-0"

**Upper Level Floor Plan**

LIN.
Br.3 12⁴x10¹
Br.2 12⁰x11³

*Copyright by designer/architect.*

## Plan #701037

**Dimensions:** 52' W x 59'4" D
**Levels:** 1
**Square Footage:** 1,782
**Bedrooms:** 3
**Bathrooms:** 2
**Foundation:** Basement
**Materials List Available:** Yes
**Price Category:** C

This home is ideal for families looking for luxury and style mixed with convenience.

**Features:**

- Great Room: This large room is enhanced by the three-sided fireplace it shares with adjacent living areas.

- Hearth Room: Enjoy the fireplace here, too, and decorate to emphasize the bayed windows.

- Kitchen: This kitchen was designed for efficiency and is flooded with natural light.

- Breakfast Area: Picture-awing windows are the highlight in this area.

- Master Suite: A boxed ceiling and walk-in closet as well as a bath with a double-vanity, whirlpool tub, shower, and window with a plant ledge make this suite a true retreat.

- Bedrooms: These lovely bedrooms are served by a luxurious full bath.

*Images provided by designer/architect.*

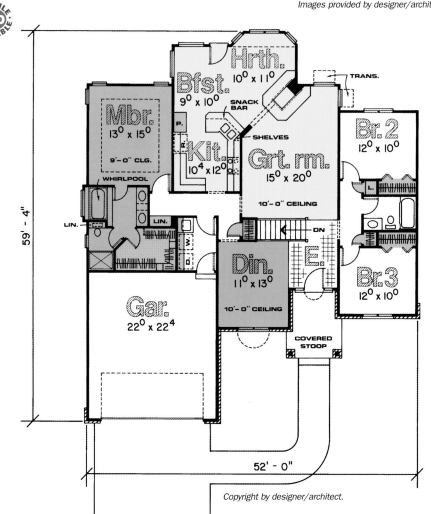

*Copyright by designer/architect.*

# Plan #701175

**Dimensions:** 50' W x 48' D
**Levels:** 1.5
**Square Footage:** 1,788
**Main Level Sq. Ft.:** 1,191
**Upper Level Sq. Ft.:** 597
**Bedrooms:** 4
**Bathrooms:** 2½
**Foundation:** Basement
**Material List Available:** Yes
**Price Category:** C

*Images provided by designer/architect.*

Thoughtful details both inside and out make this home a welcoming place for family and friends.

**Features:**

- Covered Porch: This porch provides a relaxing vantage point for watching the children play in the yard or simply unwinding after a long day.

- Kitchen: Filled with both storage and workspace, this kitchen is designed to be both efficient and elegant. The snack bar opens to the breakfast room, ideal for morning coffee and casual family meals.

- Master Suite: This secluded master suite will be your private oasis, thanks to its 9-ft. ceiling, whirlpool tub, private commode, his and her sinks, and walk-in closet.

- Secondary Bedrooms: Upstairs, you can use these three additional rooms bedrooms, home office space, or whatever your needs require.

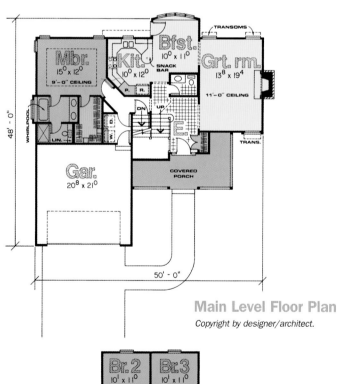

**Main Level Floor Plan**

*Copyright by designer/architect.*

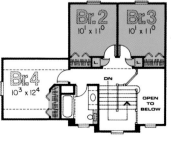

**Upper Level Floor Plan**

# Choosing Kitchen Cabinets

**W**ho can't relate to this scenario: you turn on the oven to preheat it, but wait, did you take out the large roasting pan first? How about the lasagna dish, muffin tins, pizza stone, and cookie sheets that are in there, too? Now where can you put everything that was in the oven while the casserole is baking, and the countertop is laden with the rest of tonight's dinner ingredients?

The oven, it seems, has become the catch-all for the big, awkward stuff that you can't fit into kitchen cabinets but is just too ugly to display. Besides, the countertop is where you keep the toaster oven, food processor, coffeemaker, canisters, hand mixer, portable TV, notepad, coupon file, bills, hand lotion, car keys, and your vitamins! Wouldn't life be grand if there was a place for everything and everything was in its place? Good cabinetry out-

The following article was reprinted from *The Smart Approach to Home Decorating* (Creative Homeowner 2007).

**Shorter cabinets** directly over the cooktop and sink open up the room, provide a safe distance between cabinetry and heat, and allow for decorative lighting in the form of fluorescent sconces, opposite.

**To break up the monotony** of cabinets, install some alternative storage, such as these drawer-like baskets. Take advantage of the easy access by filling them with things you use often, left.

fitted with an assortment of organizing options can help you there. It can make your kitchen more efficient and a whole lot neater while establishing a style, or "look," for the room. Keep in mind, however, that cabinetry will also consume about 40 percent of your remodeling budget, according to the NKBA. So before making any expensive decisions—or costly mistakes—investigate all of the various cabinetry options that are available to you.

## Cabinet Construction

Basically, cabinets are constructed in one of two ways: framed or frameless. Framed cabinets have a traditional look, with a full frame across the face of the cabinet box that may show between closed doors. This secures adjacent cabinets and strengthens wider cabinet boxes with a center rail. Hinges on framed cabinets may or may not be visible around doors when they are closed. The door's face may be ornamented with raised or recessed panels, trimmed or framed panels, or a framed-glass panel with or without muntins (the narrow vertical and horizontal strips of wood that divide panes of glass).

Frameless cabinets—also known as European-style cabinets, although American manufacturers also make them—are built without a face frame and sport a clean, contemporary look.

There's no trim or molding with this simple design. Close-fitting doors cover the entire front of the box; no ornamentation appears on the face of the doors; and hinges are typically hidden inside the cabinet box.

Choosing one type over another is generally a matter of taste, although framed units offer slightly less interior space. But the quality of construction is a factor that should always be taken into consideration. How do you judge it? Solid wood is too expensive for most of today's budgets, but it might be used on just the doors and frames. More typical is plywood box construction, which offers good structural support and solid wood on the doors and frames. To save money, cabinetmakers sometimes use strong plywood for support elements, such as the box and frame, and medium-density fiberboard for other parts, such as doors and drawer fronts. In yet another alternative, good-quality laminate cabinets can be made with high-quality, thick particleboard underneath the laminate finish.

There are other things to look for in cabinet construction. They include dovetail or mortise-and-tenon joinery and solidly mortised hinges. Also, make sure that the interior of every cabinet is well finished, with adjustable shelves that are a minimum $\frac{5}{8}$ inch thick to prevent bowing.

Unless you have the time and skill to build the cabinets yourself or can hire someone else to do it, you'll have to purchase them in one of four ways. Knockdown cabinetry (also known as RTA, ready to assemble) is shipped flat and, sometimes, unfinished because you put the pieces together. Stock cabinetry comes in standard sizes but limited styles and colors; it is often available on the spot or can be delivered quickly. Like stock, semi-custom cabinetry comes in standard styles, but it is manufactured to fit a homeowner's specific size and finish needs. Custom cabinetry is not limited in terms of style or size because it is built to the designer's specifications.

## Cabinet Accessories & Options

Most people would agree that no matter how much storage space they have, they need even more. The problem often isn't the amount, it's the inaccessible placement and inefficient configuration of the storage space. One of the greatest benefits today's designers and manufacturers offer is fitted and accessorized interiors that maximize even the smallest nook and cranny inside cabinets and drawers. These accommodations not

**Color makes all the difference** in a room. Here, a variety of creamy colors throughout the kitchen adds personality. Pretty green and blue cabinets are a nice change from plain white.

**An updated country style,** cabinets with sleeker lines and elegant granite counters intermingle here with the usual down-home charm and informal mix of woods and hardware.

only expand the use of space, but increase convenience and accessibility. Among them are the following:

**Appliance Garages.** Appliance garages make use of dead space in a corner, but they can be installed anywhere in the vertical space between the wall-mounted cabinet and the countertop. A tambour (rolltop) door hides small appliances such as a food processor or anything else you want within reach but hidden from view. This form of minicabinet can be equipped with an electrical outlet and can even be divided into separate sections to store more than one item. Reserve part of the appliance garage for cookbook storage, or outfit it with small drawers for little items or spices. Customize an appliance garage any way you like.

**Lazy Susans and Carousel Shelves.** These rotating shelves maximize dead corner storage and put items such as dishes or pots and pans within easy reach. A Lazy Susan rotates 360 degrees, so just spin it to find what you're looking for. Carousel shelves, which attach to two right-angled doors, rotate 270 degrees; open the doors and the shelves, which are actually attached to the doors, put any item within hand reach. Pivoting shelves are a variation on the carousel design and may or may not be door-mounted. In addition, units may be built into taller cabinets, creating a pantry that can store a lot in a small amount of space.

**Fold-Down Mixer Shelf.** This spring-loaded shelf swings up and out of a base cabinet for use, then folds down and back

**These custom cabinets** add unique options, such as pullout storage for dish linens and angled cabinets that make use of small spaces.

into the cabinet when the mixer is no longer needed, which reduces clutter by keeping the countertop clear of appliances.

**Slide-Outs and Tilt-Outs.** Installed in base cabinets, slide-out trays and racks store small appliances, linens, cans, or boxed items, while slide-out bins are good for holding onions, potatoes, grains, pet food, or potting soil—even garbage or recycling containers. A tilt-out tray is located in the often-wasted area just below the lip of the countertop in front of the sink and above base cabinet doors. It looks like a drawer but tilts open to provide a neat nook for sponges and scouring pads that look messy when left on the counter.

**Built-in Pantry Units.** These fold-out or slide-out units can be fitted into narrow areas that might otherwise remain wasted. Store dry or canned goods here. Fold-out units have door-mounted shelves and an in-cabinet shelf that pivots; slide-out units fit multiple shelves in a cabinet.

In addition to these options, check out everything that a cabinet manufacturer has to offer to make the most of a cabinet's storage capacity. Other items to look for include special racks for trays and cookie sheets, drawer inserts for organizing spices and utensils, watertight recycling bins, wine racks, fold-down recipe book rests, sliding pot racks, built-in canister drawers, and plate racks.

**Unique two-toned cabinetry** adds interest in a country kitchen, left. The appliances are integrated with the same two-toned panels and the hardware echoes the geometric design.

**Glass-fronted bins** are a colorful and convenient way to store pasta and dried beans, opposite bottom left.

**Personalize your kitchen** with cabinets made from exotic wood and finished with a custom-mixed high-gloss lacquer, opposite bottom right.

**Cabinetry** with the look of fine furniture integrates this kitchen almost seamlessly into an adjacent living space, below.

If you decide to make do with your existing cabinets, consider refitting the interiors with cabinet organizers. These plastic, plastic-coated wire, or enameled-steel racks and hangers are widely available at department stores and home centers.

Beware of the temptation to over-specialize your kitchen storage. Sizes and needs for certain items change, so be sure to allot at least 50 percent of your kitchen's storage to standard cabinets with one or more movable shelves.

## The Decorative Role of Cabinets

The look you create in your kitchen will be largely influenced by the cabinetry you select. Finding a style that suits you and how you will use your new kitchen is similar to shopping for furniture. In fact, don't be surprised to see many furniture details dressing up the cabinets on view in showrooms and home centers today.

Besides architectural elements such as fluted pilasters, corbels, moldings, and bull's-eye panels, look for details such as fretwork, rope motifs, gingerbread trim, balusters, composition ornamentation (it looks like carving), even footed cabinets that mimic freestanding furniture pieces.

If your taste runs toward less-fussy design, you'll also find handsome door and drawer styles that feature minimal or no decoration. Woods and finishes are just as varied, and range from informal looks in birch, oak, ash, and maple to rich mahogany and cherry. Laminate finishes, though less popular than they were a decade ago, haven't completely disappeared from the marketplace, but an array of colors has replaced the once-ubiquitous almond and white finishes.

## Color

Color is coming on strong on wood cabinetry, too. Accents in one, two, or more hues are pairing with natural wood tones. White-painted cabinets take on a warmer glow with tinted shades of this always popular neutral. Special "vintage" finishes, such as translucent color glazes, continue to grow in popularity, as do distressed finishing techniques, such as wire brushing and rubbed-through color that add both another dimension and the appeal of handcraftmanship, even on mass-produced items. Contemporary kitchens, which historically favor an all-white palette, are warming up with earthier neutral shades, less sterile off-whites, and wood.

If you're shy about using color on such a high-ticket item as cabinetry, try it as an accent on molding, door trim, or island cabinetry. Just as matched furniture suites have become passé in other rooms of the house, the same is true for the kitchen, where mixing several looks can add sophistication and visual interest.

## Hardware

Another way to emphasize your kitchen's decorative style is with hardware. From exquisite reproductions in brass, pewter, wrought iron, or ceramic to handsome bronze, chrome, nickel, glass, steel, plastic, rubber, wood, or stone creations, a smorgasbord of shapes and designs is available. Some pieces are highly polished; others are matte-finished, smooth, or hammered. Some are abstract or geometrical; others are simple, elegant shapes. Whimsical designs take on the forms of animals or teapots, vegetables or flowers. Even just one or two great-looking door or drawer pulls can be showstoppers in a kitchen that may otherwise be devoid of much personality. Like mixing cabinet finishes, a combination of two hardware styles—perhaps picked up from other materials in the room—makes a big design statement. As the famed architect Mies Van der Rohe once stated, "God is in the details," and the most perfect detail in your new kitchen may be the artistic hardware that you select.

Besides looks, consider the function of a pull or knob. You have to be able to grip it easily and comfortably. If your fingers or hands get stiff easily, select C- or U-shaped pulls. If you like a knob, try it out in the showroom to make sure it isn't slippery or awkward when you grab it. Knobs and pulls can be inexpensive if you can stick to unfinished ones that you can paint in an accent color picked up from the tile or wallpaper. If you don't plan to buy new cabinets, changing the hardware on old ones can redefine their style. The right knob or pull can suggest any one of a number of vintage looks or decorative styles from Colonial to Victorian to Arts and Crafts to Postmodern.

**This cabinet color,** opposite, was chosen to echo one of the colors in the granite countertop and backsplash.

**Satin-finish hardware** looks great against paint with a soft metallic sheen, while the center of each handle reflects the granite countertop, top left.

**Unique braided handles** personalize plain cabinetry, top right.

**The homeowner matched** this pattern in the adjacent accessories. Adding natural-wood accents, such as these drawer handles, helps balance the traditional and modern styles that are both in play in this kitchen, below.

## Plan #701084

**Dimensions:** 55'4" W x 56' D
**Levels:** 1
**Square Footage:** 1,806
**Bedrooms:** 3
**Bathrooms:** 2
**Foundation:** Basement;
crawl space for fee
**Material List Available:** Yes
**Price Category:** D

*Images provided by designer/architect.*

This brick ranch will be the best-looking home in the neighborhood.

**Features:**

• Great Room: This area is a great place to gather with family and friends. The 10-ft.-high ceiling and arched windows make this room bright and airy. On cold nights, gather by the warmth of the fireplace.

• Dining Room: A column off the entry defines this formal dining area. Arched windows and a 10-ft.-high ceiling add to the elegance of the space.

• Kitchen: This island kitchen will inspire the chef in the family to create a symphony at every meal. The triple window in the adjoining breakfast area floods this area with natural light.

• Master Suite: Located on the opposite side of the home from the secondary bedrooms, this private area features a 10-ft.-high ceiling in the sleeping area. The master bath boasts a compartmentalized lavatory and shower area in addition to dual vanities and a walk-in closet.

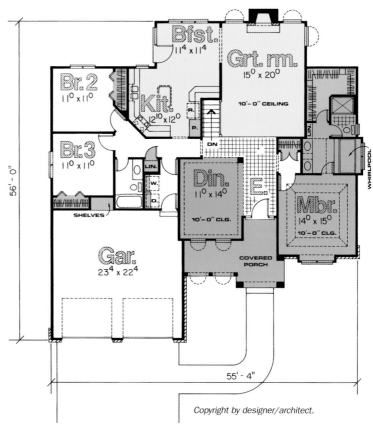

*Copyright by designer/architect.*

## Plan #701224

**Dimensions:** 61' W x 62' D
**Levels:** 1
**Square Footage:** 1,807
**Bedrooms:** 2
**Bathrooms:** 2
**Foundation:** Basement
**Material List Available:** Yes
**Price Category:** D

An abundance of clever design features help make this a residence that conveys both comfort and elegance.

**Features:**

- Kitchen: A home chef's dream, this kitchen is open to the dining room and family room. A center island serves as a spot for entertaining or quick weeknight meals, while the walk-in pantry holds all of your cooking staples.

- Family Room: Family and friends will enjoy gathering around the corner fireplace in this family room, which features a dramatic 10 ft. ceiling.

- Sunroom: Located off the family room, this cheerful sunroom provides year-round light and warmth.

- Master Suite: With its 10 ft. ceiling and his-and-hers sinks, this bedroom is the ideal spot for unwinding after a long day.

*Images provided by designer/architect.*

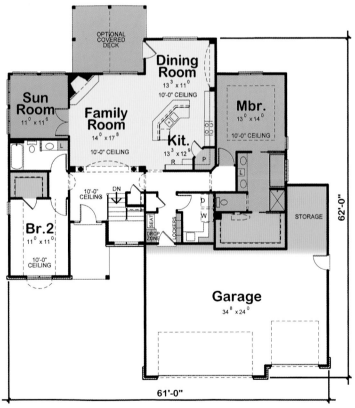

*Copyright by designer/architect.*

## Plan #701031

**Dimensions:** 64' W x 44' D
**Levels:** 1
**Square Footage:** 1,808
**Bedrooms:** 3
**Bathrooms:** 2½
**Foundation:** Basement
**Materials List Available:** Yes
**Price Category:** D

*Images provided by designer/architect.*

You'll love the way that natural light pours into this home from the gorgeous windows you'll find in room after room.

**Features:**

- Great Room: You'll notice the bayed, transom-topped window in this lovely great room as soon as you step into the home. A wet-bar makes the room a natural place for entertaining, and the see-through fireplace makes it cozy on chilly days and winter evenings.

- Kitchen: This well-designed kitchen will be a delight for everyone who cooks here, not only because of the ample counter and cabinet space but also because of its location in the home.

- Master Suite: Angled ceilings in both the bedroom and the bathroom of this suite make it feel luxurious, and the picturesque window in the bedroom gives it character. The bath includes a corner whirlpool tub where you'll love to relax at the end of the day.

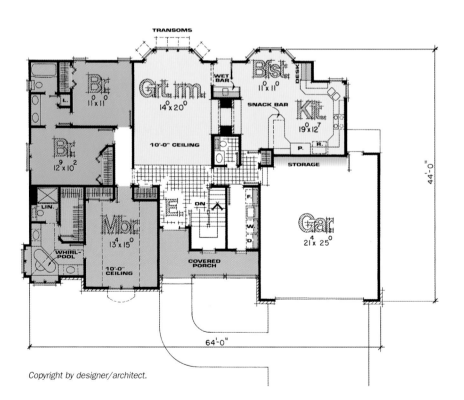

*Copyright by designer/architect.*

## Plan #701316

**Dimensions:** 50' W x 48' D

**Levels:** 2

**Square Footage:** 1,818

**Main Level Sq. Ft.:** 1,302

**Upper Level Sq. Ft.:** 516

**Bedrooms:** 3

**Bathrooms:** 2½

**Foundation:** Basement

**Materials List Available:** Yes

**Price Category:** D

*Images provided by designer/architect.*

Offering plenty of architectural style, this home is designed with the busy modern lifestyle in mind.

**Features:**

• Ceiling Height: 8 ft. unless otherwise noted.

• Great Room: This is sure to be the central gathering place of the home with its volume ceiling, abundance of windows, and its handsome fireplace.

• Kitchen: This convenient and attractive kitchen includes a snack bar that will get lots of use for impromptu family meals.

• Breakfast Area: Joined to the kitchen by the snack bar, this breakfast area will invite you to linger over morning coffee. It includes a pantry and access to the backyard.

• Master Bedroom: This private retreat offers the convenience of a walk-in closet and the luxury of its own whirlpool bath and shower.

• Computer Loft: Designed with the family computer in mind, this loft overlooks a two-story entry.

*Copyright by designer/architect.*

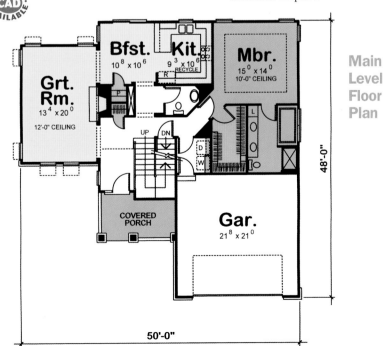

## Plan #701132

**Dimensions:** 53' W x 62' D

**Levels:** 1

**Square Footage:** 1,820

**Bedrooms:** 3

**Bathrooms:** 2

**Foundation:** Basement; crawl space or slab for fee

**Material List Available:** Yes

**Price Category:** D

*Images provided by designer/architect.*

*Copyright by designer/architect.*

**Bonus Area Floor Plan**

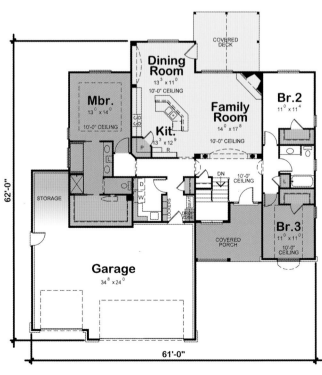

## Plan #701222

**Dimensions:** 61' W x 62' D

**Levels:** 1

**Square Footage:** 1,826

**Bedrooms:** 3

**Bathrooms:** 2

**Foundation:** Basement

**Material List Available:** Yes

**Price Category:** D

*Images provided by designer/architect.*

*Copyright by designer/architect.*

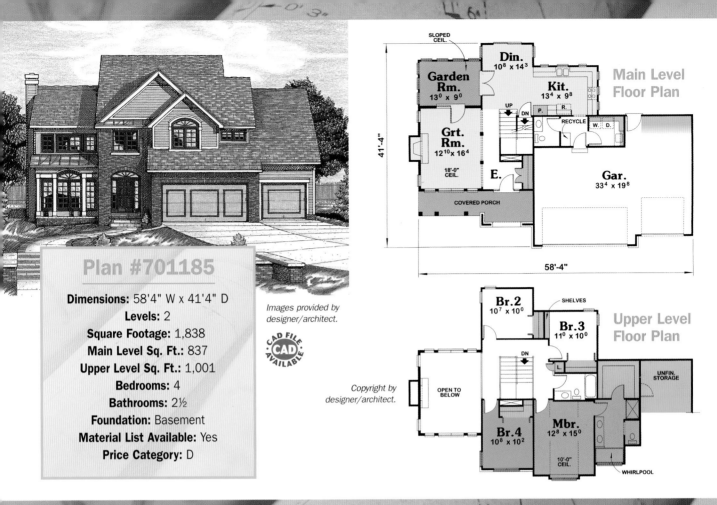

**Main Level Floor Plan**

Garden Rm. 13⁰ x 9⁰

Din. 10⁸ x 14³

Kit. 13⁴ x 9⁸

Grt. Rm. 12¹⁰ x 16⁴
18'-0" CEIL.

SLOPED CEIL.

UP
DN
RECYCLE
P.  R.
W. D.

Gar. 33⁴ x 19⁸

COVERED PORCH

E.

41'-4"

58'-4"

**Upper Level Floor Plan**

Br.2 10⁷ x 10⁰

Br.3 11⁰ x 10⁰

SHELVES

DN

OPEN TO BELOW

UNFIN. STORAGE

Br.4 10⁸ x 10²

Mbr. 12⁸ x 15⁰
10'-0" CEIL.

WHIRLPOOL

*Images provided by designer/architect.*

CAD FILE AVAILABLE

*Copyright by designer/architect.*

## Plan #701185

**Dimensions:** 58'4" W x 41'4" D

**Levels:** 2

**Square Footage:** 1,838

**Main Level Sq. Ft.:** 837

**Upper Level Sq. Ft.:** 1,001

**Bedrooms:** 4

**Bathrooms:** 2½

**Foundation:** Basement

**Material List Available:** Yes

**Price Category:** D

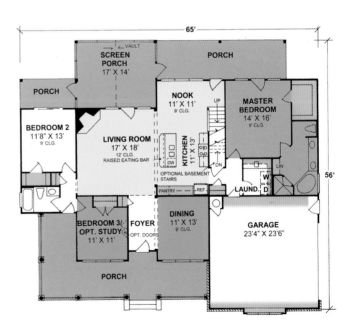

65'

SCREEN PORCH 17' X 14'
VAULT

PORCH

PORCH

NOOK 11' X 11'
9' CLG.

MASTER BEDROOM 14' X 16'
9' CLG

BEDROOM 2 11'8" X 13'
9' CLG.

LIVING ROOM 17' X 18'
12' CLG.
RAISED EATING BAR

KITCHEN 11' X 13'

UP
DN

OPTIONAL BASEMENT STAIRS

PANTRY
REF.

LAUND.
W D
LIN

56'

BEDROOM 3/ OPT. STUDY 11' X 11'

FOYER
OPT. DOORS

DINING 11' X 13'
9' CLG.

GARAGE 23'4" X 23'6"

PORCH

*Copyright by designer/architect.*

## Plan #701209

**Dimensions:** 65' W x 56' D

**Levels:** 1

**Square Footage:** 1,838

**Bedrooms:** 3

**Bathrooms:** 2

**Foundation:** Basement

**Material List Available:** Yes

**Price Category:** D

*Images provided by designer/architect.*

CAD FILE AVAILABLE

## Plan #701121

**Dimensions:** 54' W x 63' D

**Levels:** 1

**Square Footage:** 1,842

**Bedrooms:** 3

**Bathrooms:** 2

**Foundation:** Slab; basement for fee

**Material List Available:** Yes

**Price Category:** D

*Images provided by designer/architect.*

This home's multiple porch areas provide loads of extra living space for relaxing and entertaining.

**Features:**

• Porches: Perch on this home's front porch to enjoy the view or welcome the children home from school. Three connecting porches wrap around the rear of the home, while a screened-in center porch offers added protection from the elements.

Rear View

• Living Room: This breathtaking living room with corner fireplace features multiple windows that overlook the porches.

• Kitchen: The island and eating bar in this gourmet kitchen provide abundant space for entertaining and holiday meals.

• Master Suite: You'll love retreating to this master suite, thanks to its 9-ft. ceiling, direct access to porches, his and her sinks, private commode, and huge walk-in closet.

• Optional Game Room: On the second floor, a generous storage area can be transformed into a game room for family and guests.

**Bonus Area Floor Plan**

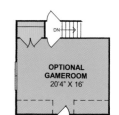

*Copyright by designer/architect.*

## Plan #701040

**Dimensions:** 44' W x 40' D

**Levels:** 2

**Square Footage:** 1,846

**Main Level Sq. Ft.:** 919

**Upper Level Sq. Ft.:** 927

**Bedrooms:** 4

**Bathrooms:** 2½

**Foundation:** Basement; crawl space or slab for fee

**Materials List Available:** Yes

**Price Category:** D

*This home, as shown in the photograph, may differ from the actual blueprints. For more detailed information, please check the floor plans carefully.*

*Images provided by designer/architect.*

You'll love the features and design in this compact but amenity-filled home.

**Features:**

• Entry: A balcony overlooks this two-story entry, where a plant shelf tops the coat closet.

• Great Room: A trio of tall windows points up the large dimensions of this room, which is sure to be the hub of your home. Arrange the

furniture to create a cozy space around the fireplace, or leave it open to the room.

• Kitchen: You'll love to work in this well-designed kitchen area.

• Master Suite: On the second floor, this master suite features a tiered ceiling and two walk-in closets. In the bath, you'll find a double vanity, whirlpool tub, and separate shower.

**Upper Level Floor Plan**

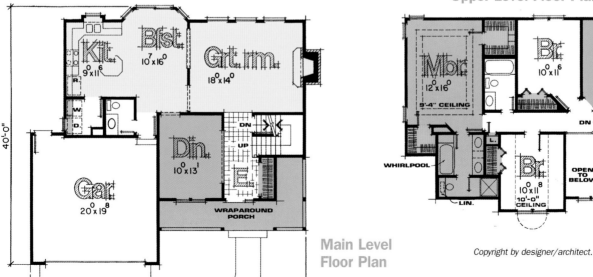

**Main Level Floor Plan**

*Copyright by designer/architect.*

## Plan #701080

**Dimensions:** 62' W x 48' D
**Levels:** 1
**Square Footage:** 1,850
**Bedrooms:** 3
**Bathrooms:** 2
**Foundation:** Basement; crawl space for fee
**Material List Available:** Yes
**Price Category:** D

*Images provided by designer/architect.*

With beautiful architectural details and abundant amenities, this home will steal your heart.

### Features:

- **Kitchen:** Keeping this kitchen cheerful are walls surrounded by transom windows, bringing the morning sun into your home. The kitchen has everything you want, including an island, a pantry, counter space to spare, and a desk area, and it opens directly into the breakfast room.

- **Dining Room:** Separated from the kitchen and breakfast room by a hallway, this dining room can adopt an air of elegance and decorum. It has a built-in hutch and, with the right furniture, can be used for family dinners and small dinner parties alike.

- **Master Suite:** This bedroom, sectioned in two, is simply a dream. Through double doors is a walk-in closet to the left, dual vanities to the front, a skylight above, and a full master bath to the right, equipped with a whirlpool tub, shower stall, and window seat. Here, "staying in" sounds romantic.

- **Secondary Bedrooms:** If three bedrooms are more than you need, Bedroom 2 will work wonderfully as a den. With transom windows bringing in the sunlight and double doors opening to the entryway, this room would be a welcoming place to entertain guests who have just arrived.

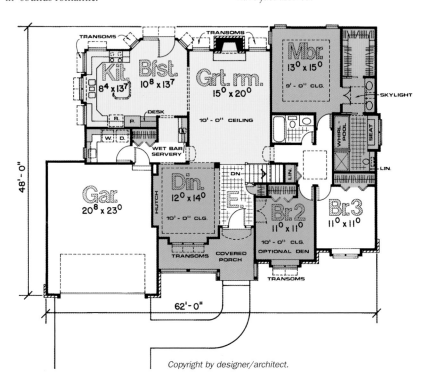

*Copyright by designer/architect.*

## Plan #701182

**Dimensions:** 59'8" W x 42'8" D
**Levels:** 1.5
**Square Footage:** 1,853
**Main Level Sq. Ft.:** 1,285
**Upper Level Sq. Ft.:** 568
**Bedrooms:** 4
**Bathrooms:** 2½
**Foundation:** Basement
**Material List Available:** Yes
**Price Category:** D

*Images provided by designer/architect.*

**Features:**

- Kitchen: This spacious kitchen's central location makes transporting groceries a breeze. The snack bar adds extra dining space and function.

- Master Suite: This large bedroom suite has it all, including his and her sinks, private commode, and gigantic walk-in closet.

- Secondary Bedrooms: On the second floor, three additional bedrooms offer plenty of closet space and a shared bathroom.

- Storage Space: This home plan provides plenty of extra storage space, making it easy to find a place for everything.

The distinctive details of this charming home were designed with your family's needs in mind.

**CAD FILE AVAILABLE**

**Main Level Floor Plan**

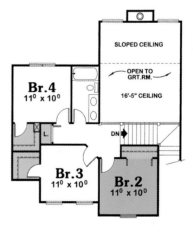

**Upper Level Floor Plan**
*Copyright by designer/architect.*

## Plan #701072

**Dimensions:** 52' W x 45'4" D
**Levels:** 1.5
**Square Footage:** 1,855
**Main Level Sq. Ft.:** 1,297
**Upper Level Sq. Ft.:** 558
**Bedrooms:** 4
**Bathrooms:** 2½
**Foundation:** Basement;
crawl space for fee
**Materials List Available:** Yes
**Price Category:** D

*Images provided by designer/architect.*

If bright, sunny rooms make you happy, you'll love the open design of this beautiful home.

**Features:**

- Great Room: Thanks to its spectacular 13-ft. ceiling and large floor plan, this great room, complete with cozy fireplace, will impress your family and friends.

- Breakfast Room: Large windows allow the sunshine to stream into this comfortable spot, ideal for morning coffee or grabbing a bite on the go.

- Master Suite: This master suite features a large walk-in closet, whirlpool bath, skylight, his and her sinks, and a 9-ft. step ceiling.

- Secondary Bedrooms: Three additional bedrooms with a shared bathroom on the second floor are perfect for siblings.

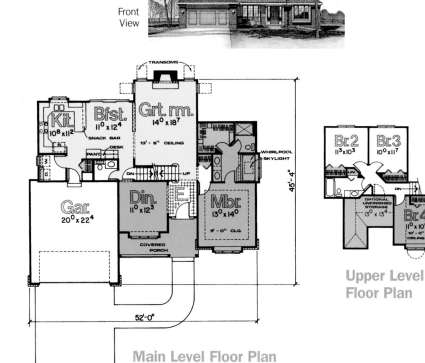

Front View

**Main Level Floor Plan**

**Upper Level Floor Plan**

*Copyright by designer/architect.*

## Plan #701097

**Dimensions:** 52' W x 47'4" D
**Levels:** 1.5
**Square Footage:** 1,858
**Main Level Sq. Ft.:** 1,405
**Upper Level Sq. Ft.:** 453
**Bedrooms:** 3
**Bathrooms:** 2½
**Foundation:** Basement;
crawl space for fee
**Material List Available:** Yes
**Price Category:** D

*Images provided by designer/architect.*

This traditional design incorporates 13-ft. ceilings and all the features you want in your home.

### Features:

• **Great Room:** Entertain your family and friends in this great room–a fireplace and wall of windows make it the perfect place for gatherings.

• **Kitchen:** Cabinets and countertops fill this kitchen, making it easy to store all of your ingredients while providing plenty of work-space for cooking.

• **Master Suite:** This master suite is suited for all of your needs. His and her sinks and a large walk-in closet add practical elements.

• **Secondary Bedrooms:** Two secondary bedrooms are upstairs, next to a large storage space.

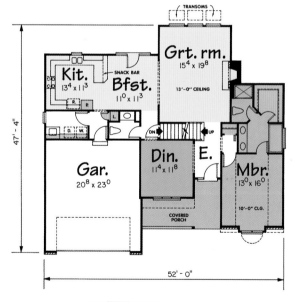

**Main Level Floor Plan**

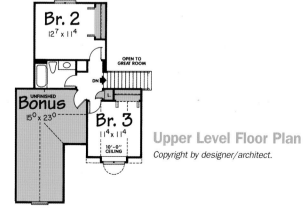

**Upper Level Floor Plan**
*Copyright by designer/architect.*

## Plan #701098

**Dimensions:** 54' W x 45'4" D
**Levels:** 1.5
**Square Footage:** 1,865
**Main Level Sq. Ft.:** 1,301
**Upper Level Sq. Ft.:** 564
**Bedrooms:** 4
**Bathrooms:** 2½
**Foundation:** Basement;
crawl space for fee
**Material List Available:** Yes
**Price Category:** D

*Images provided by designer/architect.*

### Features:

- **Porch:** This porch welcomes you home. It is the perfect spot for relaxing day or night.

- **Breakfast Room:** This breakfast room lets in the morning sunshine while you enjoy a meal at the table or at the breakfast bar. A desk ensures that stray papers and forms stay organized until you need them.

- **Master Suite:** This large master suite features a considerable walk-in closet, his and her sinks, and a separate toilet room.

- **Secondary Bedrooms:** Additional bedrooms are upstairs, the three of them share a bathroom. Also upstairs is a large storage space for those extra items.

This lovely home has an interior designed with daily living in mind, which creates an ideal environment for a growing family.

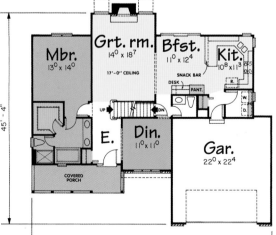

**Main Level Floor Plan**

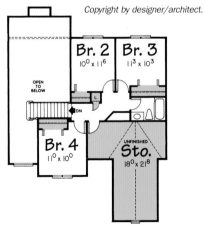

*Copyright by designer/architect.*

**Upper Level Floor Plan**

## Plan #701124

**Dimensions:** 49' W x 60' D
**Levels:** 1.5
**Square Footage:** 1,867
**Main Level Sq. Ft.:** 1,375
**Upper Level Sq. Ft.:** 492
**Bedrooms:** 3
**Bathrooms:** 2½
**Foundation:** Slab; basement for fee
**Material List Available:** Yes
**Price Category:** D

*Images provided by designer/architect.*

You'll be happy to have this magnificent home welcoming you every day.

**Features:**

- **Porches:** The front porch is perfect for relaxing or playing board games with family or friends. The porches in the back are wonderful for entertaining, especially the screened-in porch, which you can use rain or shine.

- **Great Room:** The creative decorator will find inspiration in the open design that encompasses the living room, great room, and dining room. The gorgeous 14-ft. ceiling adds to the beauty of the room and the house as a whole.

- **Master Suite:** This expansive master suite has a 9-ft. ceiling, his and her sinks, and a large closet area.

- **Optional Game Room:** Turn this space in the second floor into an optional game room, which is fun for the kids and the young at heart.

### Main Level Floor Plan

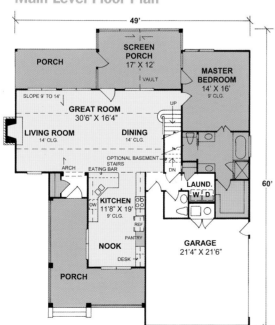

### Upper Level Floor Plan

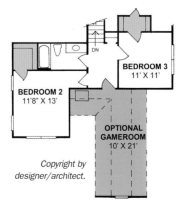

*Copyright by designer/architect.*

## Plan #701010

**Dimensions:** 52' W x 47'4" D

**Levels:** 1.5

**Square Footage:** 1,869

**Main Level Sq. Ft.:** 1,421

**Upper Level Sq. Ft.:** 448

**Bedrooms:** 3

**Bathrooms:** 2½

**Foundation:** Basement

**Materials List Available:** Yes

**Price Category:** D

*Images provided by designer/architect.*

This compact home is packed with all the amenities you'll need for a gracious lifestyle.

**Features:**

- Ceiling Height: 8 ft. except as noted.

- Great Room: A soaring ceiling and six tall transom-topped windows make this a light and airy spot for entertaining.

- Formal Dining Room: This elegant room is ideal for entertaining dinner guests.

- Breakfast Area: This sunny area shares a see-through fireplace with the great room. It's the perfect place to start the day.

- Master Suite: Here are all the features you expect to find in large luxury homes. Wake up to tall, sloped ceilings, and enjoy the corner whirlpool, separate shower, and vanity. A large walk-in closet provides plenty of wardrobe storage.

- Attached Garage: The garage provides two bays of parking plus plenty of storage space.

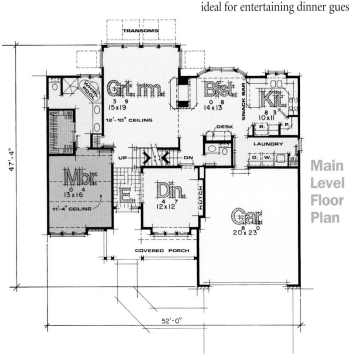

**Main Level Floor Plan**

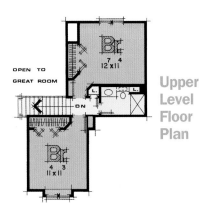

**Upper Level Floor Plan**

*Copyright by designer/architect.*

## Plan #701113

**Dimensions:** 48' W x 48' D

**Levels:** 1.5

**Square Footage:** 1,897

**Main Level Sq. Ft.:** 1,448

**Upper Level Sq. Ft.:** 449

**Bedrooms:** 3

**Bathrooms:** 2½

**Foundation:** Slab; basement for fee

**Material List Available:** Yes

**Price Category:** D

The beautiful architecture of this design will make this home a neighborhood favorite.

*This home, as shown in the photograph, may differ from the actual blueprints. For more detailed information, please check the floor plans carefully.*

*Images provided by designer/architect.*

**Features:**

- **Family Room:** With its amazing 18-ft. vaulted ceiling, this family room will be the envy of all of your neighbors, friends, and family. The large space and corner fireplace make this room perfect for entertaining.

- **Dining Room:** Host the dinner party they'll talk about for weeks in this room. A 12-ft. vaulted ceiling provides a dramatic flair to the room.

- **Kitchen:** This kitchen has everything the family chef would need, and more. It comes complete with an eating bar, a desk, and a butler's pantry for all your cooking and storage needs.

- **Master Suite:** This master suite will make you feel like royalty. A large walk-in closet, a master bath that contains a separate toilet room, and 9-ft. ceiling make it a wonderful room to wake up in every day.

**Main Level Floor Plan**

**Upper Level Floor Plan**

*Copyright by designer/architect.*

## Plan #701140

**Dimensions:** 62' W x 68'8" D

**Levels:** 1

**Square Footage:** 1,899

**Bedrooms:** 2

**Bathrooms:** 2½

**Foundation:** Basement; crawl space or slab for fee

**Material List Available:** Yes

**Price Category:** D

*Images provided by designer/architect.*

This craftsman-style home elegant, but practical enough for your daily life.

**Features:**

• Kitchen: Cook to your heart's content in this kitchen, complete with a large pantry and workspace big enough for your dinner and all the side dishes. The connecting eating area opens out to a covered porch, ideal for meals outside.

• Dining Room: This dining room is wonderful for entertaining loved ones.

• Master Suite: This master suite is perfect for unwinding after a long day. The bedroom has a 10-ft. ceiling, large walk-in closet, his and her sinks, separate toilet room, and large tub.

• Optional Lower Level: Always wanted extra entertainment rooms? This lower level includes a media room, lounge area, and bar — great for guests or your family to relax in and enjoy.

*Copyright by designer/architect.*

## Plan #701001

**Dimensions:** 56' W x 58' D

**Levels:** 1

**Square Footage:** 1,911

**Bedrooms:** 3

**Bathrooms:** 2

**Foundation:** Basement

**Materials List Available:** Yes

**Price Category:** D

*Images provided by designer/architect.*

Detailed, soaring ceilings and top-notch amenities set this distinctive home apart.

**Features:**

- Ceiling Height: 8 ft. except as noted.

- Formal Dining Room: The entry enjoys a pleasing view of this dining room's detailed 12-ft. ceiling and picture window.

- Great Room: At the back of the home, a see-through fireplace in this great room is joined by a built-in entertainment center.

- Hearth Room: This bayed room shares the see-through fireplace with the great room.

- Master Suite: Enjoy the stars and the sun in the private bath's whirlpool and separate shower. The bath features the same decorative ceiling as the dining room.

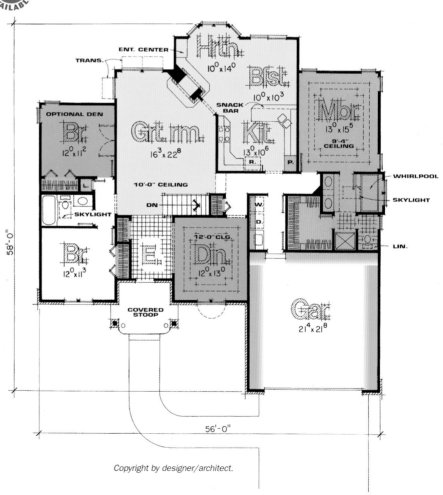

*Copyright by designer/architect.*

Images provided by designer/architect.

CAD FILE AVAILABLE

Copyright by designer/architect.

## Plan #701211

**Dimensions:** 57' W x 58' D

**Levels:** 1

**Square Footage:** 1,915

**Bedrooms:** 3

**Bathrooms:** 2

**Foundation:** Basement

**Material List Available:** Yes

**Price Category:** D

---

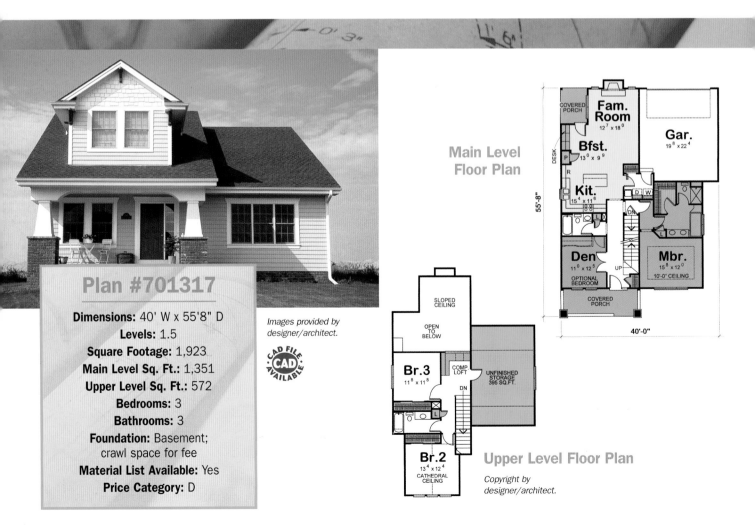

Images provided by designer/architect.

CAD FILE AVAILABLE

**Main Level Floor Plan**

**Upper Level Floor Plan**

Copyright by designer/architect.

## Plan #701317

**Dimensions:** 40' W x 55'8" D

**Levels:** 1.5

**Square Footage:** 1,923

**Main Level Sq. Ft.:** 1,351

**Upper Level Sq. Ft.:** 572

**Bedrooms:** 3

**Bathrooms:** 3

**Foundation:** Basement; crawl space for fee

**Material List Available:** Yes

**Price Category:** D

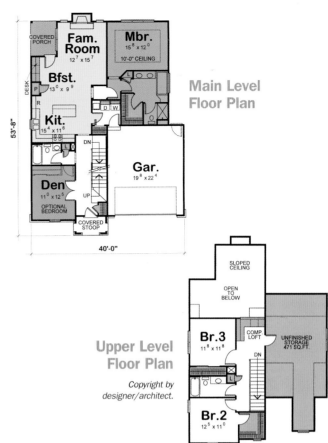

**Main Level Floor Plan**

*Images provided by designer/architect.*

**CAD FILE AVAILABLE**

## Plan #701325

**Dimensions:** 40' W x 53'8" D

**Levels:** 1.5

**Square Footage:** 1,928

**Main Level Sq. Ft.:** 1,356

**Upper Level Sq. Ft.:** 572

**Bedrooms:** 3

**Bathrooms:** 3

**Foundation:** Basement

**Material List Available:** Yes

**Price Category:** D

**Upper Level Floor Plan**

*Copyright by designer/architect.*

---

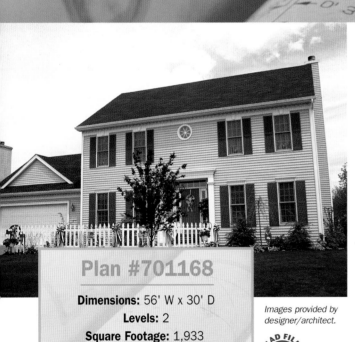

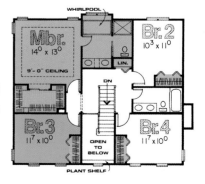

**Main Level Floor Plan**

*Images provided by designer/architect.*

**CAD FILE AVAILABLE**

## Plan #701168

**Dimensions:** 56' W x 30' D

**Levels:** 2

**Square Footage:** 1,933

**Main Level Sq. Ft.:** 941

**Upper Level Sq. Ft.:** 992

**Bedrooms:** 4

**Bathrooms:** 2½

**Foundation:** Basement

**Material List Available:** Yes

**Price Category:** D

**Upper Level Floor Plan**

*Copyright by designer/architect.*

## Plan #701160

**Dimensions:** 64' W x 52' D
**Levels:** 1
**Square Footage:** 1,948
**Bedrooms:** 3
**Bathrooms:** 2½
**Foundation:** Basement
**Material List Available:** Yes
**Price Category:** D

*Images provided by designer/architect.*

*This home, as shown in the photograph, may differ from the actual blueprints. For more detailed information, please check the floor plans carefully.*

This stately and traditional ranch home will be a joy to come home to.

**Features:**

- Great Room: With its 10-ft.-high ceiling and fireplace, this great room is the perfect place to entertain guests or relax after dinner.

- Kitchen: You won't run out of space in this kitchen. It features a center island, wet bar, and pantry room. The attached breakfast room is filled with windows to start your day with sunshine.

- Master Suite: You'll never want to leave this master suite with its expansive walk-in closet, whirlpool bath, separate toilet area, and his and her sinks.

- Secondary Bedrooms: The ample closet space and a shared bathroom make these two extra bedrooms perfect for the kids.

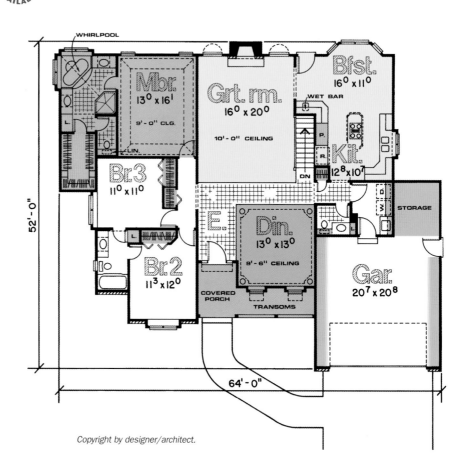

*Copyright by designer/architect.*

## Plan #701302

**Dimensions:** 56'8" W x 53' D

**Levels:** 1

**Square Footage:** 1,948

**Bedrooms:** 1

**Bathrooms:** 2

**Foundation:** Slab

**Material List Available:** Yes

**Price Category:** C

*Images provided by designer/architect.*

This one-story home is beautifully designed to meet your needs.

**Features:**

- Great Room: Located at the heart of the home, this great room is the perfect place to entertain family or guests. Conveniently located next to the kitchen, it opens out to a patio so that the party can spill outdoors if necessary.

- Kitchen: A curved island separates this room from the dining room, creating a perfect place to keep food and drinks for guests. The kitchen features a walk-in pantry and plenty of counter space for all of your food preparation needs.

- Master Suite: Amenities in this master suite include a window seat, a vaulted ceiling, his and her sink, and a spacious walk-in closet.

- Flex Room: This room can serve a number of needs, such as becoming an additional bedroom, a guest room, or a library.

*Copyright by designer/architect.*

## Plan #701127

**Dimensions:** 67' W x 51' D
**Levels:** 1.5
**Square Footage:** 1,980
**Main Level Sq. Ft.:** 1,467
**Upper Level Sq. Ft.:** 513
**Bedrooms:** 3
**Bathrooms:** 2½
**Foundation:** Crawl space;
basement for fee
**Material List Available:** Yes
**Price Category:** D

*Images provided by designer/architect.*

This farmhouse's wide front porch is inviting to friends and neighbors throughout your community.

**Features:**

- Porches: The front porch welcomes visitors to your home, providing ample space to sit, have a drink, and talk. Around the back, two porches provide space for entertaining or relaxing. The screened-in porch is perfect if the weather turns.

- Kitchen: This kitchen is open to the living room and nook, making it wonderful for conversations throughout the rooms or if you need to transport food throughout. The raised eating bar is great for snacks or as a buffet at parties.

- Master Suite: Enjoy the amenities in this master suite, including direct access to the rear porch, a spacious walk-in closet, and his-and-her sinks.

- Study: This flexible room can serve a variety of needs, such as being a home office, a study, or an additional bedroom for children or guests.

## Main Level Floor Plan

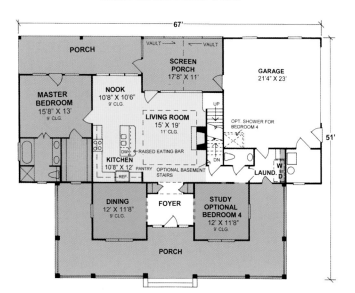

## Upper Level Floor Plan

*Copyright by designer/architect.*

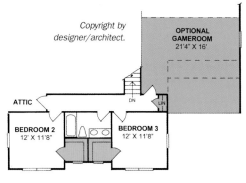

# Plan #701103

**Dimensions:** 62' W x 42'6" D
**Levels:** 1.5
**Square Footage:** 1,984
**Main Level Sq. Ft.:** 1,487
**Upper Level Sq. Ft.:** 497
**Bedrooms:** 3
**Bathrooms:** 2½
**Foundation:** Slab; basement for fee
**Material List Available:** Yes
**Price Category:** D

**Features:**

- Living Room: This two-story gathering area is available for family and friends. The fireplace adds a focal point to the room.

- Kitchen: This peninsula kitchen features a raised bar open to the breakfast area. The breakfast area boasts French doors that lead to the future rear deck.

- Master Suite: Residing on the main level is this beautiful retreat, which boasts a tray ceiling. The master bath features dual vanities, whirlpool tub, and a separate toilet area.

- Upper Level: Two secondary bedrooms are found on this level. A large full bathroom is centrally located for easy access.

A stone and stucco exterior give this home an elegant look.

## Main Level Floor Plan

## Upper Level Floor Plan

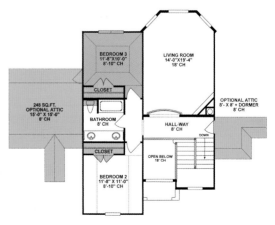

*Copyright by designer/architect.*

## Plan #701220

**Dimensions:** 65' W x 70' D

**Levels:** 1

**Square Footage:** 1,991

**Bedrooms:** 1

**Bathrooms:** 2½

**Foundation:** Slab

**Material List Available:** Yes

**Price Category:** D

*Images provided by designer/architect.*

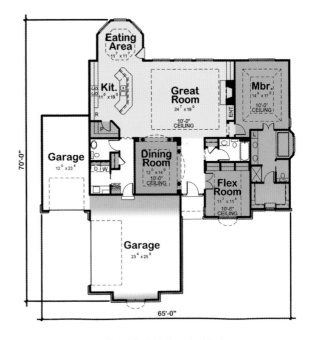

*Copyright by designer/architect.*

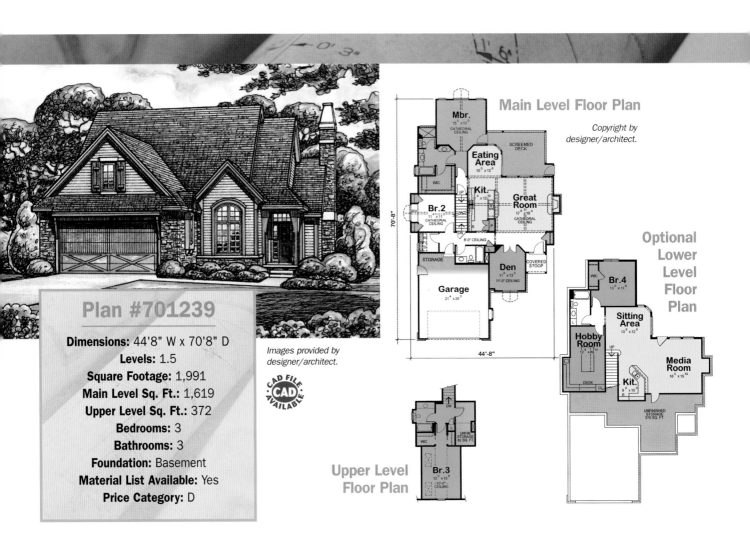

## Plan #701239

**Dimensions:** 44'8" W x 70'8" D

**Levels:** 1.5

**Square Footage:** 1,991

**Main Level Sq. Ft.:** 1,619

**Upper Level Sq. Ft.:** 372

**Bedrooms:** 3

**Bathrooms:** 3

**Foundation:** Basement

**Material List Available:** Yes

**Price Category:** D

*Images provided by designer/architect.*

**Main Level Floor Plan**

*Copyright by designer/architect.*

**Optional Lower Level Floor Plan**

**Upper Level Floor Plan**

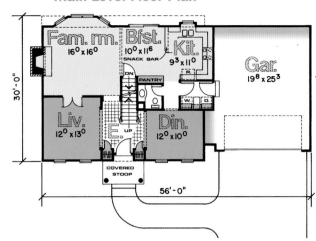

## Main Level Floor Plan

*Images provided by designer/architect.*

## Plan #701076

**Dimensions:** 56' W x 30' D
**Levels:** 2
**Square Footage:** 1,993
**Main Level Sq. Ft.:** 1,000
**Upper Level Sq. Ft.:** 993
**Bedrooms:** 4
**Bathrooms:** 2½
**Foundation:** Basement; crawl space for fee
**Material List Available:** Yes
**Price Category:** D

### Upper Level Floor Plan

*Copyright by designer/architect.*

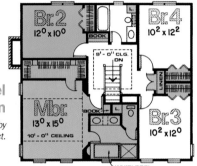

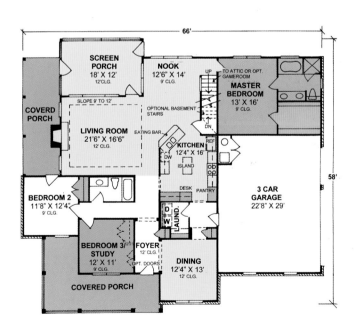

## Plan #701207

**Dimensions:** 66' W x 58' D
**Levels:** 1
**Square Footage:** 1,995
**Bedrooms:** 3
**Bathrooms:** 2
**Foundation:** Basement
**Material List Available:** Yes
**Price Category:** B

*Images provided by designer/architect.*

*This home, as shown in the photograph, may differ from the actual blueprints. For more detailed information, please check the floor plans carefully.*

### Optional Gameroom

*Copyright by designer/architect.*

## Plan #701030

**Dimensions:** 64' W x 50' D
**Levels:** 1
**Square Footage:** 1,996
**Bedrooms:** 2
**Bathrooms:** 2
**Foundation:** Basement;
crawl space for fee
**Materials List Available:** Yes
**Price Category:** D

*Images provided by designer/architect.*

This compact design includes features usually reserved for larger homes and has styling that is typical of more-exclusive home designs.

### Features:

- **Entry:** As you enter this home, you'll see the formal living and dining rooms—both with special ceiling detailing—on either side.

- **Great Room:** Located in the rear of the home for convenience, this great room is likely to be your favorite spot. The fireplace is framed by transom-topped windows, so you'll love curling up here, no matter what the weather or time of day.

- **Kitchen:** Ample counter and cabinet space make this kitchen a dream in which to work.

- **Master Suite:** A tray ceiling and lovely corner windows create an elegant feeling in the bedroom, and two walk-in closets make it easy to keep this space tidy and organized. The private bath has a skylight, corner whirlpool tub, and two separate vanities.

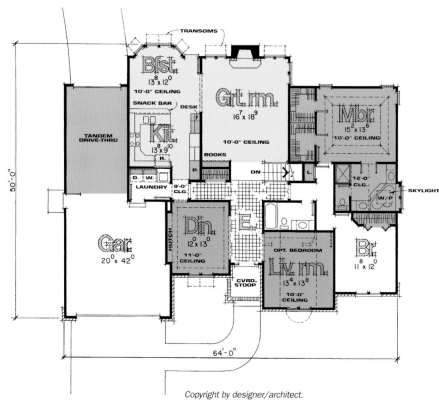

*Copyright by designer/architect.*

## Plan #701187

**Dimensions:** 54' W x 50'8" D
**Levels:** 1.5
**Square Footage:** 1,996
**Main Level Sq. Ft.:** 1,398
**Upper Level Sq. Ft.:** 598
**Bedrooms:** 4
**Bathrooms:** 2½
**Foundation:** Basement
**Material List Available:** Yes
**Price Category:** D

*Images provided by designer/architect.*

If you've been looking for a plan that combines traditional good looks with the comfort of a contemporary home, you'll love this design.

**Features:**

• **Covered Porch:** Greet guests under the shade of this covered porch, where you can sit and chat or watch the children playing in the front yard.

• **Kitchen:** Search no longer for a kitchen that combines space with efficiency. Large

countertops provide a sizeable workspace, while the pantry stores items for later use. The spacious snack bar connects to the breakfast room, where windows allow you to enjoy the sunlight while drinking your morning coffee.

• **Master Suite:** This spacious master suite has all of the amenities you need to fully relax, including a 10-ft.-ceiling, large walk-in closet, separate toilet area, and his and her sinks.

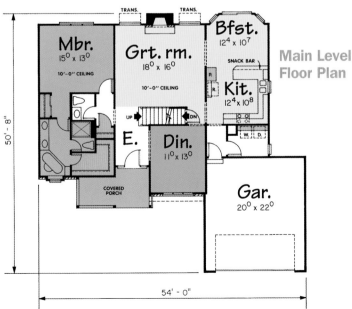

**Main Level Floor Plan**

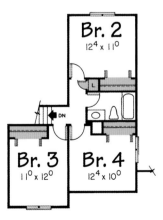

**Upper Level Floor Plan**

*Copyright by designer/architect.*

## Plan #701054

**Dimensions:** 55'4" W x 37'8" D
**Levels:** 2
**Square Footage:** 1,998
**Main Level Sq. Ft.:** 1,093
**Upper Level Sq. Ft.:** 905
**Bedrooms:** 3
**Bathrooms:** 2½
**Foundation:** Basement
**Materials List Available:** Yes
**Price Category:** D

*Images provided by designer/architect.*

You'll love the open design of this comfortable home if sunny, bright rooms make you happy.

**Features:**

• Entry: Walk into this two-story entry, and you're sure to admire the open staircase and balcony from the upper level.

• Dining Room: To the left of the entry, you'll see this dining room, with its special ceiling detail and built-in display cabinet.

• Living Room: Located immediately to the right, this living room features a charming bay window.

• Family Room: French doors from the living room open into this sunny space, where a handsome fireplace takes center stage.

• Kitchen: Combined with the breakfast area, this kitchen features an island cooktop, a large pantry, and a built-in desk.

**Main Level Floor Plan**

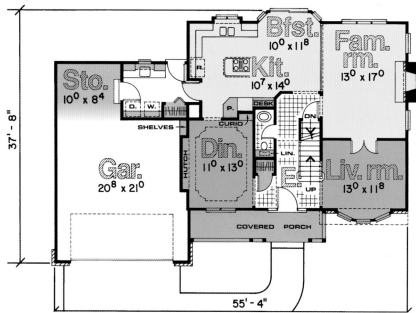

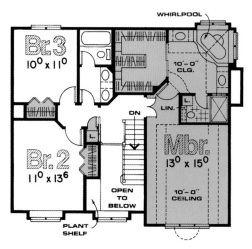

**Upper Level Floor Plan**

*Copyright by designer/architect.*

## Plan #701011

**Dimensions:** 52' W x 47'4" D
**Levels:** 1.5
**Square Footage:** 1,999
**Main Level Sq. Ft.:** 1,421
**Upper Level Sq. Ft.:** 578
**Bedrooms:** 4
**Bathrooms:** 2½
**Foundation:** Basement
**Materials List Available:** Yes
**Price Category:** D

*This home, as shown in the photograph, may differ from the actual blueprints. For more detailed information, please check the floor plans carefully.*

*Images provided by designer/architect.*

Hipped roofs and a trio of gables bring distinction to this plan.

**Features:**

- Ceiling Height: 8 ft.

- Open Floor Plan: The rooms flow into each other and are flanked by an abundance of windows. The result is a light and airy space that seems much larger than it really is.

- Formal Dining Room: Here is the perfect room for elegant entertaining.

- Breakfast Nook: This bright, bayed nook is the perfect place to start the day. It's also great for intimate get-togethers.

- Great Room: The family will enjoy gathering in this spacious area.

- Bedrooms: This large master suite, along with three secondary bedrooms and an extra room, provides plenty of room for a growing family.

- Attached Garage: The garage provides two bays of parking plus plenty of storage space.

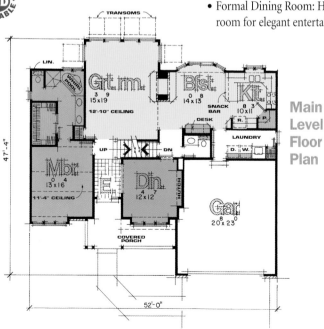

**Main Level Floor Plan**

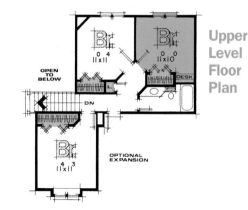

**Upper Level Floor Plan**

*Copyright by designer/architect.*

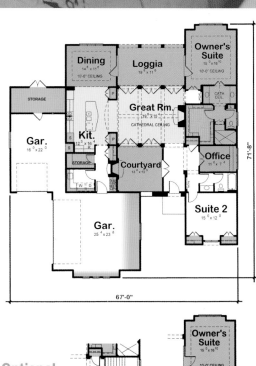

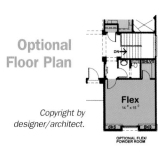

## Plan #701297

**Dimensions:** 67' W x 71'8" D

**Levels:** 1

**Square Footage:** 2,012

**Bedrooms:** 2

**Bathrooms:** 2

**Foundation:** Basement

**Material List Available:** Yes

**Price Category:** D

*Images provided by designer/architect.*

**CAD FILE AVAILABLE**

### Optional Floor Plan

*Copyright by designer/architect.*

---

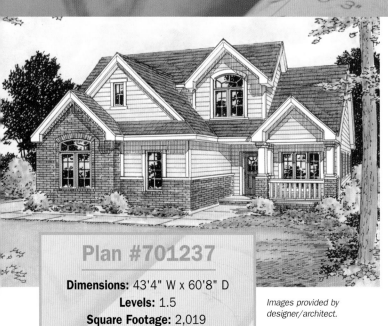

## Plan #701237

**Dimensions:** 43'4" W x 60'8" D

**Levels:** 1.5

**Square Footage:** 2,019

**Main Level Sq. Ft.:** 1,503

**Upper Level Sq. Ft.:** 516

**Bedrooms:** 3

**Bathrooms:** 2½

**Foundation:** Basement

**Material List Available:** Yes

**Price Category:** D

*Images provided by designer/architect.*

**CAD FILE AVAILABLE**

**Main Level Floor Plan**

**Upper Level Floor Plan**

*Copyright by designer/architect.*

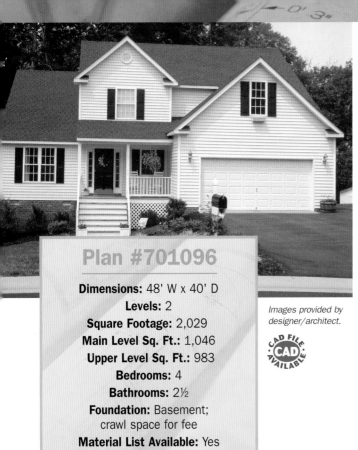

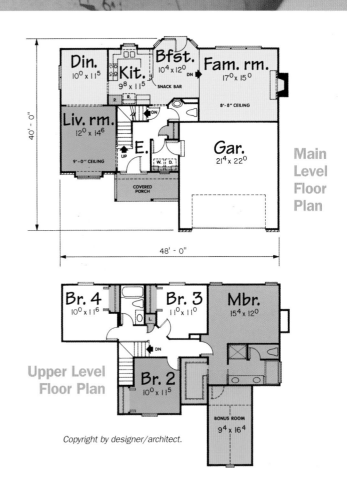

**Main Level Floor Plan**

**Upper Level Floor Plan**

*Images provided by designer/architect.*

*Copyright by designer/architect.*

## Plan #701096

**Dimensions:** 48' W x 40' D

**Levels:** 2

**Square Footage:** 2,029

**Main Level Sq. Ft.:** 1,046

**Upper Level Sq. Ft.:** 983

**Bedrooms:** 4

**Bathrooms:** 2½

**Foundation:** Basement; crawl space for fee

**Material List Available:** Yes

**Price Category:** D

---

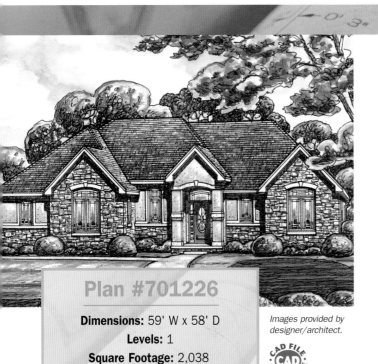

**Main Level Floor Plan**

**Optional Lower Level Floor Plan**

*Images provided by designer/architect.*

*Copyright by designer/architect.*

## Plan #701226

**Dimensions:** 59' W x 58' D

**Levels:** 1

**Square Footage:** 2,038

**Bedrooms:** 3

**Bathrooms:** 2

**Foundation:** Basement

**Material List Available:** Yes

**Price Category:** D

## Plan #701195

**Dimensions:** 69'5" W x 63'6" D

**Levels:** 1

**Square Footage:** 2,040

**Bedrooms:** 4

**Bathrooms:** 3

**Foundation:** Basement

**Material List Available:** Yes

**Price Category:** D

Elegant pillars and interesting architectural details enhance this wonderful home.

**CAD FILE AVAILABLE** CAD

### Features:

- **Porches:** The two porches at the front and the rear of the house provide wonderful spaces to sit and relax, or to have a conversation with friends.

- **Family Room:** This large family room has a cathedral ceiling and is perfect for entertaining guests. The fireplace provides an inviting place for people to gather.

- **Kitchen:** This kitchen will be a favorite of the family chef. Its long counterspaces and rectangular island are perfect for cooking. The attached breakfast room is a great place to gather for a meal and soak in the sunshine from the large windows.

- **Master Suite:** You will never want to leave this octagonal master bedroom. It has direct access to the back porch, a large walk-in closet, separate toilet area, tub, and his and her sinks.

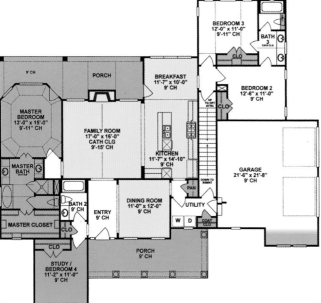

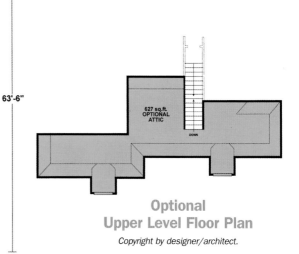

**Optional Upper Level Floor Plan**

*Copyright by designer/architect.*

## Plan #701320

**Dimensions:** 40' W x 55' D
**Levels:** 1.5
**Square Footage:** 2,051
**Main Level Sq. Ft.:** 1,497
**Upper Level Sq. Ft.:** 554
**Bedrooms:** 3
**Bathrooms:** 2½
**Foundation:** Basement; crawl space for fee
**Material List Available:** Yes
**Price Category:** D

Multiple roof lines add to the charm of this home.

**Features:**

- Family Room: This room is sure to be your family's headquarters, thanks to the sloped ceiling, central location, and cozy fireplace.

- Kitchen: This island kitchen with double sink includes a snack bar that is open to the family room. The walk-in pantry provides ample storage space, and the nearby computer niche comes in handy when planning meals.

- Master Suite: For the sake of privacy, this retreat is located on the main floor away from the secondary bedrooms. The large walk-in closet and luxurious private bath are welcome amenities.

- Garage: This front-loading, two-car garage can keep your cars out of the weather.

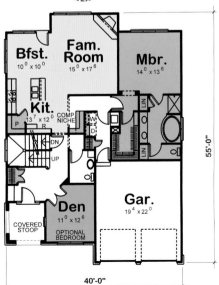

**Main Level Floor Plan**

*Copyright by designer/architect.*

**Upper Level Floor Plan**

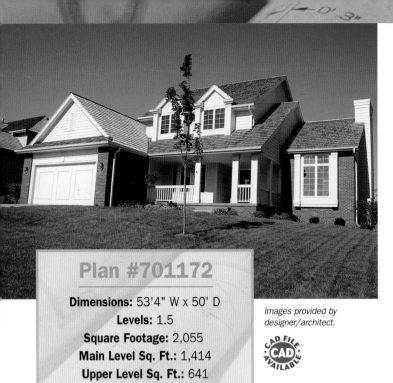

## Plan #701172

**Dimensions:** 53'4" W x 50' D

**Levels:** 1.5

**Square Footage:** 2,055

**Main Level Sq. Ft.:** 1,414

**Upper Level Sq. Ft.:** 641

**Bedrooms:** 4

**Bathrooms:** 2½

**Foundation:** Basement

**Material List Available:** Yes

**Price Category:** D

*Images provided by designer/architect.*

**Main Level Floor Plan**

**Upper Level Floor Plan**

*Copyright by designer/architect.*

## Plan #701181

**Dimensions:** 73'4" W x 56'8" D

**Levels:** 1

**Square Footage:** 2,057

**Bedrooms:** 3

**Bathrooms:** 2

**Foundation:** Basement

**Material List Available:** Yes

**Price Category:** D

*Images provided by designer/architect.*

*Copyright by designer/architect.*

## Plan #701214

**Dimensions:** 67' W x 59' D

**Levels:** 1

**Square Footage:** 2,065

**Bedrooms:** 3

**Bathrooms:** 2½

**Foundation:** Basement

**Material List Available:** Yes

**Price Category:** D

*Images provided by designer/architect.*

**Optional Basement Level Floor Plan**

*Copyright by designer/architect.*

## Plan #701155

**Dimensions:** 66' W x 56' D

**Levels:** 1

**Square Footage:** 2,068

**Bedrooms:** 3

**Bathrooms:** 2½

**Foundation:** Basement

**Material List Available:** Yes

**Price Category:** D

*Images provided by designer/architect.*

*This home, as shown in the photograph, may differ from the actual blueprints. For more detailed information, please check the floor plans carefully.*

*Copyright by designer/architect.*

## Plan #701255

**Dimensions:** 95'4" W x 44'2" D

**Levels:** 1

**Square Footage:** 2,069

**Bedrooms:** 3

**Bathrooms:** 2½

**Foundation:** Basement

**Material List Available:** Yes

**Price Category:** D

This angled ranch-style home will be sure to stand out in your neighborhood.

*Images provided by designer/architect.*

### Features:

- **Kitchen:** This large gorgeous kitchen features a pantry, a center island, and open access to the family room, where guests can sit and relax under an 11-ft. ceiling.

- **Master Suite:** You'll be sure to love this master suite, with its 10-ft. ceiling, separate toilet room, his and her sinks, and large walk-in closet, so you'll never have to fight over closet space again.

- **Secondary Bedrooms:** Two secondary bedrooms that share a bathroom occupy the same wing as the master suite.

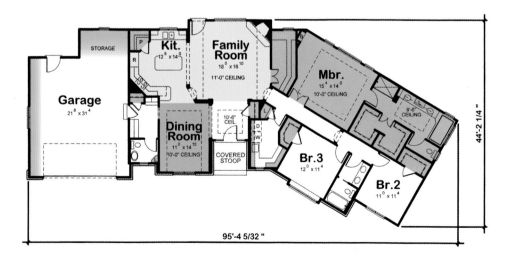

**Bonus Area Floor Plan**

*Copyright by designer/architect.*

## Plan #701278

**Dimensions:** 67' W x 58' D

**Levels:** 1

**Square Footage:** 2,069

**Bedrooms:** 3

**Bathrooms:** 2

**Foundation:** Basement

**Material List Available:** Yes

**Price Category:** D

Spacious and distinctive, the amenities of this home cater to family life.

*Images provided by designer/architect.*

**Features:**

• Family Room: Under its soaring cathedral ceiling, this room contains a two-sided fireplace and an entertainment center for all of your stay-at-home activities.

• Hearth Room: Relax in this hearth room, which is open to the kitchen and dining room. Guests and family can enjoy the two-sided fireplace that is connected to the family room.

• Master Suite: You'll love this spacious master suite with his and her sinks, separate toilet room, and large walk-in closet.

• Garage: This three-car garage and extra storage area is perfect for your cars and those extra items, such as bicycles, tennis rackets, and kiddy pools.

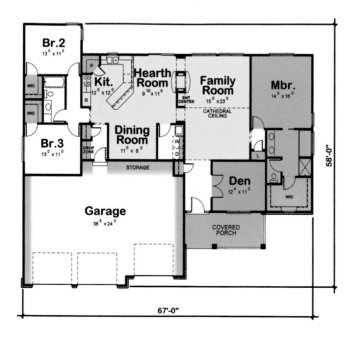

## Optional Guest Suite Floor Plan

Adds Additional 340 Sq. Ft.

*Copyright by designer/architect.*

## Plan #701041

**Dimensions:** 46' W x 41'5" D
**Levels:** 2
**Square Footage:** 2,078
**Main Level Sq. Ft.:** 1,113
**Upper Level Sq. Ft.:** 965
**Bedrooms:** 4
**Bathrooms:** 2½
**Foundation:** Basement
**Materials List Available:** Yes
**Price Category:** D

This lovely home has an unusual dignity, perhaps because its rooms are so well-proportioned and thoughtfully laid out.

### Features:

- **Gathering Room:** This room is sunken, giving it an unusually cozy, comfortable feeling. Its abundance of windows let natural light stream in during the day, and the fireplace warms it when the weather's chilly.

- **Dining Room:** This dining room links to the parlor beyond through a cased opening.

- **Parlor:** A tall, angled ceiling highlights a large, arched window that's the focal point of this room.

- **Breakfast Area:** A wooden rail visually links this bayed breakfast area to the family room.

- **Master Suite:** A roomy walk-in closet adds a practical touch to this luxurious suite. The bath features a skylight, whirlpool tub, and separate shower.

### Main Level Floor Plan

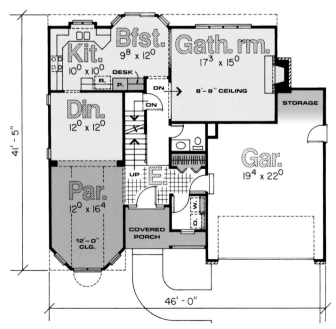

### Upper Level Floor Plan

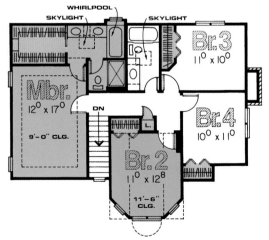

# Plan #701279

**Dimensions:** 67' W x 58' D
**Levels:** 1
**Square Footage:** 2,081
**Bedrooms:** 3
**Bathrooms:** 2
**Foundation:** Basement
**Material List Available:** Yes
**Price Category:** D

*Images provided by designer/architect.*

You and your guests will appreciate the amenities in this attractive home.

**Features:**

- Family Room: You and your guests will love the cathedral ceiling, entertainment center, and two-way fireplace in this room.

- Kitchen: This spacious kitchen is perfect for the home chef, with lots of counter space and a large pantry for all of your ingredients. The kitchen opens up to the hearth room, where you can enjoy the two-way fireplace.

- Master Suite: Luxuriate in this roomy master suite with his and her sinks, separate toilet, and spacious walk-in closet.

- Secondary Bedrooms: Both secondary bedrooms feature walk-in closets. They share a bathroom, making it the perfect setup for siblings.

*Copyright by designer/architect.*

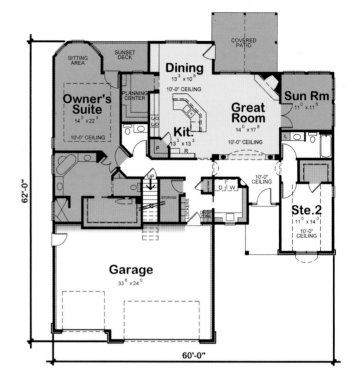

## Plan #701223

**Dimensions:** 60' W x 62' D

**Levels:** 1

**Square Footage:** 2,083

**Bedrooms:** 2

**Bathrooms:** 2½

**Foundation:** Basement

**Material List Available:** Yes

**Price Category:** D

*Images provided by designer/architect.*

CAD FILE AVAILABLE

*Copyright by designer/architect.*

## Plan #701154

**Dimensions:** 44' W x 48' D

**Levels:** 2

**Square Footage:** 2,085

**Main Level Sq. Ft.:** 1,062

**Upper Level Sq. Ft.:** 1,023

**Bedrooms:** 4

**Bathrooms:** 2½

**Foundation:** Basement

**Material List Available:** Yes

**Price Category:** D

*Images provided by designer/architect.*

CAD FILE AVAILABLE

**Main Level Floor Plan**

**Upper Level Floor Plan**

*Copyright by designer/architect.*

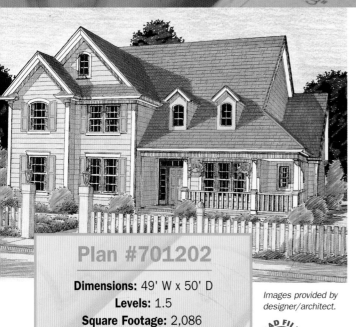

## Plan #701202

**Dimensions:** 49' W x 50' D
**Levels:** 1.5
**Square Footage:** 2,086
**Main Level Sq. Ft.:** 1,383
**Upper Level Sq. Ft.:** 703
**Bedrooms:** 4
**Bathrooms:** 3
**Foundation:** Basement
**Material List Available:** Yes
**Price Category:** D

*Images provided by designer/architect.*

CAD FILE AVAILABLE

**Main Level Floor Plan**

**Upper Level Floor Plan**

*Copyright by designer/architect.*

---

## Plan #701245

**Dimensions:** 71' W x 62' D
**Levels:** 1
**Square Footage:** 2,099
**Bedrooms:** 3
**Bathrooms:** 2½
**Foundation:** Basement
**Material List Available:** Yes
**Price Category:** D

*Images provided by designer/architect.*

CAD FILE AVAILABLE

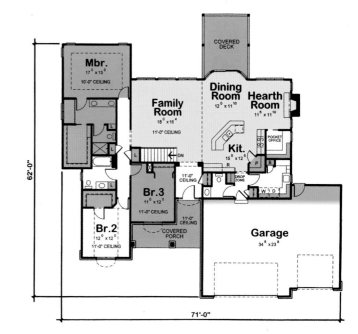

*Copyright by designer/architect.*

## Plan #701055

**Dimensions:** 50' W x 40' D

**Levels:** 2

**Square Footage:** 2,103

**Main Level Sq. Ft.:** 1,082

**Upper Level Sq. Ft.:** 1,021

**Bedrooms:** 4

**Bathrooms:** 2½

**Foundation:** Basement

**Materials List Available:** Yes

**Price Category:** D

You'll love the comfort and the unusual design details you'll find in this home.

**Features:**

- **Entry:** A T-shaped staircase frames this two-story entry, giving both visual interest and convenience.

- **Family Room:** Bookcases frame the lovely fireplace here, so you won't be amiss by decorating to create a special reading nook.

- **Breakfast Area:** Pass through the cased opening between the family room and this breakfast area for convenience.

- **Kitchen:** Combined with the breakfast area, this kitchen features an island, pantry, and desk.

- **Master Suite:** On the upper floor, this suite has a walk-in closet and a bath with sunlit whirlpool tub, separate shower, and double vanity. A window seat makes the bedroom especially cozy, no matter what the outside weather.

## Main Level Floor Plan

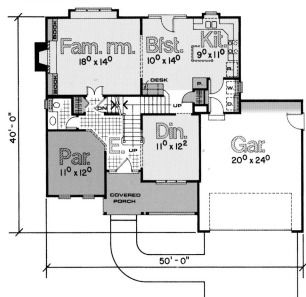

## Upper Level Floor Plan

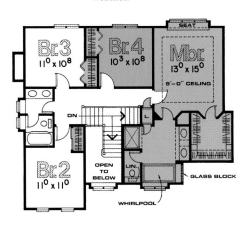

*Copyright by designer/architect.*

## Plan #701075

**Dimensions:** 64' W x 52' D
**Levels:** 1.5
**Square Footage:** 2,115
**Main Level Sq. Ft.:** 1,505
**Upper Level Sq. Ft.:** 610
**Bedrooms:** 4
**Bathrooms:** 2½
**Foundation:** Basement;
crawl space for fee
**Materials List Available:** Yes
**Price Category:** D

This contemporary home is not only beautifully designed on the outside; it has everything you need on the inside. It will be the envy of the neighborhood.

*Images provided by designer/architect.*

**Features:**

• Great Room: The cathedral ceiling and cozy fireplace strike a balance that creates the perfect gathering place for family and friends. An abundance of space allows you to tailor this room to your needs.

• Kitchen/Breakfast Room: This combined area features a flood of natural light, workspace to spare, an island with a snack bar, and a door that opens to the backyard, creating an ideal space for outdoor meals and gatherings.

• Dining Room: A triplet of windows projecting onto the covered front porch creates a warm atmosphere for formal dining.

• Master Bedroom: Away from the busy areas of the home, this master suite is ideal for shedding your daily cares and relaxing in a romantic atmosphere. It includes a full master bath with skylight, his and her sinks, a stall shower, a whirlpool tub, and a walk-in closet.

• Second Floor: Three more bedrooms and the second full bathroom upstairs give you plenty of room for a large family. Or if you only need two extra rooms, use the fourth bedroom as a study or entertainment area for the kids.

**Upper Level Floor Plan**

*Copyright by designer/architect.*

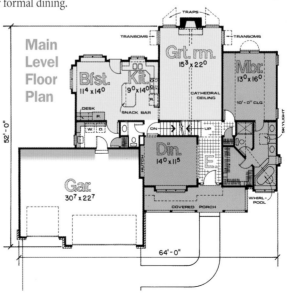

**Main Level Floor Plan**

## Plan #701115

**Dimensions:** 66' W x 54' D

**Levels:** 1

**Square Footage:** 2,126

**Bedrooms:** 3

**Bathrooms:** 2

**Foundation:** Slab; basement for fee

**Material List Available:** Yes

**Price Category:** D

*Images provided by designer/architect.*

This home is as beautiful inside as it is outside, with little details that will truly make it feel unique.

**Features:**

- Porches: The front porch is perfect for welcoming guests to your home, or greeting the children after school. After dinner, relax on the rear porch while watching the stars.

- Family Room: A beautiful 12-ft. ceiling, windows to the porch, and three-way fire place make this room wonderful for relaxing with friends and family.

- Kitchen: This kitchen's efficient layout is sure to delight the family chef. A large workspace, pantry, and center island make meal prep a pleasure. The eating area and snack bar are perfect for quick meals or catching up with the family. The three-way fireplace can be enjoyed from here in the kitchen, the nook, or the family room.

- Master Suite: You will never want to leave this master suite, with its windowed bedroom, 9-ft. ceiling, mirror bypass, toilet, tub, and his and her sinks.

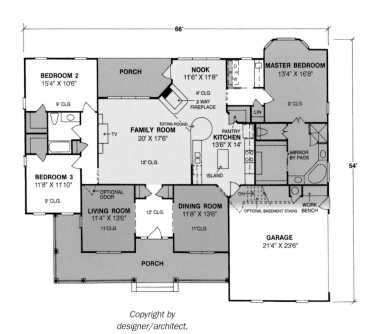

*Copyright by designer/architect.*

## Plan #701081

**Dimensions:** 55'4" W x 37'8" D
**Levels:** 2
**Square Footage:** 2,131
**Main Level Sq. Ft.:** 1,093
**Upper Level Sq. Ft.:** 1,038
**Bedrooms:** 4
**Bathrooms:** 2½
**Foundation:** Basement;
crawl space for fee
**Materials List Available:** Yes
**Price Category:** D

*Images provided by designer/architect.*

A gorgeous contemporary exterior design and an extravagant interior will combine to make this home your favorite place to be.

### Features:

- **Family Room:** This spacious family area gives you room to entertain friends and family alike. Through French doors is the living room, which can add to that space or become your home office, made even more ideal by the glow from the bay windows.

- **Kitchen-Dining Areas:** This L-shaped kitchen, with ample storage and workspace and an island range, is open to the breakfast area to create a space that simplifies the morning chaos. The kitchen also moves into a formal dining area, complete with hutch and curio, which looks out onto the covered porch for peaceful dinners.

- **Master Bedroom:** Located far from the daily hubbub, this master bedroom is your private hideaway. Attached is a full bathroom with stall shower, his and her sinks, a whirlpool tub, and a unique walk-in closet that gives both of you plenty of space.

- **Secondary Bedrooms:** Three bedrooms sit down the hall from the master, sharing the second full bathroom (with dual sinks to simplify the mornings). If three is one too many for you, use the versatile last bedroom as a study or entertainment space.

### Main Level Floor Plan

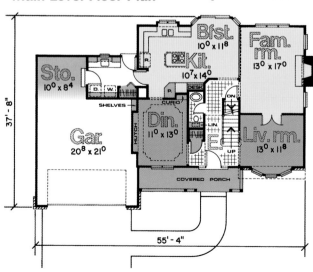

### Upper Level Floor Plan

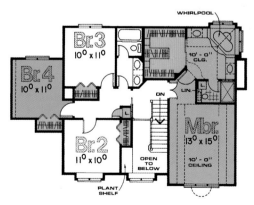

*Copyright by designer/architect.*

## Plan #701068

**Dimensions:** 74'4" W x 58' D

**Levels:** 1

**Square Footage:** 2,133

**Bedrooms:** 3

**Bathrooms:** 2½

**Foundation:** Basement;
crawl space for fee

**Material List Available:** Yes

**Price Category:** D

Images provided by
designer/architect.

Copyright by designer/architect.

## Plan #701153

**Dimensions:** 70' W x 54' D

**Levels:** 1

**Square Footage:** 2,149

**Bedrooms:** 3

**Bathrooms:** 2½

**Foundation:** Basement

**Material List Available:** Yes

**Price Category:** D

Images provided by
designer/architect.

Copyright by
designer/architect.

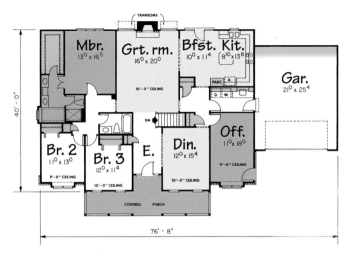

## Plan #701186

**Dimensions:** 76'8" W x 40' D

**Levels:** 1

**Square Footage:** 2,151

**Bedrooms:** 3

**Bathrooms:** 2½

**Foundation:** Basement

**Material List Available:** Yes

**Price Category:** D

*Images provided by designer/architect.*

*Copyright by designer/architect.*

---

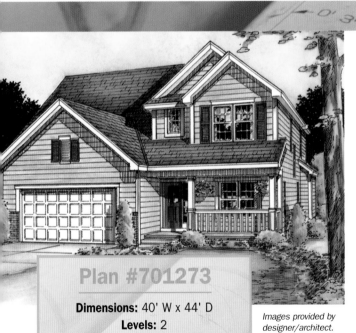

**Main Level Floor Plan**

## Plan #701273

**Dimensions:** 40' W x 44' D

**Levels:** 2

**Square Footage:** 2,155

**Main Level Sq. Ft.:** 1,075

**Upper Level Sq. Ft.:** 1,080

**Bedrooms:** 3

**Bathrooms:** 2½

**Foundation:** Basement

**Material List Available:** Yes

**Price Category:** D

*Images provided by designer/architect.*

**Upper Level Floor Plan**

*Copyright by designer/architect.*

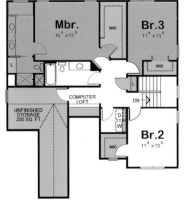

## Main Level Floor Plan

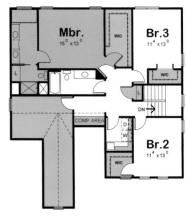

## Upper Level Floor Plan

## Plan #701272

**Dimensions:** 40' W x 44' D
**Levels:** 2
**Square Footage:** 2,168
**Main Level Sq. Ft.:** 1,075
**Upper Level Sq. Ft.:** 1,093
**Bedrooms:** 3
**Bathrooms:** 2½
**Foundation:** Basement
**Material List Available:** Yes
**Price Category:** D

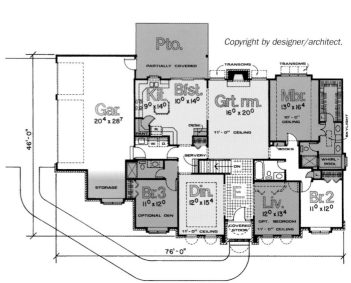

Kitchen

## Plan #701078

**Dimensions:** 76' W x 46' D
**Levels:** 1
**Square Footage:** 2,172
**Bedrooms:** 4
**Bathrooms:** 3
**Foundation:** Basement; crawl space for fee
**Material List Available:** Yes
**Price Category:** D

## Plan #701303

**Dimensions:** 48' W x 63' D

**Levels:** 1

**Square Footage:** 2,160

**Bedrooms:** 2

**Bathrooms:** 2

**Foundation:** Slab

**Material List Available:** Yes

**Price Category:** D

*Images provided by designer/architect.*

CAD FILE AVAILABLE · CAD

*Copyright by designer/architect.*

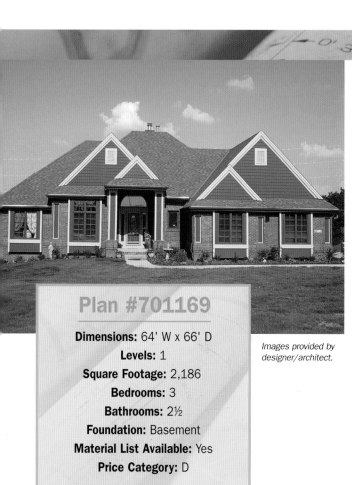

## Plan #701169

**Dimensions:** 64' W x 66' D

**Levels:** 1

**Square Footage:** 2,186

**Bedrooms:** 3

**Bathrooms:** 2½

**Foundation:** Basement

**Material List Available:** Yes

**Price Category:** D

*Images provided by designer/architect.*

*Copyright by designer/architect.*

## Plan #701260

**Dimensions:** 54'4" W x 47'4" D
**Levels:** 1.5
**Square Footage:** 2,196
**Main Level Sq. Ft.:** 1,497
**Upper Level Sq. Ft.:** 699
**Bedrooms:** 4
**Bathrooms:** 2½
**Foundation:** Basement
**Material List Available:** Yes
**Price Category:** D

*Images provided by designer/architect.*

**Features:**

- Great Room: Your family and guests will love this room, with its extraordinary 14-ft. ceiling that is open to the second floor and its cozy fireplace.

- Kitchen: This kitchen has everything you'd need at arm's reach, yet is spacious enough for the home cook to comfortably cook a large meal or be assisted by little helping hands. The connecting dinette is a wonderful place to have a snack.

- Master Suite: The perfect oasis away from the rest of the world, this master suite features a spacious walk-in closet, large tub, and his and her sinks.

- Secondary Bedrooms: Upstairs, three secondary bedrooms share a bathroom and plentiful storage area.

You'll fall in love with this charming home with its beautiful architecture.

**CAD FILE AVAILABLE** CAD

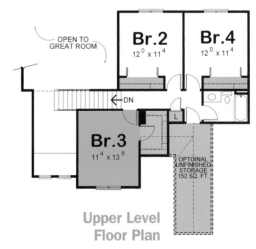

*Copyright by designer/architect.*

## Plan #701089

**Dimensions:** 50' W x 44' D
**Levels:** 2
**Square Footage:** 2,198
**Main Level Sq. Ft.:** 1,179
**Upper Level Sq. Ft.:** 1,019
**Bedrooms:** 4
**Bathrooms:** 3½
**Foundation:** Basement; crawl space or slab for fee
**Material List Available:** Yes
**Price Category:** D

Enter through the covered stoop into a house that is designed to suit all of your family's needs.

**Features:**

- **Family Room:** This large great room is accentuated by a beautiful fireplace.

- **Kitchen:** Find a place for all of your cooking equipment and utensils in this well-appointed kitchen.

- **Breakfast Room:** Connected to the kitchen, this breakfast room opens out to the backyard for easy access to snacks and drinks during playtime.

- **Master Suite:** Located near the secondary bedrooms, this master suite features a large living space and a luxurious bath that includes double sinks and large tub.

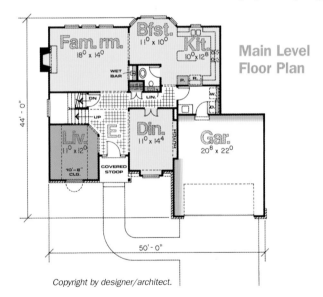

**Main Level Floor Plan**

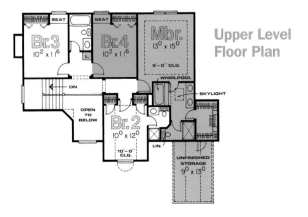

**Upper Level Floor Plan**

# Flexibility

**W**ith the aging of America and boomerang children, a house plan that can combine bedroom and a private bath makes a great suite. If the situation changes, the rooms can be used for other needs. Even more accommodating, some homeowners are utilizing a pair of adjacent secondary bedrooms as an in-law suite. Such arrangements offer considerable privacy, with the in-law suite offering both a sleeping area and its own living space as well.

## Four-Seasons Room

Bringing the outside in and views to the outside are important to many people. Many of us work in an office all day, so we like to incorporate outside living into our lives at home. Whether the area is screened in, enclosed with windows, or just an open patio, it is an important element to daily living.

When asked "what is your favorite place in your home?" a surprising number of people answer their porch or deck. If you can identify with this group, consider adding (operable) windows all around your outdoor living space along with supplemental baseboard heating, enabling you to enjoy this space anytime!

## Kids' Playroom

Whether it is your own family, company with children, or neighborhood kids, it is always important that you find a place for a playroom. It helps with everyone's sanity to keep the noise and toys away from adults.

Ironically, a kids playroom just might be one of your most prized luxuries in your new home. By having most of their toys, games, puzzles, etc. in this one room, keeping the rest of the house presentable is an achievable reality!

**Large windows, patio doors, and sliders** do a good job of opening the home to the outside.

**Rooms such as this**, top, can be used as formal dining rooms, or a den or home office.

**Families who home school** need a dedicated space for lessons and study, above.

## Home-Schooling Room

Increasingly popular, home-schooling parents have a particular challenge with today's more open home designs—the need for privacy so their kids can concentrate on their studies or tests. When planning this space, consider storage, workspaces, lighting (especially natural light) and computer hookups.

Ideally, a room in the home can be dedicated to schooling. More often, it will double as a school room and serve another purpose at other times, so make sure the space is flexible. Pay particular attention to floor coverings if school or other activities are likely to include messy projects, crafts, and the like.

## Craft/Gardening Areas

When it comes to unwinding from our hurried lives or pursuing something we really enjoy, many people like to relax with a special hobby or craft. How many times do you have a project spread out on the kitchen or dining room table? An area out of public view would take the stress out of constant picking up. Therefore, having room to pursue these and other hobbies in and of itself can contribute to the flexibility of your home, especially if works in progress can be left undisturbed.

The primary considerations for such spaces are related to the type of activity. Gardening, for example, is ideally suited for an area with a sink in it and close to an outside door. Sewing and needlework projects are enhanced by high light levels. Woodworking fits well with concrete floors for easy cleanup plus plenty of electrical outlets for various power tools.

Whatever your favorite pursuit, what things could you do with your home which would enhance the experience? How about special task lighting? This is sometimes a hard area to identify, simply because we learn to cope with the shortcomings inherent to our present situation. The answers lie in things that frustrate you when engaged in these activities.

## Bedroom/Bath Arrangements for Blended Families

Blending families can be a difficult task, but picking a home plan that has been designed to address bedroom/bath needs makes the task so much easier.

Especially when combining boys and girls from two families into one new family, thought needs to be given regarding bedroom and bathroom accommodations. Everyone needs a sense of privacy and a sense of space which they can call their own. And when it comes to sharing a bathroom, dual lavatories are a big plus, as is a toilet/shower area separate from the lavs.

## Home Offices (His and Her)

Kevin and Tina both work at home. Sharing an office is not working, so they found a plan that gives them his and her offices. They can work in their own spaces but more than that; it makes for a pleasant marriage.

People who succeed in working from home attest to the importance of having a dedicated home office space where they can focus on their work. Today's economy coupled with downsizing and early retirement is giving birth to numerous cottage industries.

The type of work you do out of your home will dictate your space needs. Pay careful attention to storage and any special wiring, as well as privacy.

## Formal Dining

Candlelight, soft music, ample room for guests, and great conversation make dinner parties a delight. The formal dining room also makes an excellent backdrop for a great dining room suite. Because  entertaining inevitably involves food, look at how your home enhances the dining experience. Be mindful of seating, which always becomes an issue. Homes designed with an open floorplan, especially ones in which the dining room flows uninterrupted into a great room, offer numerous entertaining options.

## Room to Grow

An item no one wants to think about is outgrowing their home. But the reality is that family situations change and our needs and wants for space in the home change, too. The solution? Unfinished areas of the home, especially on a second level or over a garage or in a basement.

You may not need this space when you first move into your home, but it will give you room to add a bedroom, media room, playroom, etc. Families can grow into these spaces and configure them as the need arises, without having the initial cost of finishing the space affecting their mortgage qualifications or mortgage payment.

**"Change is all around us."** That has become the norm in American society. And as our lives change, we begin to appreciate homes that were designed to adapt to our changing situations. It's called flexible design.

To some extent, we've all grown up with the flexible concept, such as when we turned a spare bedroom into a TV room by replacing the bed with a sofa and chair. But flexible design goes further than that—having a lot to do with how rooms are accessed and what other rooms they are adjacent to. While flexible living doesn't change the footprint of a home, it does encourage looking for ways to change spaces to meet a particular need. It typically also involves minor changes to the design, such as adding, removing, or repositioning doors, closets, and shelving.

The home plan shown below illustrates the flex room concept well. This efficient design works nicely for many buyer profiles, from singles to couples to smaller families. It will also accommodate larger families when built on a basement foundation and part of the basement space is finished.

A flex room is so labeled to suggest buyers themselves determine how the space will be used. Many people would envision the flex room in this home used as a third bedroom. (See the illustration below.) When doing so, the passage to the kitchen is eliminated and the entrance into this space is via an alcove and door conveniently placed near the bathroom. Statistics also show that after being launched out on their own half of our adult children return home within 30 months, sometimes bringing a spouse or child back with them. Middle adulthood may also mean moving in aging parents no longer able to live independently. With the adjacent bath, this flex room converts nicely as a modest suite.

Another likely utilization of the flex space in this design would be as a formal dining room. At 14 x 10 feet, the room is nicely proportioned for an oval table. The entry pillars, 10-foot-high boxed ceiling, and double window enhance the dining experience, as does the easy kitchen connection.

A quick review of this home plan elicited uses ranging from media room, library, and music room to a home-schooling room. If a media room, extra soundproofing meas-

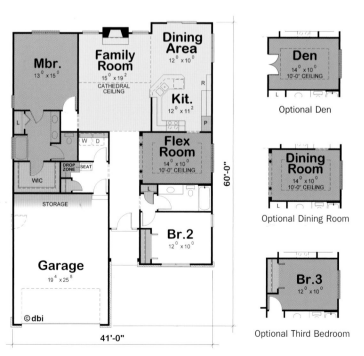

**The flex room** can lead to any one of a number of possible configurations, including those shown above right.

ures will mean some of the guys can be in there watching the big game, while others enjoy conversation in the family room and kitchen. Home schoolers, on the other hand, would appreciate plenty of shelving. For even more flexibility, a Murphy bed (one that folds up into the wall) or a day bed means the same space can serve multiple purposes as needed.

But more common was to hear people express their intention that the flex space would become a den or home office. Abundant natural light has been shown to enhance concentration and reduce stress, so in addition to the double window, consider adding a skylight. In addition to eliminating the passageway to the kitchen, a pair of full-lite French doors could be added to close off the space when privacy is desired.

You may also want to consider turning bedroom #2, the flex room, and bath into a full guest suite. Well-separated from the master suite, either bedroom #2 or the flex room can function as the actual bedroom, with the other room being a private living space for your guest, boomerang child, or elderly parent. This arrangement also services another emerging trend—an elderly or widowed sibling coming to live with you.

Designs that embody such flexibility are in demand by homebuyers. How you intend to use the space is entirely up to you. But thinking about how a home's design can adapt to your future needs should be a prime consideration before you build.

**The flex room** is a great locations for a home office, den, or private library, right.

**Media rooms** are becoming more and more popular. Plan for the proper electrical connections if considering one, below.

# Homes for Today's Blended Families

**Her Plans** at a Glance™
- Storing
- Entertaining
- Flexible Living
- De-Stressing

**T**he Brady Bunch gave us a few laughs as well as insights into issues families face as they try to unite two families as one through remarriage. Certainly, the Brady's housekeeper, Alice, helped smooth over some of the inevitable conflict. While most of us do not enjoy the luxury of a live-in housekeeper, there are steps which can be taken when building or remodeling a home that can reduce the angst of bringing two families together.

Moms know their girls spend a lot of time in the bathroom – which usually doubles as their dressing, hair care, and makeup center. Girls need space to keep these items, as well as other feminine products. Boys generally don't give bathrooms much consideration (as evidenced by the toilet seat being left up, as well as dirty clothes and wet towels strewn about.)

Of course, separate baths for each of the kids bedrooms would be ideal, but the expense and space required can make it impractical. Still, parents of blended families have legitimate concerns, especially if boys and girls from different backgrounds will be sharing the same bath area.

Compartmentalized baths are a welcome solution! A traditional compartmentalized bath places a door between the sink/vanity and the toilet/tub area, allowing two family members to use the bath area at the same time. As secondary baths in some designs have grown larger, two sinks reduces stress when several people are getting ready at the same time.

Even better is the emerging solution of having vanity/sink areas private to each secondary bedroom, with private access to a shared toilet/tub area. This is especially welcome if one of the kids is a "cleanie" and the other a "messy," as they can have their sink/vanity area to their liking!

The occasional child presents different challenges. Imagine having your 6-year-old daughter, Mandy, who lives with you only on weekends and for a month during the summer. First and foremost is her emotional well-being. In this regard, stability and familiarity are paramount.

Mandy needs a place in the home that is hers, even if the room is used for other purposes while she is away. Ideally, Mandy's room should be on par with other children's bedrooms in your home so that she doesn't feel like a second-class family member. She also needs a place for her things and ideally a place where she can keep projects in progress, such as half-finished puzzles or other creations.

A room that functions as a home office or hobby area during the week is an excellent solution, particularly when outfitted with a daybed or Murphy bed, one which folds up into the wall

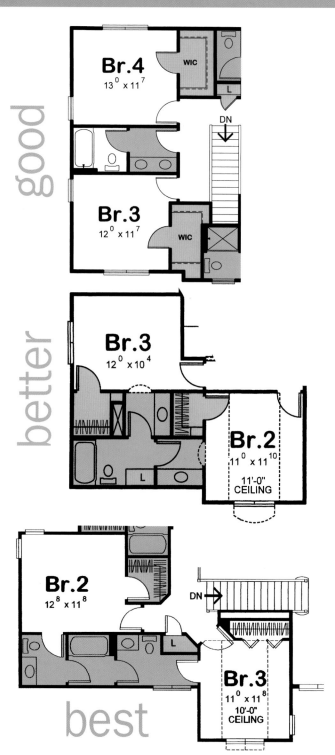

**Each of these three floor plans** illustrates bathroom options for the blended family.

**Good,** a typical compartmentalized bath.
**Better,** a bath with vanities in each bedroom.
**Best,** half-baths in each bedroom with a shared bathing area.

when not in use. A walk-in closet for Mandy's room provides numerous creative opportunities. While she's younger, this area can double as Mandy's private play space. Consider a drywall opening into the closet area from the bedroom—a window, into that space. As she grows, this space will naturally fill with Mandy's things.

Parents, particularly parents in blended families, want to interact with all of the children and allow the kids to spend time together. Open floor plans, especially designs where the kitchen is open to the family room, enhance opportunities for communication—even if the parent is just working in the kitchen while keeping an eye on what the kids are doing. Of course, children need privacy as well. All parents share the experience of arguments with kids over music volume coming from bedrooms. Insulating interior bedroom walls and using solid core doors are a sure way to set your homes apart in the minds of these buyers.

Even laundry rooms are a design consideration for blended families. No one wants to see another family member's undergarments. While laundry rooms which double as the entry to the home from the garage are common, many buyers prefer designs where the laundry area can be closed off.

**Finished bonus rooms,** above are perfect play areas for children who do not live in the house full time. They can leave their games and projects as is between visits.

**Open floor plans** are ideal for blended families, or any family, as parents can keep an eye on everyone easily, below.

# De-Stressing

**A**fter a long and hectic day, find personal space to decompress is as important as breathing. If reading or watching a little TV is how you like to unwind, a sitting area in the master bedroom or a cozy hearth room may be the perfect answer. Enjoy nature? Then covered outdoor living spaces will be high on your list. If you like to work off stress by working out, an exercise room works for you!

## Large Pantry

As a nation, we're cooking less, but not eating less. Some grew up in homes where a hot cooked breakfast was the daily norm. Today, a bowl of cereal, toast, or a granola bar might be more common. That means an increasing need for storage for prepared foods.

Do you need space for your bread maker, indoor grill, food processor, or mixer? Don't let clutter on your countertop stress you, put them in the pantry.

In addition to making pantries bigger, there's an evolving industry helping to make pantries more organized through innovative storage solutions. With items organized and on display, we can quickly scan the pantry before a restocking trip to the grocery store, saving both time and the aggravation of returning home only to find you forgot something.

## Rear Foyer

A funny thing happened over the past couple decades. The door in from the garage became our principal entry to the home. Sure, a formal front entry to greet guests is important and is often a focal point of the home's design, but we're becoming increasingly comfortable with family and friends coming through the garage.

An emerging trend is to think of the entry from the garage as a rear foyer. And just as you probably wouldn't make your laundry room a part of your front entryway, you probably don't want folks traipsing past piles of laundry on their way in from the garage. Note: you may want to modify your home plan if originally designed with the laundry/mudroom entry connecting the garage with the rest of the house.

Our research revealed nothing is more stressful for moms than getting the family out the door on time in the morning with everything they need. Rear foyers may offer solutions such as lockers for each of the kids and even walk-in closets. A bench for removing shoes is also popular.

## Drop Zone

Mail, keys, cell phones, cameras—wouldn't it be great to have a convenient place to drop our stuff so it doesn't end up as kitchen clutter, or worse? Today's hot new concept: the drop zone. Typically made to match kitchen cabinetry and 3 to 4 feet in width, drop zones often incorporate a recharging center, mail sorting area, drop-off counter, and cabinets and drawers for everything from flashlights to sunglasses.

Some drop zones are designed with doors behind which everything is concealed. They may include one or more locking cabinet doors or drawers for expensive items such as a camcorder or notebook PC. They may also double as a family message center when outfitted with cork board or a white write-on board.

Stress-free living includes knowing you'll never lose your

**Luxurious baths** are great places to de-stress.

keys again and where your fully charged cell phone is when you leave the house.

## Split Bedrooms

After a stressful day at work, retreat to the master suite which is separated from secondary bedrooms for privacy. Designers typically try to buffer the master bedroom from other bedrooms by careful placement of closets, hallways, and baths.

As opposed to designing a bedroom wing for the home, one-story designs in which the secondary bedrooms are situated far from the master bedroom are becoming more popular.

## Walk-In Shower

Because they are used everyday in our time-starved society, showers are becoming the focal point of many bathrooms. As showers are getting bigger in today's homes, they are also getting more luxurious. Multiple shower heads are commonplace, as are seats in the shower.

How long does it take for clear shower doors to show white streaks? Low-maintenance showers are in demand, as well as walk-in showers which have no shower door to make cleaning easier. If your shower does require a door, look at the frameless versions which are elegant and easier to clean.

## Split Vanities

Women take more time in the morning in the bathroom getting ready than men do. And a fair amount of that time is spent leaning over the countertop. Split vanities provide handy storage solutions for items each spouse uses daily, keeping your vanity neat and organized. And if one partner likes things clean and orderly while the other doesn't even notice this type of thing, neither will be annoyed at the condition of their vanity area.

Recognizing that men are on average several inches taller than women, building the vanities to be different heights is another aspect of a comfortable, de-stressing bath.

## Garden/Whirlpool Tubs

When asked about what they would like to do to de-stress after a long day, many women envision taking a relaxing bath. The experience is both soothing and rejuvenating—especially when surrounded by aromatic candles and pretty soaps.

Standard tubs have given way to soaking tubs and whirlpool tubs. Look at the height of the tub in terms of getting in and out. Stepping up or sinking the tub 7 or 8 inches lower than the surrounding floor make it easier to get in and out of the tub.

Another aspect to consider is if there is a window over the tub. Privacy is as important as natural light. How easy will it be to reach over the tub and close the shades? You may want to opt for glass block or for the new privacy glass windows which go from clear to opaque at the flip of a switch.

**Choose furniture** for outdoor living areas based on comfort and the ability to stand up to the elements.

## Craft/Gardening Area

How many times do you have a project spread out on the kitchen or dining room table? An area out of public view would take the stress out of constantly cleaning up. Having room in the home to pursue these and other hobbies can contribute to de-stressing, especially if works can be left undisturbed.

The primary considerations for such spaces are related to the type of activity. Gardening is ideally suited for an area with a sink in it and being close to an outside door. Sewing and needlework projects are enhanced by high light levels. Woodworking fits well with concrete floors for easy cleanup, plus plenty of electrical outlets for various power tools.

## Outdoor Living

Most people long to spend time outdoors. This is good as research shows being outside is beneficial for both our physical and mental health.

Like many other product decisions, balancing cost, aesthetics, low maintenance, and durability are principal considerations for porches, decks, and patios. But these same aspects also apply to landscaping and irrigation, exterior lighting, play structures, and other backyard decisions.

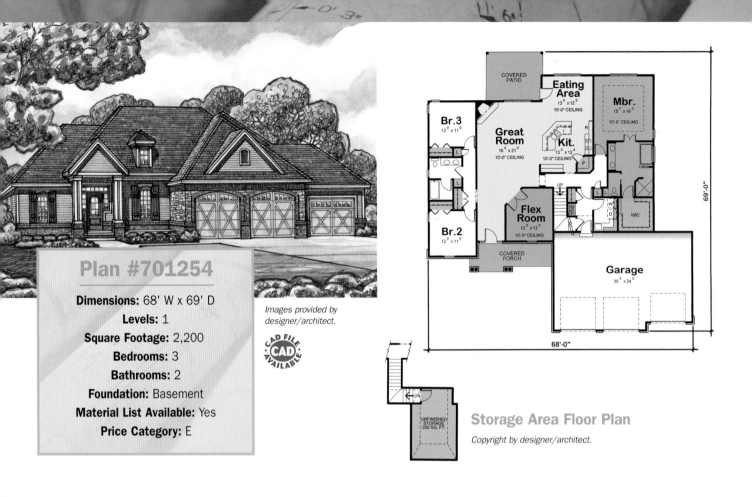

## Plan #701254

**Dimensions:** 68' W x 69' D

**Levels:** 1

**Square Footage:** 2,200

**Bedrooms:** 3

**Bathrooms:** 2

**Foundation:** Basement

**Material List Available:** Yes

**Price Category:** E

*Images provided by designer/architect.*

**CAD FILE AVAILABLE**

**Storage Area Floor Plan**

*Copyright by designer/architect.*

## Plan #701196

**Dimensions:** 68' W x 54'4" D

**Levels:** 1

**Square Footage:** 2,203

**Bedrooms:** 3

**Bathrooms:** 3

**Foundation:** Basement

**Material List Available:** Yes

**Price Category:** E

*Images provided by designer/architect.*

**CAD FILE AVAILABLE**

**Bonus Area Floor Plan**

*Copyright by designer/architect.*

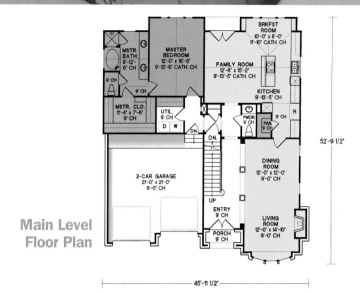

## Main Level Floor Plan

BRKFST ROOM
10' X 8'-0"
11'-10" CATH. CH

MASTER BEDROOM
12'-0" X 16'-6"
9'-12'-6" CATH. CH

FAMILY ROOM
12'-6" X 15'-2"
9'-13'-5" CATH. CH

MSTR. BATH
9'-12'-6" CH
9' CH

KITCHEN
9'-13'-5" CH

MSTR. CLO.
11'-4" X 7'-6"
9' CH

UTIL.
9' CH
D W

PWDR
9' CH

PAN
9' CH

DN.

UP

DINING ROOM
12'-0" X 12'-0"
9'-0" CH

2-CAR GARAGE
21'-0" X 21'-0"
9'-0" CH

ENTRY
9' CH

LIVING ROOM
12'-0" X 14'-10"
9'-0" CH

PORCH
9' CH

52'-9 1/2"

45'-11 1/2"

*Images provided by designer/architect.*

### Plan #701321

**Dimensions:** 45'11½" W x 52'9½" D

**Levels:** 1.5

**Square Footage:** 2,214

**Main Level Sq. Ft.:** 1,576

**Upper Level Sq. Ft.:** 638

**Bedrooms:** 3

**Bathrooms:** 2½

**Foundation:** Slab

**Material List Available:** Yes

**Price Category:** E

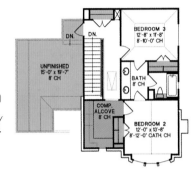

## Upper Level Floor Plan

DN.

DN.

BEDROOM 3
12'-8" X 11'-8"
8'-10'-0" CH

UNFINISHED
15'-0" X 19'-7"
8' CH

BATH
8' CH

COMP. ALCOVE
8' CH

BEDROOM 2
12'-0" X 13'-8"
8'-12'-0" CATH. CH

*Copyright by designer/architect.*

### Plan #701212

**Dimensions:** 59' W x 63' D

**Levels:** 1

**Square Footage:** 2,218

**Bedrooms:** 4

**Bathrooms:** 3

**Foundation:** Slab

**Material List Available:** Yes

**Price Category:** E

*Images provided by designer/architect.*

59'

SCREEN PORCH
20' X 10'
11' CLG.

MASTER BEDROOM
13'8" X 16'6"
11' CLG.

LIVING ROOM
20' X 16'6"
11' CLG.

BEDROOM 3
15' X 11'
8' CLG.

BEDROOM 2
11' X 14'
9' CLG.

KITCHEN
14'8" X 12'
ISLAND

BEDROOM 4
11' X 12'6"
8' CLG.

3 CAR GARAGE
28' X 24'

NOOK
10' X 11'
11' CLG.

DINING
11' X 13'

PORCH

63'

OPT. GAMEROOM
15' X 20'4"
8' CLG.
ADDS 325 SQ. FT.

## Optional Gameroom

*Copyright by designer/architect.*

## Plan #701139

**Dimensions:** 54' W x 44' D
**Levels:** 2
**Square Footage:** 2,219
**Main Level Sq. Ft.:** 1,132
**Upper Level Sq. Ft.:** 1,087
**Bedrooms:** 4
**Bathrooms:** 2½
**Foundation:** Basement; crawl space for fee
**Material List Available:** Yes
**Price Category:** E

*Images provided by designer/architect.*

Country charm abounds in this lovely home.

**Features:**

• Entry: The central location of this large entry allows access to the dining room or great room. The area features a handy closet.

• Great Room: This gathering area features a 10-ft.-high ceiling and large windows, which allow plenty of natural light into the space.

• Upper Level: Three bedrooms and the master suite occupy this level. The master suite features a tray ceiling and a well-appointed bath.

• Garage: A front-loading two-car garage with additional storage completes the floor plan.

Front View

### Main Level Floor Plan

*Copyright by designer/architect.*

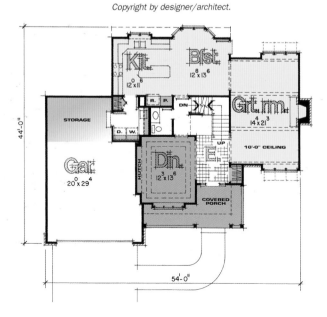

### Upper Level Floor Plan

# Plan #701308

**Dimensions:** 92'8" W x 59'4" D
**Levels:** 1
**Square Footage:** 2,223
**Bedrooms:** 1
**Bathrooms:** 2½
**Foundation:** Basement; crawl space for fee
**Materials List Available:** Yes
**Price Category:** E

CAD FILE AVAILABLE

This home features a flowing, open floor plan coupled with an abundance of amenities.

**Features:**

- Ceiling Height: 8 ft. unless otherwise noted.

- Foyer: This elegant entry features a curved staircase and a view of the formal dining room.

- Formal Dining Room: Magnificent arched openings lead from the foyer into this dining room. The boxed ceiling adds to the architectural interest.

- Great Room: A wall of windows, a see-through fireplace, and built-in entertainment center make this the perfect gathering place.

- Covered Deck: The view of this deck, through the wall of windows in the great room, will lure guests out to this large deck.

- Hearth Room: This room share a panoramic view with the eating area.

- Kitchen: This kitchen features a corner pantry, a built-in desk, and a curved island.

## Main Level Floor Plan

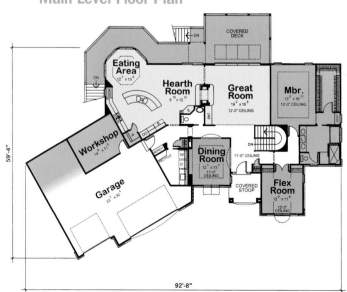

## Optional Basement Level Floor Plan

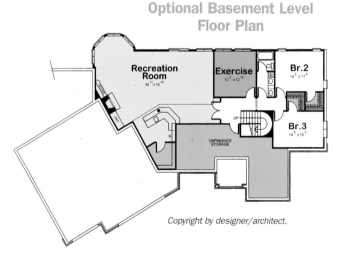

## Plan #701107

**Dimensions:** 63'3" W x 48'7" D
**Levels:** 1.5
**Square Footage:** 2,237
**Main Level Sq. Ft.:** 1,776
**Upper Level Sq. Ft.:** 461
**Bedrooms:** 3
**Bathrooms:** 2½
**Foundation:** Slab; basement for fee
**Material List Available:** Yes
**Price Category:** E

*Images provided by designer/architect.*

This stunning design is beautiful on the outside, and lovely and functional on the inside.

**CAD FILE AVAILABLE**

**Features:**

- **Living Room:** This 18-ft.-high, two-story living room will be the envy of all of your friends and neighbors. The gorgeous full-height windows will allow for abundant sunshine and an unobstructed view.

- **Kitchen:** Culinary experts and household cooks alike will find everything they need in this kitchen, which opens out to the sunny breakfast area.

- **Raised Study:** The perfect place for children to do their homework, or for you to get extra office work done, this raised study is in a convenient location and is large enough for multiple purposes.

- **Master Suite:** Relax in this large master suite with 9-ft. ceiling, large tub, separate toilet room, walk-in closet, and his and her sinks.

**Main Level Floor Plan**

**Upper Level Floor Plan**

## Plan #701206

**Dimensions:** 52' W x 49' D
**Levels:** 1.5
**Square Footage:** 2,241
**Main Level Sq. Ft.:** 1,455
**Upper Level Sq. Ft.:** 786
**Bedrooms:** 4
**Bathrooms:** 2½
**Foundation:** Basement
**Material List Available:** Yes
**Price Category:** E

This wonderful home is spacious enough for your whole family.

CAD FILE AVAILABLE

*Images provided by designer/architect.*

**Features:**

- Living Room: Entertain guests in this spacious living room, complete with a fireplace.

- Kitchen: The eating bar and center island are just some of the amenities in this beautiful kitchen, with open access to the nook that connects to the porch for outdoor dining.

- Master Suite: This roomy master suite is conveniently located next to the laundry room, so you won't need to carry clothing up and down stairs. The master bath features a large walk-in closet, his and her sinks, a separate toilet room, and a tub.

- Secondary Bedrooms: Three additional bedrooms are located upstairs, across from the optional game room. A shared bath features his and her sinks and a separate toilet room; cutting down on the time deciding whose turn it is to use the bathroom.

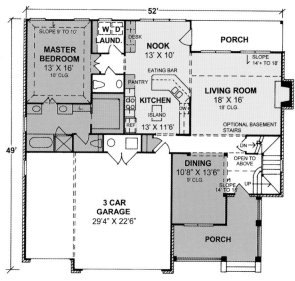

**Main Level Floor Plan**

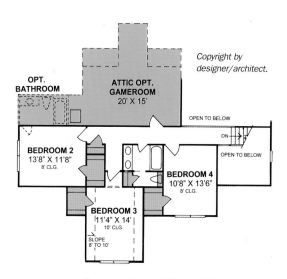

*Copyright by designer/architect.*

**Upper Level Floor Plan**

## Plan #701229

**Dimensions:** 64' W x 64' D
**Levels:** 1
**Square Footage:** 2,242
**Bedrooms:** 2
**Bathrooms:** 2½
**Foundation:** Basement
**Material List Available:** Yes
**Price Category:** E

This charming home is accompanied by exquisite architecture.

CAD FILE AVAILABLE

**Features:**

- **Family Room:** Lined with windows, your family will love this sunny space with 10-ft.-high ceilings, an entertainment center, and access to the backyard.

- **Kitchen:** This roomy kitchen opens out to the dining room and family room, and features an island for holding food or quick meals.

- **Master Suite:** Luxurious and filled with amenities, this master suite features a bedroom area with a 10-ft.-high stepped ceiling; a bathroom featuring a tub, separate toilet area, and his and her sinks; and a massive walk-in closet with a dresser and bench inside.

- **Optional Lower Level:** Your family and guests will never be bored in this basement. Create an exercise room, a media room, a game room, and a bar.

*Copyright by designer/architect.*

**Optional Lower Level Floor Plan**

## Plan #701048

**Dimensions:** 50' W x 48' D
**Levels:** 2
**Square Footage:** 2,248
**Main Level Sq. Ft.:** 1,568
**Upper Level Sq. Ft.:** 680
**Bedrooms:** 4
**Bathrooms:** 2½
**Foundation:** Slab;
crawl space or basement for fee
**Materials List Available:** Yes
**Price Category:** E

*Images provided by designer/architect.*

*This home, as shown in the photograph, may differ from the actual blueprints. For more detailed information, please check the floor plans carefully.*

This design is wonderful for any family but has features that make it ideal for one with teens.

**Features:**

• **Family Room:** A vaulted ceiling gives a touch of elegance here and a corner fireplace makes it comfortable, especially when the weather's cool.

• **Living Room:** Both this room and the dining room have a formal feeling, but don't let that stop you from making them a family gathering spot.

• **Kitchen:** A built-in desk, butler's pantry, and a walk-in pantry make this kitchen easy to organize. The breakfast nook shares an angled eating bar with the family room.

• **Master Suite:** A walk-in closet and corner whirlpool tub and shower make this suite feel luxurious.

**Main Level Floor Plan**

*Copyright by designer/architect.*

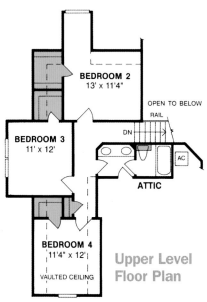

**Upper Level Floor Plan**

## Plan #701120

**Dimensions:** 80' W x 59' D
**Levels:** 1.5
**Square Footage:** 2,252
**Main Level Sq. Ft.:** 1,736
**Upper Level Sq. Ft.:** 516
**Bedrooms:** 4
**Bathrooms:** 3
**Foundation:** Slab; crawl space for fee
**Materials List Available:** Yes
**Price Category:** E

This classic farmhouse is just what you have been searching for.

**Features:**

- Front Porch: Invite the neighbors over to sit on this fabulous porch and enjoy a glass of lemonade as the kids play in the front yard.

- Kitchen: This large kitchen is open into the breakfast nook and features an eating bar. The laundry room and access to the garage are just off the kitchen.

- Master Suite: This private retreat, designed just for the two of you, features access to the rear porch. The large walk-in closet has plenty of space for your clothes.

- Garage: This large three-car garage is ready to hold whatever you need to store.

*Images provided by designer/architect.*

Upper Level Floor Plan

Front View

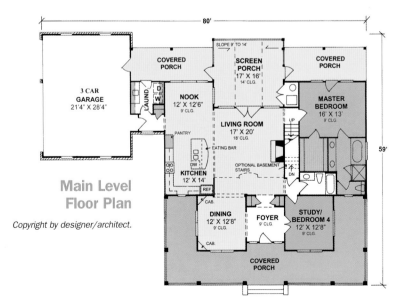

Main Level Floor Plan

*Copyright by designer/architect.*

## Plan #701216

**Dimensions:** 53' W x 78' D

**Levels:** 1

**Square Footage:** 2,255

**Bedrooms:** 2

**Bathrooms:** 2

**Foundation:** Basement

**Material List Available:** Yes

**Price Category:** E

This house's design makes it perfect for empty nesters.

*Images provided by designer/architect.*

**Features:**

- Kitchen: The family chef will love this airy kitchen. Open to the eating area that leads to the covered porch, it is perfect for a meal outside or for relaxing after dinner.

- Great Room: Entertain two or twenty in this great room, with its 11-ft.-high ceiling, entertainment center, fireplace, and bar.

- Library: Curl up with a book in this library, boasting an 11-ft.-high step ceiling and convenient location to the rest of the house.

- Master Suite: Forget sharing in this master suite! Two walk-in closets and his and her sinks are only a few luxurious features of the suite. An 11-ft.-high ceiling, tub, and separate toilet area add lavishness and convenience.

- Optional Lower Level: You'll never have to spend money on a movie ticket again with this home theater. A family room adds another place to relax, featuring a kitchenette and entertainment center.

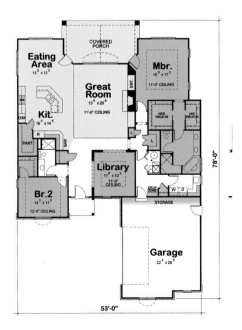

**Optional Lower Level Floor Plan**

*Copyright by designer/architect.*

## Plan #701230

**Dimensions:** 48' W x 40' D

**Levels:** 2

**Square Footage:** 2,255

**Main Level Sq. Ft.:** 1,065

**Upper Level Sq. Ft.:** 1,190

**Bedrooms:** 4

**Bathrooms:** 2½

**Foundation:** Slab

**Material List Available:** Yes

**Price Category:** E

*Images provided by designer/architect.*

The open design of this home allows for abundant sunshine and spacious rooms.

**Features:**

- **Family Room:** Seat your loved ones easily in this gracious family room, which features multiple windows and corner fireplace.

- **Kitchen:** You and your guests can still carry on a conversation in this kitchen even while you are checking on the side dishes. The kitchen is open to the dining and family rooms, so serving is easy.

- **Master Suite:** It's easy to relax and unwind in this master suite, with its 9-ft.-high ceiling, spacious walk-in closet, and dual sinks.

- **Secondary Bedrooms:** Down the hall from the master suite, three additional bedrooms share a bathroom that includes his and her sinks and a separate toilet room, making morning bathroom time go a bit smoother.

## Main Level Floor Plan

## Upper Level Floor Plan

*Copyright by designer/architect.*

## Plan #701016

**Dimensions:** 46' W x 48' D
**Levels:** 2
**Square Footage:** 2,270
**Main Level Sq. Ft.:** 1,150
**Upper Level Sq. Ft.:** 1,120
**Bedrooms:** 4
**Bathrooms:** 2½
**Foundation:** Basement
**Materials List Available:** Yes
**Price Category:** E

*Images provided by designer/architect.*

With its wraparound porch, this home evokes the charm of a traditional home.

**Features:**

- Ceiling Height: 8 ft.

- Foyer: The dramatic two-story entry enjoys views of the formal dining room and great room. A second floor balcony overlooks the entry and a plant shelf.

- Formal Dining Room: This gracious room is perfect for family holiday gatherings and for more formal dinner parties.

- Great Room: All the family will want to gather in this comfortable, informal room which features bay windows, an entertainment center, and a see-through fireplace.

- Breakfast Area: Conveniently located just off the great room, the bayed breakfast area features a built-in desk for household bills and access to the backyard.

- Kitchen: An island is the centerpiece of this kitchen. Its intelligent design makes food preparation a pleasure.

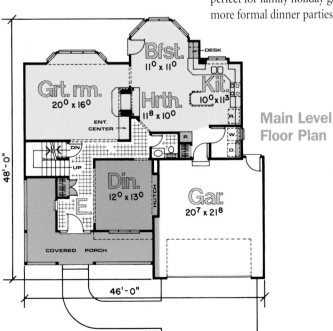

**Main Level Floor Plan**

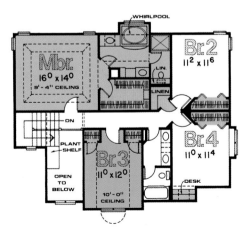

**Upper Level Floor Plan**

*Copyright by designer/architect.*

## Plan #701134

**Dimensions:** 68'8" W x 63' D
**Levels:** 1
**Square Footage:** 2,274
**Bedrooms:** 3
**Bathrooms:** 2½
**Foundation:** Slab; basement for fee
**Material List Available:** Yes
**Price Category:** E

This stately home has a convenient design perfect for your whole family.

*Images provided by designer/architect.*

**Features:**

- Kitchen: This well-designed kitchen opens out to the great room and eating area, providing your family and guests with multiple areas to gather. Large parties can spill out onto the covered porch.

- Master Suite: You won't believe the size and luxury of this master suite. A 10-ft. ceiling graces the bedroom, which opens to the

bathroom complete with a separate toilet room, tub, and his and her sinks. A large walk-in closet gives you a place for all of your clothing and accessories.

- Optional Lower Level: Enhance your living area with this optional lower-level plan. The basement plan includes an office, a family room, a bar, and an eating area.

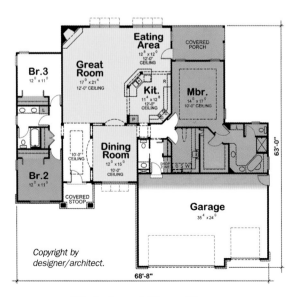

**Main Level Floor Plan**

Alternate
Master Bath

Optional
Basement
Stairs

Optional Lower Level
Floor Plan

## Plan #701150

**Dimensions:** 54' W x 50' D
**Levels:** 1.5
**Square Footage:** 2,276
**Main Level Sq. Ft.:** 1,551
**Upper Level Sq. Ft.:** 725
**Bedrooms:** 4
**Bathrooms:** 2½
**Foundation:** Basement
**Material List Available:** Yes
**Price Category:** E

*Images provided by designer/architect.*

This distinctive home has unique architectural details that are sure to make it stand out in your neighborhood.

### Features:

- **Great Room:** Sit back with friends and family in front of the fireplace in this great room. The 10½- ft. ceiling provides a feeling of expansiveness.

- **Kitchen:** This well-designed kitchen will satisfy your resident chef, with its spacious work area and center island. The kitchen opens out to the breakfast room, which makes it a wonderful and sunny place to enjoy a cup of coffee.

- **Master Suite:** You'll appreciate the extra details in this master suite, with its step ceiling, separate toilet room, skylight, his and her sinks, whirlpool tub, and walk-in closet.

- **Secondary Bedrooms:** The three other bedrooms are perfect for the kids. A shared bathroom features dual sinks and a clothing chute, eliminating many trips to the laundry room.

**Main Level Floor Plan**

**Upper Level Floor Plan**

*Copyright by designer/architect.*

## Plan #701077

**Dimensions:** 72' W x 56' D
**Levels:** 1
**Square Footage:** 2,276
**Bedrooms:** 3
**Bathrooms:** 2½
**Foundation:** Basement;
crawl space for fee
**Material List Available:** Yes
**Price Category:** E

This charming country home is filled with ingenious design and sumptuous spaces.

**Features:**

- **Great Room:** This spacious entertainment area can be kept formal for guests while the den holds all of the embarrassing family clutter.

- **Kitchen:** Uniquely laid out, this kitchen includes two pantries, a desk, a snack bar, and an adjacent wet bar. Transitioning right into the breakfast area means more natural light for the kitchen and simple shifting from meal preparation to dining.

- **Master Suite:** This master bedroom was planned with couples in mind. His and her closets and vanities simplify getting ready. A built-in entertainment center, whirlpool tub, and separate shower stall are added bonuses.

- **Secondary Bedrooms:** In a space all their own, these bedrooms have ample closet space, a nearby full bathroom, and are identically sized to keep siblings from squabbling.

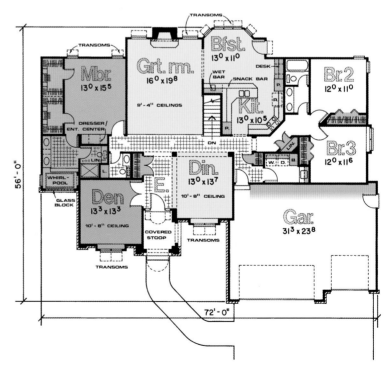

## Plan #701083

**Dimensions:** 54' W x 52' D
**Levels:** 1.5
**Square Footage:** 2,277
**Main Level Sq. Ft.:** 1,570
**Upper Level Sq. Ft.:** 707
**Bedrooms:** 4
**Bathrooms:** 2½
**Foundation:** Basement; crawl space for fee
**Material List Available:** Yes
**Price Category:** E

*Images provided by designer/architect.*

This country-style home, with its classic wraparound porch, is just the plan you have been searching for.

**Features:**

- Entry: This two-story entry gives an open and airy feeling when you enter the home. A view into the dining room and great room adds to the open feeling.

- Great Room: This grand gathering area with cathedral ceiling is ready for your friends and family to come and visit. The fireplace, flanked by large windows, adds a cozy feeling to the space.

- Kitchen: The chef in the family will love how efficiently this island kitchen was designed. An abundance of cabinets and counter space is always a plus.

- Master Suite: This main level oasis will help you relieve all the stresses from the day. The master bath boasts dual vanities and a large walk-in closet.

- Secondary Bedrooms: Three generously sized bedrooms occupy the upper level. The full bathroom is located for easy access to all three bedrooms.

**Main Level Floor Plan**

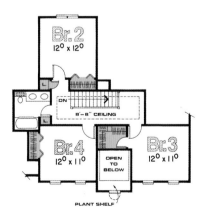

**Upper Level Floor Plan**

*Copyright by designer/architect.*

*Images provided by designer/architect.*

**Plan #701298**

**Dimensions:** 68' W x 62'8" D

**Levels:** 1

**Square Footage:** 2,279

**Bedrooms:** 2

**Bathrooms:** 3½

**Foundation:** Basement

**Material List Available:** Yes

**Price Category:** E

Copyright by
designer/architect.

**Bonus Level
Floor Plan**

**Plan #701063**

**Dimensions:** 65'4" W x 48'8" D

**Levels:** 2

**Square Footage:** 2,282

**Main Level Sq. Ft.:** 1,597

**Upper Level Sq. Ft.:** 685

**Bedrooms:** 4

**Bathrooms:** 2½

**Foundation:** Basement

**Materials List Available:** Yes

**Price Category:** E

*Images provided by designer/architect.*

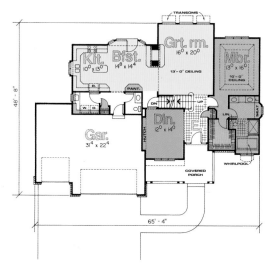

**Main
Level
Floor
Plan**

Copyright by
designer/architect.

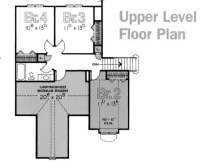

**Upper Level
Floor Plan**

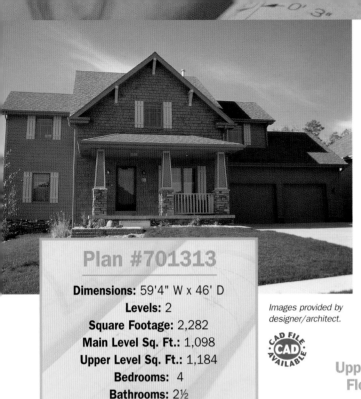

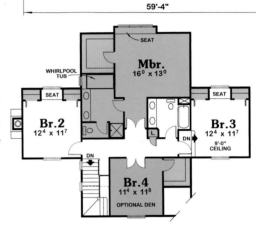

## Plan #701313

**Dimensions:** 59'4" W x 46' D

**Levels:** 2

**Square Footage:** 2,282

**Main Level Sq. Ft.:** 1,098

**Upper Level Sq. Ft.:** 1,184

**Bedrooms:** 4

**Bathrooms:** 2½

**Foundation:** Basement; crawl space or slab for fee

**Materials List Available:** Yes

**Price Category:** E

*Images provided by designer/architect.*

**CAD FILE AVAILABLE**

**Main Level Floor Plan**

**Upper Level Floor Plan**

*Copyright by designer/architect.*

---

## Plan #701322

**Dimensions:** 56' W x 52' D

**Levels:** 1.5

**Square Footage:** 2,308

**Main Level Sq. Ft.:** 1,654

**Upper Level Sq. Ft.:** 654

**Bedrooms:** 4

**Bathrooms:** 2½

**Foundation:** Basement

**Material List Available:** Yes

**Price Category:** E

*Images provided by designer/architect.*

*This home, as shown in the photograph, may differ from the actual blueprints. For more detailed information, please check the floor plans carefully.*

**CAD FILE AVAILABLE**

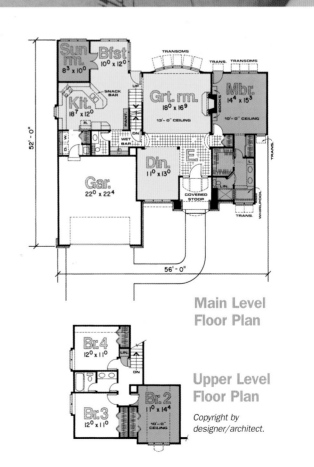

**Main Level Floor Plan**

**Upper Level Floor Plan**

*Copyright by designer/architect.*

## Plan #701035

**Dimensions:** 64' W x 57'2" D

**Levels:** 1

**Square Footage:** 2,311

**Bedrooms:** 3

**Bathrooms:** 2½

**Foundation:** Basement

**Materials List Available:** Yes

**Price Category:** E

*Images provided by designer/architect.*

## Plan #701166

**Dimensions:** 64'8" W x 62' D

**Levels:** 1

**Square Footage:** 2,317

**Bedrooms:** 2

**Bathrooms:** 2½

**Foundation:** Basement

**Material List Available:** Yes

**Price Category:** E

*Images provided by designer/architect.*

CAD FILE AVAILABLE

**Optional Basement Level Floor Plan**

*Copyright by designer/architect.*

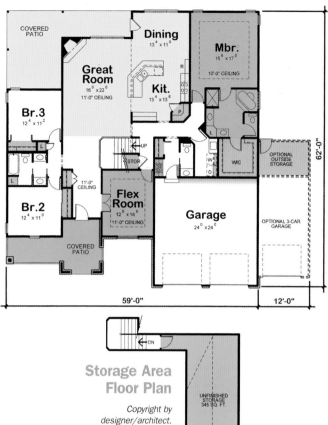

## Plan #701257

**Dimensions:** 59' W x 62' D

**Levels:** 1

**Square Footage:** 2,327

**Bedrooms:** 3

**Bathrooms:** 2½

**Foundation:** Basement

**Material List Available:** Yes

**Price Category:** E

*Images provided by designer/architect.*

**CAD FILE AVAILABLE**

### Storage Area Floor Plan

UNFINISHED STORAGE 345 SQ. FT.

*Copyright by designer/architect.*

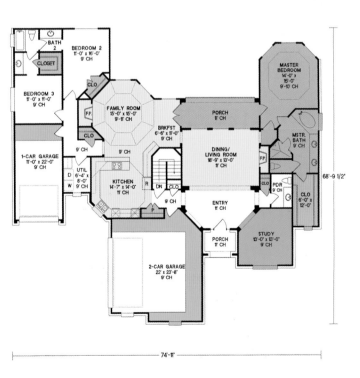

## Plan #701110

**Dimensions:** 74'11" W x 68'9½" D

**Levels:** 1

**Square Footage:** 2,331

**Bedrooms:** 3

**Bathrooms:** 2½

**Foundation:** Slab; basement for fee

**Material List Available:** Yes

**Price Category:** E

*Images provided by designer/architect.*

**CAD FILE AVAILABLE**

*Copyright by designer/architect.*

## Plan #701188

**Dimensions:** 62'8" W x 47'4" D
**Levels:** 1.5
**Square Footage:** 2,029
**Main Level Sq. Ft.:** 1,411
**Upper Level Sq. Ft.:** 618
**Bedrooms:** 4
**Bathrooms:** 2½
**Foundation:** Basement
**Material List Available:** Yes
**Price Category:** D

*Images provided by designer/architect.*

This home is well designed and will add to the function and convenience of your life.

**Features:**

- **Great Room:** This stunning great room is the perfect place to entertain your guests. With its 13-ft.-high ceiling and fireplace, it is spacious and cozy at the same time.

- **Kitchen:** Lined with counter space and storage, this kitchen features a pantry and a snack bar connecting to the breakfast room, perfect for quick meals or as a buffet or bar.

- **Master Suite:** You'll love the convenience of this master suite, with its roomy design and details such as his and her sinks, walk-in closet, and separate toilet area.

- **Secondary Bedrooms:** Three additional bedrooms and a shared bathroom are located upstairs, creating a perfect environment for siblings.

### Main Level Floor Plan

### Upper Level Floor Plan

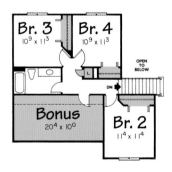

*Copyright by designer/architect.*

# Plan #701306

**Dimensions:** 54' W x 45'4" D
**Levels:** 2
**Square Footage:** 2,339
**Main Level Sq. Ft.:** 1,665
**Upper Level Sq. Ft.:** 674
**Bedrooms:** 4
**Bathrooms:** 2½
**Foundation:** Basement
**Materials List Available:** Yes
**Price Category:** E

This home is designed for gracious living and is distinguished by many architectural details.

**Features:**

- Ceiling Height: 8 ft. unless otherwise noted.

- Foyer: This is truly a grand foyer with a dramatic ceiling that soars to 18 ft.

- Great Room: The foyer's 18-ft. ceiling extends into the great room where an open staircase adds architectural windows. Warm yourself by the fireplace that is framed by windows.

- Kitchen: An island is the centerpiece of this handsome and efficient kitchen that features a breakfast area for informal family meals. The room also includes a handy desk.

- Private Wing: The master suite and study are in a private wing of the house.

- Room to Expand: In addition to the three bedrooms, the second level has an unfinished storage space that can become another bedroom or office.

**CAD FILE AVAILABLE**

## Main Level Floor Plan

## Upper Level Floor Plan

## Plan #701056

**Dimensions:** 56'8" W x 48' D
**Levels:** 2
**Square Footage:** 2,340
**Main Level Sq. Ft.:** 1,701
**Upper Level Sq. Ft.:** 639
**Bedrooms:** 4
**Bathrooms:** 2½
**Foundation:** Basement; slab for fee
**Materials List Available:** Yes
**Price Category:** E

*Images provided by designer/architect.*

You'll love this cheerful home, with its many large windows that let in natural light and cozy spaces that encourage family gatherings.

**Features:**

- Entry: Use the built-in curio cabinet here to display your best collector's pieces.
- Den: French doors from the entry lead to this room, with its built-in bookcase and triple-wide, transom-topped window.

- Great Room: The 14-ft. ceiling in this room accentuates the floor-to-ceiling windows that frame the raised-hearth fireplace.
- Kitchen: Both the layout and the work space make this room a delight for any cook.
- Master Suite: The bedroom has a tray ceiling for built-in elegance. A skylight helps to light the master bath, and an oval whirlpool tub, separate shower, and double vanity provide a luxurious touch.

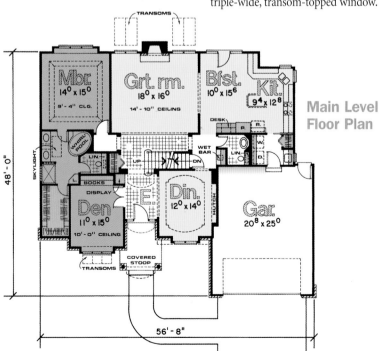

**Main Level Floor Plan**

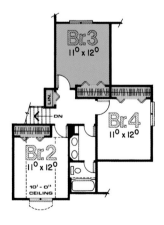

**Upper Level Floor Plan**

*Copyright by designer/architect.*

## Plan #701046

**Dimensions:** 57'4" W x 30' D
**Levels:** 2
**Square Footage:** 2,345
**Main Level Sq. Ft.:** 1,000
**Upper Level Sq. Ft.:** 1,345
**Bedrooms:** 4
**Bathrooms:** 3½
**Foundation:** Basement
**Materials List Available:** Yes
**Price Category:** E

*This home, as shown in the photograph, may differ from the actual blueprints. For more detailed information, please check the floor plans carefully.*

*Images provided by designer/architect.*

Imagine owning a home with a Colonial-styled exterior and a practical, amenity-filled interior with both formal and informal areas.

**Features:**

- Family Room: This room will be the heart of your home. A bay window lets you create a special nook for reading or quiet conversation, and a fireplace begs for a circle of comfortable chairs or soft cushions around it.

- Living Room: Connected to the family room by a set of French doors, you can use this room for formal entertaining or informal family fun.

- Kitchen: This kitchen has been designed for efficient work patterns. However, the snack bar that links it to the breakfast area beyond also invites company while the cook is working.

- Master Suite: Located on the second level, this suite features an entertainment center, a separate sitting area, built-in dressers, two walk-in closets, and a whirlpool tub.

## Main Level Floor Plan

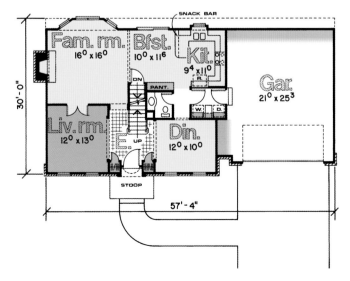

## Upper Level Floor Plan

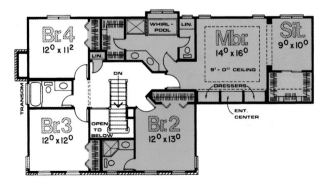

*Copyright by designer/architect.*

## Plan #701180

**Dimensions:** 50' W x 44' D
**Levels:** 2
**Square Footage:** 2,349
**Main Level Sq. Ft.:** 1,199
**Upper Level Sq. Ft.:** 1,150
**Bedrooms:** 4
**Bathrooms:** 3½
**Foundation:** Basement
**Material List Available:** Yes
**Price Category:** E

*Images provided by designer/architect.*

*This home, as shown in the photograph, may differ from the actual blueprints. For more detailed information, please check the floor plans carefully.*

**CAD FILE AVAILABLE**

This attractive traditional home is filled with details and conveniences to enhance your lifestyle.

**Features:**

• Family Room: Friends and family alike will appreciate this beautiful family room for its fireplace, wet bar, and comfortable atmosphere.

• Kitchen: This kitchen is open to the breakfast room and has plenty of work and storage space for the family cook.

• Master Suite: You'll love waking up in this master suite, with its 9-ft.-high ceiling, his and her sinks, separate toilet area, and large walk-in closet.

• Secondary Bedrooms: Three extra bedrooms share two bathrooms, making the arrangement perfect for siblings or to be used as guest rooms.

*Copyright by designer/architect.*

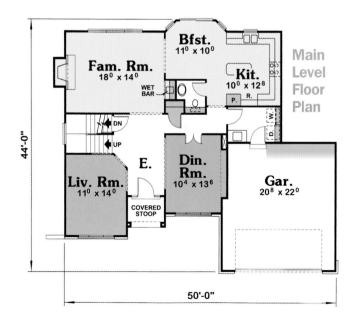

**Main Level Floor Plan**

**Upper Level Floor Plan**

## Plan #701013

**Dimensions:** 54' W x 50' D

**Levels:** 2

**Square Footage:** 2,353

**Main Level Sq. Ft.:** 1,653

**Upper Level Sq. Ft.:** 700

**Bedrooms:** 4

**Bathrooms:** 2½

**Foundation:** Basement

**Materials List Available:** Yes

**Price Category:** E

*Images provided by designer/architect.*

The dramatic two-story entry with bent staircase is the first sign that this is a gracious home.

**Features:**

- Ceiling Height: 8 ft. except as noted.

- Great Room: A row of transom-topped windows and a tall, beamed ceiling add a sense of spaciousness to this family gathering area.

- Formal Dining Room: The bayed window helps make this an inviting place to entertain.

- See-through Fireplace: This feature spreads warmth and coziness throughout the informal areas of the home.

- Breakfast Area: This sunny area shares a see-through fireplace with the great room. It's the perfect place to start the day.

- Master Suite: Here are all the features you expect to find in large luxury homes. Wake up to tall, sloped ceilings, and enjoy the corner whirlpool, separate shower, and vanity. A large walk-in closet provides plenty of wardrobe storage.

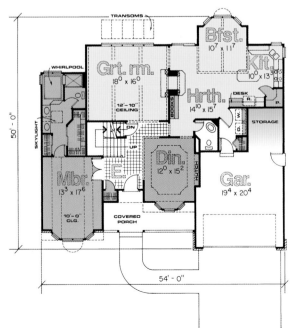

**Main Level Floor Plan**

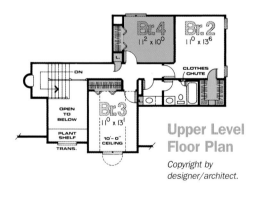

**Upper Level Floor Plan**

*Copyright by designer/architect.*

## Plan #701318

**Dimensions:** 48' W x 49' D

**Levels:** 2

**Square Footage:** 2,354

**Main Level Sq. Ft.:** 1,207

**Upper Level Sq. Ft.:** 1,147

**Bedrooms:** 4

**Bathrooms:** 3½

**Foundation:** Basement

**Materials List Available:** Yes

**Price Category:** E

*Images provided by designer/architect.*

Careful attention to traffic flow in this open layout result in a convenient and comfortable home.

**Features:**

- Ceiling Height: 8 ft. unless otherwise noted.

- Family Room: This sunny room is perfectly suited for family activities.

- Breakfast Area: You'll want to linger over breakfast in this sunlight-filled bayed area that flows into the family room.

- Kitchen: The breakfast area flows into this kitchen, which features a pantry and center island that doubles as a snack bar.

- Dining Room. Corner columns lend elegance to this room, making it perfect for formal entertaining as well as family gatherings.

- Computer Loft: This loft, designed to accommodate the family computer, overlooks the two-story entry.

- Master Suite: This comfortable retreat offers a walk-in closet, bathtub, and separate shower.

**Main Level Floor Plan**

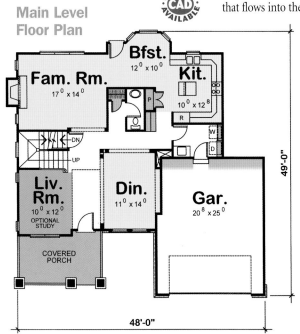

**Upper Level Floor Plan**

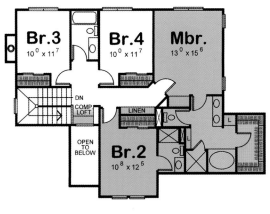

*Copyright by designer/architect.*

## Plan #701101

**Dimensions:** 75' W x 52' D
**Levels:** 1.5
**Square Footage:** 2,361
**Main Level Sq. Ft.:** 1,649
**Upper Level Sq. Ft.:** 712
**Bedrooms:** 3
**Bathrooms:** 2½
**Foundation:** Slab; basement for fee
**Material List Available:** Yes
**Price Category:** E

Interesting architecture and elegant details make this home inviting and memorable.

**Features:**

- Porches: At the front of the house, a porch greets guests and provides a shady spot to catch up on reading or to chat. A sun deck extends almost the full length of the back of the home, making it great for parties or relaxing outdoors.

- Living Room: This uniquely shaped living room has a stunning 18-ft. ceiling open to the second floor. The fireplace, two-story windows, and entertainment center make it perfect for entertaining guests.

- Kitchen: This efficiently designed kitchen allows for the resident chef to maneuver easily. The center island bridges the kitchen and the breakfast room, making it a wonderful place to eat a meal.

- Master Suite: This bedroom is both elegant and relaxing, opening up to a master bath that includes a walk-in closet, large tub, separate toilet room, and his and her sinks.

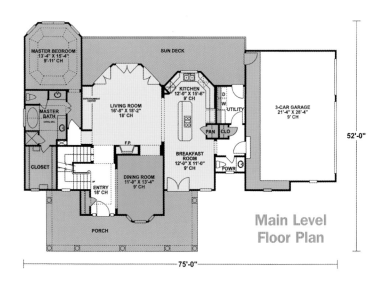

**Main Level Floor Plan**

**Upper Level Floor Plan**

*Copyright by designer/architect.*

## Plan #701208

**Dimensions:** 83' W x 56' D
**Levels:** 1.5
**Square Footage:** 2,382
**Main Level Sq. Ft.:** 1,862
**Upper Level Sq. Ft.:** 520
**Bedrooms:** 3
**Bathrooms:** 2
**Foundation:** Basement
**Material List Available:** Yes
**Price Category:** E

*Images provided by designer/architect.*

This wonderful farmhouse provides ample space for relaxing either inside or out.

**Features:**

- **Porches:** Four sprawling porches allow for endless activities outside. The screened-in porch is the perfect place to enjoy the changing seasons.

- **Kitchen:** This kitchen is wonderful for the home cook. An eating bar provides extra counter space and a place for quick snacks.

- **Master Suite:** This large master suite includes a 9-ft.-high ceiling, his and her sinks, a tub, a separate area for the toilet, and a spacious walk-in closet.

- **Study:** Convert this room into a home office or a study place for the children. Use it to suit your family's needs.

**Main Level Floor Plan**

**Upper Level Floor Plan**

*Copyright by designer/architect.*

## Plan #701050

**Dimensions:** 56' W x 49' D
**Levels:** 2
**Square Footage:** 2,384
**Main Level Sq. Ft.:** 1,616
**Upper Level Sq. Ft.:** 768
**Bedrooms:** 4
**Bathrooms:** 2½
**Foundation:** Slab; basement for fee
**Materials List Available:** Yes
**Price Category:** E

*Images provided by designer/architect.*

This design is ideal if you want a generously sized home now and room to expand later.

**Features:**

- **Living Room:** Your eyes will be drawn towards the ceiling as soon as you enter this lovely room. The ceiling is vaulted, giving a sense of grandeur, and a graceful balcony from the second floor adds extra interest to this room.

- **Kitchen:** Designed with lots of counter space to make your work convenient, this kitchen also shares an eating bar with the breakfast nook.

- **Breakfast Nook:** Eat here or go out to the adjoining private porch where you can enjoy your meal in the morning sunshine.

- **Master Suite:** The bayed area in the bedroom makes a picturesque sitting area. French doors in the bedroom open to a private bath that's fitted with a bathtub, separate shower, two vanities, and a walk-in closet.

### Main Level Floor Plan

### Upper Level Floor Plan

*Copyright by designer/architect.*

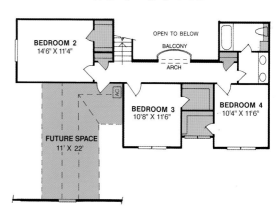

## Plan #701149

**Dimensions:** 54' W x 42' D

**Levels:** 2

**Square Footage:** 2,387

**Main Level Sq. Ft.:** 1,303

**Upper Level Sq. Ft.:** 1,084

**Bedrooms:** 4

**Bathrooms:** 2½

**Foundation:** Basement

**Material List Available:** Yes

**Price Category:** E

*Images provided by designer/architect.*

The exterior of this traditional home is filled with windows to capture the sunlight.

**Features:**

- Kitchen: This spacious kitchen provides many amenities to the home cook, including a snack bar and a salad sink. The connecting breakfast room is a beautiful and sunny haven to start your day.

- Family Room: Relax with family and friends in this large, well-appointed room.

- Master Suite: This master suite is truly an oasis, with its 11-ft. ceiling, walk-in closet, his and her sinks, and whirlpool bathtub.

- Secondary Bedrooms: Across the hall from the master suite, three additional bedrooms share a bathroom with dual sinks, making the morning rush a bit less stressful.

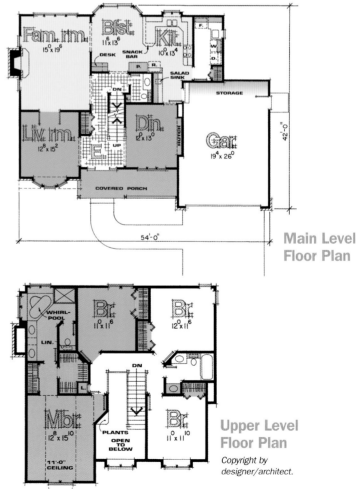

**Main Level Floor Plan**

**Upper Level Floor Plan**

*Copyright by designer/architect.*

## Plan #701242

**Dimensions:** 58' W x 68' D

**Levels:** 1

**Square Footage:** 2,390

**Bedrooms:** 2

**Bathrooms:** 2½

**Foundation:** Basement

**Material List Available:** Yes

**Price Category:** E

*Images provided by designer/architect.*

Visually stunning inside and out, you'll love the ample room and amenities this home provides.

**CAD FILE AVAILABLE**

**Features:**

- **Kitchen:** This open kitchen allows easy access to the eating area and great room. The island is perfect for quick snacks or extra workspace.

- **Office:** Tucked behind the kitchen, this office is a wonderful private retreat for work.

- **Master Suite:** Under a 10-ft. ceiling, you'll find a large bedroom area with access to the

back porch. The bath features a separate toilet room, spacious walk-in closet, and tub.

- **Porch:** This covered porch is accessible through the eating area and the master bedroom, making it perfect for a meal outside or simply relaxing at the end of the day.

**Main Level Floor Plan**

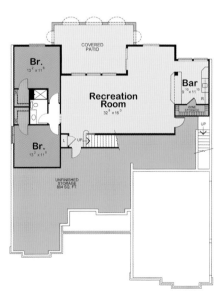

**Optional Lower Level Floor Plan**

*Copyright by designer/architect.*

## Plan #701309

**Dimensions:** 54' W x 49'10" D
**Levels:** 2
**Square Footage:** 2,391
**Main Level Sq. Ft.:** 1,697
**Upper Level Sq. Ft.:** 694
**Bedrooms:** 4
**Bathrooms:** 2½
**Foundation:** Basement
**Material List Available:** Yes
**Price Category:** E

*Images provided by designer/architect.*

*This home, as shown in the photograph, may differ from the actual blueprints. For more detailed information, please check the floor plans carefully.*

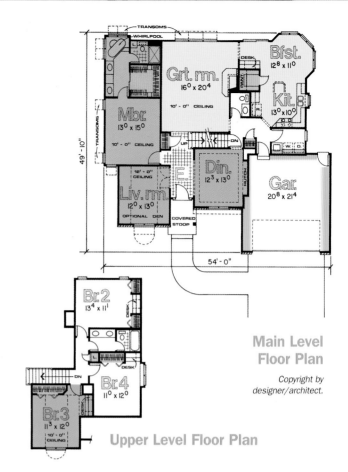

**Main Level Floor Plan**

*Copyright by designer/architect.*

**Upper Level Floor Plan**

## Plan #701252

**Dimensions:** 59' W x 44' D
**Levels:** 2
**Square Footage:** 2,400
**Main Level Sq. Ft.:** 1,161
**per Level Sq. Ft.:** 1,239
**Bedrooms:** 4
**Bathrooms:** 3½
**Foundation:** Basement
**Material List Available:** Yes
**Price Category:** E

*Images provided by designer/architect.*

**Main Level Floor Plan**

**Upper Level Floor Plan**

*Copyright by designer/architect.*

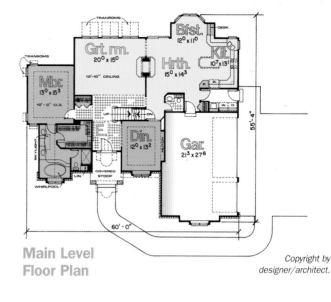

**Main Level
Floor Plan**

## Plan #701157

**Dimensions:** 60' W x 55'4" D
**Levels:** 1.5
**Square Footage:** 2,405
**Main Level Sq. Ft.:** 1,733
**Upper Level Sq. Ft.:** 672
**Bedrooms:** 4
**Bathrooms:** 2½
**Foundation:** Basement
**Material List Available:** Yes
**Price Category:** E

*Images provided by
designer/architect.*

Kitchen

**Upper Level
Floor Plan**

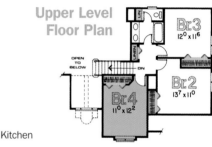

## Plan #701311

**Dimensions:** 58' W x 42'8" D
**Levels:** 2
**Square Footage:** 2,417
**Main Level Sq. Ft.:** 1,162
**Upper Level Sq. Ft.:** 1,255
**Bedrooms:** 4
**Bathrooms:** 2½
**Foundation:** Basement
**Materials List Available:** Yes
**Price Category:** E

*Images provided by
designer/architect.*

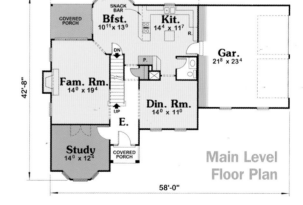

**Main Level
Floor Plan**

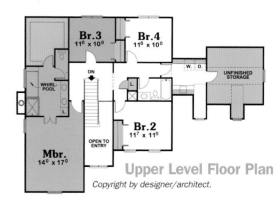

**Upper Level Floor Plan**

## Plan #701267

**Dimensions:** 40' W x 46' D

**Levels:** 2

**Square Footage:** 2,429

**Main Level Sq. Ft.:** 1,044

**Upper Level Sq. Ft.:** 1,385

**Bedrooms:** 4

**Bathrooms:** 2½

**Foundation:** Slab;
crawl space or basement for fee

**Material List Available:** Yes

**Price Category:** E

*Images provided by designer/architect.*

**Main Level Floor Plan**

**Upper Level Floor Plan**

*Copyright by designer/architect.*

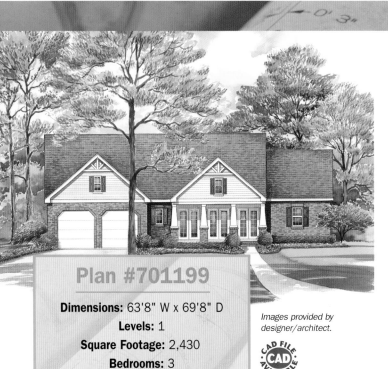

## Plan #701199

**Dimensions:** 63'8" W x 69'8" D

**Levels:** 1

**Square Footage:** 2,430

**Bedrooms:** 3

**Bathrooms:** 2½

**Foundation:** Basement

**Material List Available:** Yes

**Price Category:** E

*Images provided by designer/architect.*

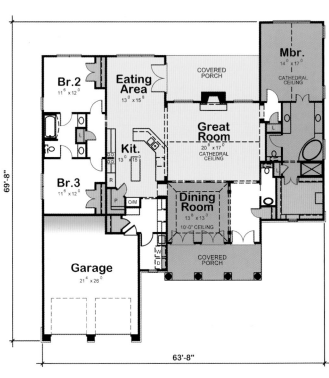

*Copyright by designer/architect.*

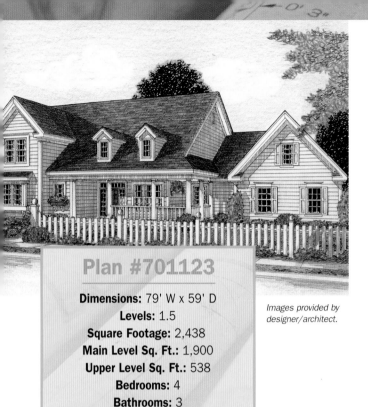

**Main Level Floor Plan**

**Upper Level Floor Plan**

## Plan #701123

**Dimensions:** 79' W x 59' D
**Levels:** 1.5
**Square Footage:** 2,438
**Main Level Sq. Ft.:** 1,900
**Upper Level Sq. Ft.:** 538
**Bedrooms:** 4
**Bathrooms:** 3
**Foundation:** Slab; basement for fee
**Material List Available:** Yes
**Price Category:** E

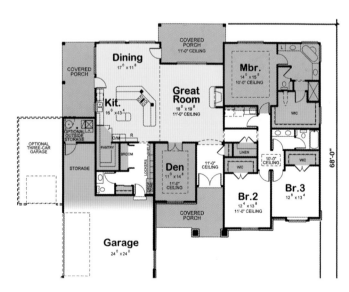

**Optional Floor Plan**

## Plan #701253

**Dimensions:** 69' W x 68' D
**Levels:** 1
**Square Footage:** 2,449
**Bedrooms:** 3
**Bathrooms:** 2½
**Foundation:** Basement
**Material List Available:** Yes
**Price Category:** E

## Plan #701032

**Dimensions:** 66' W x 68' D
**Levels:** 1
**Square Footage:** 2,456
**Bedrooms:** 3
**Bathrooms:** 2½
**Foundation:** Basement
**Materials List Available:** Yes
**Price Category:** E

*Images provided by designer/architect.*

If you're looking for a home that gives comfort at every turn, this could be the one.

**Features:**

- **Entry:** Airy and open, this entry imparts a welcoming feeling.

- **Great Room:** You'll love the style built into this centrally located room. A row of transom-topped windows adds natural light, and a fireplace gives it character.

- **Dining Room:** Just off the entry for convenience, this formal room has a boxed ceiling that accentuates its interesting angled shape.

- **Gathering Room:** This lovely room features an angled ceiling, snack bar, built-in entertainment center, built-in desk, and abundance of windows. A door leads to the large, covered rear porch with skylights.

- **Master Suite:** Relax in comfort after a long day, or sit on the adjoining, covered rear porch to enjoy the evening breezes.

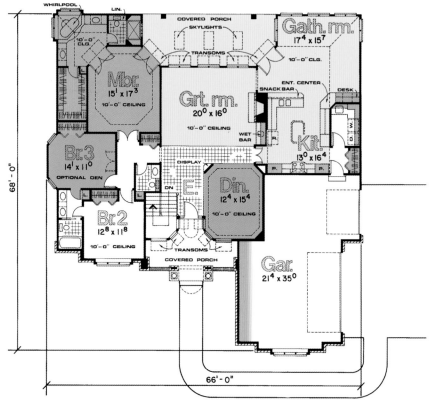

*Copyright by designer/architect.*

## Plan #701243

**Dimensions:** 58'8" W x 62' D
**Levels:** 1.5
**Square Footage:** 2,476
**Main Level Sq. Ft.:** 1,863
**Upper Level Sq. Ft.:** 613
**Bedrooms:** 3
**Bathrooms:** 2½
**Foundation:** Basement
**Material List Available:** Yes
**Price Category:** E

**Features:**

- **Great Room:** Enjoy this large room by relaxing in front of the fireplace with friends and family.

- **Kitchen:** The large walk-in pantry and center island makes preparing meals in this kitchen a pleasure. The room is open to the eating area.

- **Master Suite:** With his and her sinks and a large walk-in closet, the generous size of this master suite makes getting ready in the morning a breeze.

- **Secondary Bedrooms:** Upstairs, two loft bedrooms and a Jack-and-Jill bathroom give kids some privacy from each other.

With its eye-catching exterior, this home is perfect for you and your family.

**Main Level Floor Plan**

*Copyright by designer/architect.*

**Upper Level Floor Plan**

## Plan #701015

**Dimensions:** 64' W x 46' D
**Levels:** 2
**Square Footage:** 2,480
**Main Level Sq. Ft.:** 1,369
**Upper Level Sq. Ft.:** 1,111
**Bedrooms:** 4
**Bathrooms:** 2½
**Foundation:** Basement
**Materials List Available:** Yes
**Price Category:** E

*Images provided by designer/architect.*

Tapered columns and an angled stairway give this home a classical style.

**Features:**

• Ceiling Height: 8 ft.

• Living Room: Just off the dramatic two-story entry is this distinctive living room, with its tapered columns, transom-topped windows, and boxed ceiling.

• Formal Dining Room: The tapered columns, transom-topped windows, and boxed ceiling found in the living room continue into this gracious dining space.

• Family Room: Located on the opposite side of the house from the living room and dining room, the family room features a beamed ceiling and fireplace framed by windows.

• Kitchen: An island is the centerpiece of this convenient kitchen.

• Master Suite: Upstairs, a tiered ceiling and corner windows enhance the master bedroom, which is served by a pampering bath.

### Main Level Floor Plan

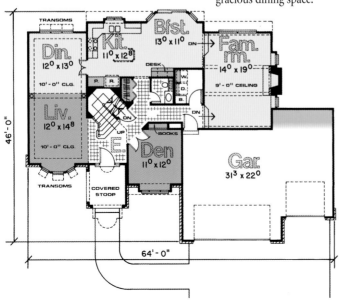

### Upper Level Floor Plan

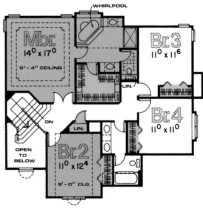

*Copyright by designer/architect.*

## Plan #701256

**Dimensions:** 63' W x 70' D
**Levels:** 1
**Square Footage:** 2,485
**Bedrooms:** 2
**Bathrooms:** 2½
**Foundation:** Basement
**Material List Available:** Yes
**Price Category:** E

*Images provided by designer/architect.*

This beautiful home comes with a multitude of floor-plan options to satisfy your family's needs.

**Features:**

• **Kitchen:** This spacious kitchen with its cathedral ceiling is as beautiful as it is functional. A large amount of counter space, along with a pantry and center island, will please the home cook.

• **Apartment Suite:** Wonderful for in-laws or live-in help, this apartment suite is complete with a bedroom, bathroom, living room, and kitchenette. Alternatively, this area can be changed to two bedrooms for the children.

• **Master Suite:** You won't have to share in this master suite. A large bedroom area opens up to a master bathroom with his and her sinks and walk-in closets.

• **Garage:** Large enough for the cars and storage, this three-car garage has access to both the outdoors and inside the house, making those trips with the grocery bags a bit easier.

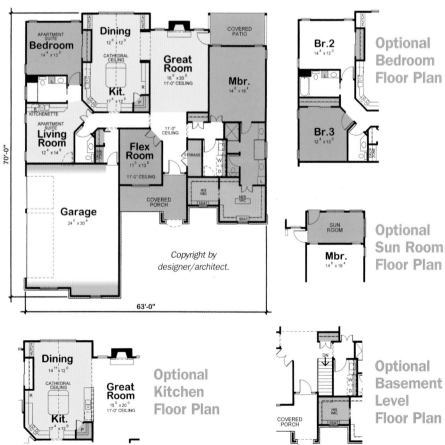

## Plan #701045

**Dimensions:** 68'8" W x 47'8" D
**Levels:** 2
**Square Footage:** 2,486
**Main Level Sq. Ft.:** 1,829
**Upper Level Sq. Ft.:** 657
**Bedrooms:** 4
**Bathrooms:** 2½
**Foundation:** Basement
**Materials List Available:** Yes
**Price Category:** E

*Images provided by designer/architect.*

Enjoy the natural light that streams through the many lovely windows in this well-designed home.

**Features:**

• Living Room: This room is sure to be your family's headquarters, thanks to the lovely 15-ft. ceiling, stacked windows, central location, and cozy fireplace.

• Dining Room: A boxed ceiling adds formality to this well-positioned room.

• Kitchen: The island cooktop in this kitchen is so large that it includes a snack bar area. A pantry gives ample storage space, and a built-in desk—where you can set up a computer station or a record-keeping area—adds efficiency.

• Master Suite: For the sake of privacy, this master suite is located on the opposite side of the home from the other living areas. You'll love the roomy bedroom and luxuriate in the private bath with its many amenities.

## Main Level Floor Plan

*Copyright by designer/architect.*

## Upper Level Floor Plan

## Plan #701130

**Dimensions:** 59' W x 58' D
**Levels:** 1.5
**Square Footage:** 2,487
**Main Level Sq. Ft.:** 2,019
**Upper Level Sq. Ft.:** 468
**Bedrooms:** 4
**Bathrooms:** 3
**Foundation:** Slab; basement for fee
**Material List Available:** Yes
**Price Category:** E

*Images provided by designer/architect.*

Both eye-catching and attractive, you will love to call this house your home.

**Features:**

- **Screen Porch:** This porch is wonderful for relaxing with friends or family, rain or shine.

- **Living Room:** Relax with friends and family under the 12-ft. ceiling in this large living room. The corner fireplace adds a cozy touch.

- **Kitchen:** This kitchen is both spacious and functional for the home cook. An eating bar adds space for either working or snacking, and the attached nook is a wonderful spot for a casual meal with the family. The nook leads out to the screened-in porch, making it perfect for outdoor meals.

- **Master Suite:** You will be happy to wake up every morning in this master suite. A 9-ft. ceiling, his and her sinks, a separate room for the toilet, and a spacious walk-in closet are just a few of the amenities provided in this room.

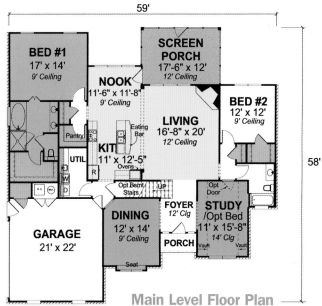

**Main Level Floor Plan**

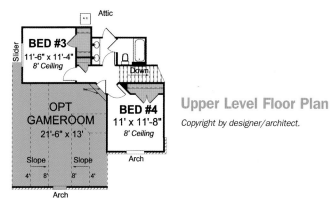

**Upper Level Floor Plan**

*Copyright by designer/architect.*

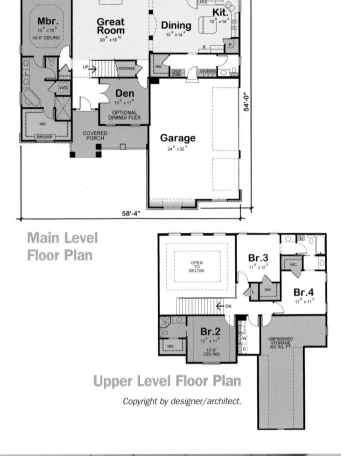

## Main Level Floor Plan

## Upper Level Floor Plan

*Copyright by designer/architect.*

## Plan #701251

**Dimensions:** 58'4" W x 54' D

**Levels:** 1.5

**Square Footage:** 2,495

**Main Level Sq. Ft.:** 1,664

**Upper Level Sq. Ft.:** 831

**Bedrooms:** 4

**Bathrooms:** 3½

**Foundation:** Basement

**Material List Available:** Yes

**Price Category:** E

*Images provided by designer/architect.*

CAD FILE AVAILABLE

---

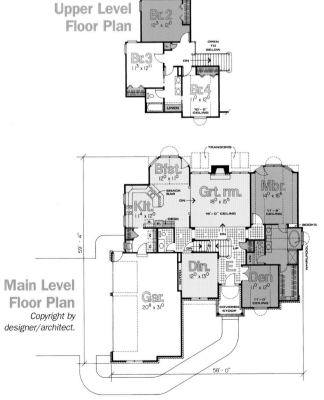

## Upper Level Floor Plan

## Main Level Floor Plan

*Copyright by designer/architect.*

## Plan #701087

**Dimensions:** 58' W x 59'4" D

**Levels:** 1.5

**Square Footage:** 2,496

**Main Level Sq. Ft.:** 1,777

**Upper Level Sq. Ft.:** 719

**Bedrooms:** 4

**Bathrooms:** 2½

**Foundation:** Basement; crawl space for fee

**Material List Available:** Yes

**Price Category:** E

*Images provided by designer/architect.*

CAD FILE AVAILABLE

Images provided by designer/architect.

Copyright by designer/architect.

## Plan #701003

**Dimensions:** 76' W x 55'4" D
**Levels:** 1
**Square Footage:** 2,498
**Bedrooms:** 4
**Bathrooms:** 2½
**Foundation:** Basement; crawl space or slab for fee
**Materials List Available:** Yes
**Price Category:** E

---

**Main Level Floor Plan**

Copyright by designer/architect.

## Plan #701227

**Dimensions:** 50' W x 44' D
**Levels:** 2
**Square Footage:** 2,499
**Main Level Sq. Ft.:** 1,178
**Upper Level Sq. Ft.:** 1,321
**Bedrooms:** 4
**Bathrooms:** 2½
**Foundation:** Basement
**Material List Available:** Yes
**Price Category:** E

Images provided by designer/architect.

CAD FILE AVAILABLE

**Optional Main Level Floor Plan**

**Upper Level Floor Plan**

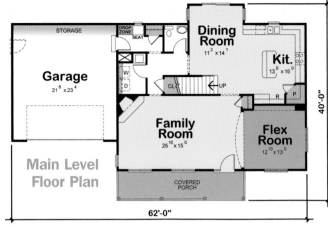

STORAGE

DROP ZONE
SEAT

**Dining Room**
11³ x 14¹

**Kit.**
13⁰ x 16⁰

W D

CL

UP

**Garage**
21⁸ x 23⁴

**Main Level Floor Plan**

**Family Room**
25¹⁰ x 15⁰

**Flex Room**
12¹⁰ x 13⁰

R P

COVERED PORCH

40'-0"

62'-0"

## Plan #701289

**Dimensions:** 62' W x 40' D

**Levels:** 2

**Square Footage:** 2,501

**Main Level Sq. Ft.:** 1,248

**Upper Level Sq. Ft.:** 1,253

**Bedrooms:** 4

**Bathrooms:** 2½

**Foundation:** Basement

**Material List Available:** Yes

**Price Category:** E

*Images provided by designer/architect.*

CAD FILE CAD AVAILABLE

*Copyright by designer/architect.*

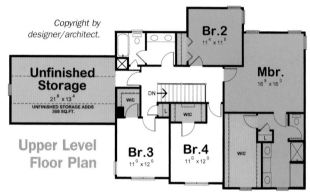

**Br.2**
11⁴ x 11⁶

**Unfinished Storage**
21⁸ x 13⁴
UNFINISHED STORAGE ADDS 308 SQ.FT.

**Mbr.**
16⁸ x 16⁰

WIC

DN

L

WIC

**Upper Level Floor Plan**

**Br.3**
11⁰ x 12⁰

**Br.4**
11⁰ x 12⁰

WIC

L

## Plan #701177

**Dimensions:** 84' W x 70'8" D

**Levels:** 1

**Square Footage:** 2,504

**Bedrooms:** 3

**Bathrooms:** 2½

**Foundation:** Basement

**Material List Available:** Yes

**Price Category:** E

*Images provided by designer/architect.*

CAD FILE CAD AVAILABLE

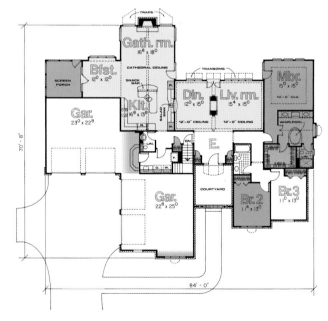

TRAPS

**Gath. rm.**
16⁸ x 18⁰
CATHEDRAL CEILING

**Bfst.**
12⁰ x 12⁰

SCREEN PORCH

SNACK BAR

TRANSOMS

**Mbr.**
15⁰ x 15⁰
10'-0" CLG

**Gar.**
23⁰ x 22⁸

**Kit.**
16⁸ x 13⁰

SALAD BOARD

**Din.**
12⁰ x 15⁰
12'-0" CEILING

**Liv. rm.**
15⁴ x 15⁰
12'-0" CEILING

WHIRLPOOL

DN

UP

70'-8"

**Gar.**
22⁸ x 25⁰

COURTYARD

**Br. 2**
11⁴ x 13⁰

**Br. 3**
11⁰ x 13⁰

84'-0"

*Copyright by designer/architect.*

**Main Level Floor Plan**

- Storage
- Garage 21⁸ x 23⁴
- Drop Zone / Seat
- Dining Room 11³ x 14¹
- Kit. 13⁰ x 16⁰
- W / D
- Family Room 25¹⁰ x 15⁰
- Flex Room 12¹⁰ x 13⁰
- Covered Porch
- 62'-0"
- 40'-0"

**Upper Level Floor Plan**

- Br.2 11⁴ x 11⁶
- Unfinished Storage 15⁸ x 13⁴ (UNFINISHED STORAGE ADDS 241 SQ. FT.)
- Mbr. 16⁸ x 16⁰
- Br.3 11⁰ x 14⁰
- Br.4 11⁰ x 11⁰

*Copyright by designer/architect.*

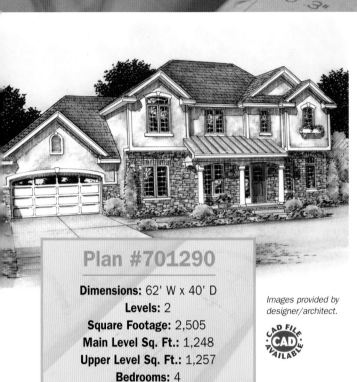

*Images provided by designer/architect.*

# Plan #701290

**Dimensions:** 62' W x 40' D
**Levels:** 2
**Square Footage:** 2,505
**Main Level Sq. Ft.:** 1,248
**Upper Level Sq. Ft.:** 1,257
**Bedrooms:** 4
**Bathrooms:** 2½
**Foundation:** Basement
**Material List Available:** Yes
**Price Category:** E

**CAD FILE AVAILABLE**

---

*Images provided by designer/architect.*

# Plan #701238

**Dimensions:** 59'4" W x 88' D
**Levels:** 1
**Square Footage:** 2506
**Bedrooms:** 3
**Bathrooms:** 2½
**Foundation:** Basement
**Material List Available:** Yes
**Price Category:** E

**CAD FILE AVAILABLE**

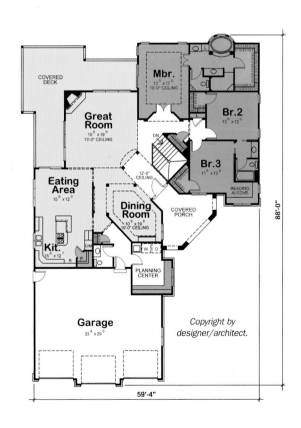

- Covered Deck
- Mbr. 13⁰ x 17⁰ 10'-0" CEILING
- Great Room 19⁶ x 19⁰ 13'-0" CEILING
- Br.2 13⁵ x 12⁰
- Br.3 11⁶ x 13⁶
- Reading Alcove
- 12'-0" CEILING
- Eating Area 15⁰ x 12⁰
- Dining Room 10⁰ x 19⁸ 10'-0" CEILING
- Covered Porch
- Kit. 15⁰ x 12⁰
- W / D
- Planning Center
- Garage 33⁴ x 29⁰
- 88'-0"
- 59'-4"

*Copyright by designer/architect.*

# Storage

Her Plans
at a Glance™
○ Storing
○ Entertaining
○ Flexible Living
○ De-Stressing

**W**Have you ever met someone who had too much storage space in their home? It's probably never happened. For many of us, the lack of space, disorganization, and clutter become significant sources of stress. In fact, according to published studies, Americans on average lose up to 150 hours every year looking for lost or misplaced items. Take control over your life and give yourself a little more time by addressing the storage opportunities of your home.

**Linens.** One of the hallmarks of a well-thought-out home plan is linen storage. Typically located in or near bath areas, the linen closets and cabinets need to be an adequate size for extra pillows, comforters and sheet sets, as well as towels and washcloths? So many linens are oversized: towels, bedding, blankets. You don't want to have to default to using other bathroom storage, taking away from places for blow dryers and personal care items.

**Bikes, Lawnmowers, and Sporting Equipment.** Its no secret that garages are getting bigger, and today's larger vehicles are only part of the reason why. Four bicycles, golf clubs, every kind of ball imaginable, skates, scooters—all in a pile—yuck!

Adequate storage makes the mess go away. Today's garage systems help organize your garage and your life by having a place for tools, gardening supplies, sporting goods, etc.

**Sizable Bedroom Closets.** "More closet space" is one of the most often mentioned reasons for buying a new home. Stuff multiplies—we're not sure how! But in addition to bigger closets, closet systems can actually help you organize and store twice as many items as the standard rod and shelf approach. Ventilated (wire) closet hanging systems have become very popular due to its flexibility and the ability for air to move between clothes and through shelving—keeping clothes fresher longer.

**Games, Holiday Decorations.** It's the day after Thanksgiving, and it's time for holiday decorations to come out. But where are they? Mixed up with the St. Patrick's Day, Valentine's Day, and Halloween decorations.

**The secret to good storage** is to have the right space for the items you want to store.

**When planning kitchen storage,** above, it is best to keep items near where they will be used.

**An organized closet,** right, keeps everything within easy reach.

**Use all available space,** such as turning the usually wasted area at the top of the sink cabinet into sponge storage, below.

From Christmas trees and lights to board games, we want convenient places to keep our stuff. Storage solutions may include closets or unfinished areas of the home.

**Kitchen Storage.** Table settings for twelve, pots and pans, the 36-cup coffee maker, a dozen cans of tuna, and gourmet cookbooks! Large families and packrats need lots of storage in the kitchen.

With the kitchen as the activity hub in most homes, more thought should go into storage and serving issues. Will items be stored near where they will be used? What about big pots and pans? Or pretty dishware and other items you would like to display? Pantry storage for prepared foods? Only you know how you want your kitchen to function, so talk with a kitchen-cabinet specialist regarding products and solutions available to create your dream kitchen.

**Cell Phones, Keys, Umbrellas, Mail.** A drop zone. Everybody needs one, and everybody has one. It's just that too many of us use a kitchen island, breakfast table, or other area that just happens to be convenient to drop off keys, pocket change, the mail, cell phones, etc. Eliminate unsightly clutter by putting in a cabinet near the entry from the garage to organize these things. Be sure to incorporate a recharging center for cell phones and the video camera. You may also want to add a tall space for hanging umbrellas and a cork board or write-on board to turn this into a message center as well.

Stress-free living includes knowing you'll never lose your keys again or fully charged cell phone when you leave the house.

**Long-Term Storage.** Johnny's history is often in a box—baby clothes, first report card, birthday cards, a brilliant essay, all kinds of awards. Until Johnny is old enough to take them off your hands, you have a storage challenge.

Items with tremendous personal value, but infrequently accessed, need dry, long-term storage. Garage storage or unfinished areas of the home can be ideal long-term storage spots. Be sure to use the right kind of containers—as cardboard boxes can deteriorate and contribute to a musty basement smell.

**Bulk Items/Cleaning Supplies.** We all love a good bargain, but where do you keep the jumbo 12-roll pack of paper towels or cleaning supplies, some of which need to be stored out of the reach of children?

Ideally you would like to keep these items close to where they will be used. Convenient to the kitchen, a walk-in coat closet off the garage entry offers shelving for such items, while in the laundry room, a broom closet, and generous cabinetry offer plenty of additional storage.

**Everyday Coats, Shoes, and Boots.** If you live in a cold winter climate, have a larger family or entertain frequently, you'll appreciate adequate coat storage easily accessed from the front door, garage entry, or both.

Nothing is more stressful than getting the family out the door with everything they need on time in the morning. If you have lockers near the garage entry, that's where the kids will find their lunches (or lunch money), backpacks, and gym clothes.

## Garage Storage

Today's garages are so much more than simply a place where cars are kept. As with homes overall, garages have become larger and are serving more purposes. In addition to auto supplies, garages are 'home' to lawn and garden products, tools, sports equipment, wintertime products, paint, and much more.

If when parked in the garage, your daily commute to your car weaves around bikes, steps over garden tools, and dodges dodge balls, you're not alone. In fact, the stress associated with this reality has given rise to garage storage and organization systems becoming one of the hottest markets in both new construction and remodeling. The promise of a neat, tidy, organized garage is compelling both rationally and emotionally.

Whether you are building a new home, or looking to reorganize the garage of your existing home, the first step is to identify any activity zones, such as a workbench or a gardening center, as these may dictate specialized storage needs. Second, determine what you really want to keep in the garage. With an existing home that means throwing some stuff away. Be prepared– you just may need to rent a dumpster for all that stuff that's been collecting in your garage.

Knowing the activity zones and items which will be stored in the garage is the first step in designing your storage solution. With blueprints (or garage measurements) in hand, identify spaces along the walls which don't interfere with opening the doors on your cars or walkways into the house. Sometimes there are also storage opportunities between parked vehicles or even overhead if your garage has a high ceiling.

Because keeping the garage reasonably clean is important from many perspectives, including safety, pest control, and overall appearance, you'll want to get most items up and off the floor. Various garage-wall storage systems are available, offering space for tools, shelving, cabinetry, and sporting goods. Mobile storage—wheeled storage cabinets, for example—address the same need as these units are easily moved to clean around them.

The choice of open shelving versus cabinet storage is often comes down to aesthetics, personal preference, and price. But another consideration should be child safety. Sharp or dangerous items (pesticides, for example) are best kept in cabinets concealed from curious eyes. Ideally, these cabinets would be lockable.

Sporting goods, particularly bicycles, present their own challenges. With an active family, these frequently used items need to be readily available. But what do you do with four bikes? Garage organization suppliers offer numerous solutions which help store bikes out of the way, many times off the floor, yet are easily accessible.

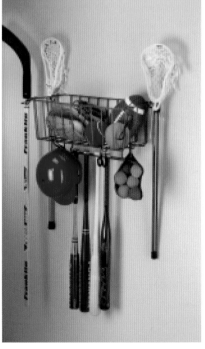

**Store sports equipment,** above, where you can retrieve it easily.

**Wall-storage systems,** opposite top and above, keep tools and the like off of the floor.

**Different types of shelving,** right, accommodate different types of items. Choose lockable cabinets for fertilizers, pesticides, and painting products.

The far end of the garage (when parked, the wall closest to your car's front bumper) offers a special storage opportunity, particularly for less frequently needed and larger items. Deep cabinets can be mounted high enough on the wall so that when you pull your car in, the hood clears underneath these cabinets.

Also, many innovative overhead storage products are becoming available. These solutions are ideal for seasonal storage (where do you store the Christmas lights and decorations for the other eleven months?) At the same time, you must consider safe accessibility. Climbing ladders to retrieve heavy or bulky items is obviously unwise.

Though not strictly storage, one final issue merits its own consideration—guys who spend a lot of time in the garage pursuing hobbies or even watching TV while playing cards. If that's

you, don't overlook heating (keeping your favorite space usable year-round); refrigeration (cold beverages, not frozen beverages); and even where to put the cable TV jack.

One final tip if you are going to install a garage storage system in your present home: after the dumpster is hauled away, you just might want to rent a U-Haul truck to store everything else from your garage during the installation of your new storage system.

Garage storage and organization systems are an excellent investment for your own sanity and peace of mind. They may also be an amenity that helps you someday resell your home for a higher price and in a quicker time frame. You'll never regret spending a little extra time carefully planning this aspect of your home.

# Plan to Entertain

**Her Plans**
at a Glance™

Storing
Entertaining
Flexible Living
De-Stressing

Candle light, soft music, ample room for guests, and great conversation make dinner parties a delight. Whether it's a formal dinner party or a family holiday dinner, memories are intertwined with meals together. The main things to look for are space, proximity to the kitchen, and flexibility. Is the dining area a comfortable size for the table, chairs, and hutch, if you have one? Is it close to the kitchen, reducing steps when carrying hot dishes or clearing the table? Should you desire privacy, can the space be closed off? If you have larger gatherings, are there two dining areas, perhaps the kids are at one table with the adults at another. Or does your dining space flow openly into an adjacent space for additional seating?

In addition, flooring choices, color, wall textures, ceiling treatments, and window coverings are primary considerations. In addition to the aesthetics, look at maintenance issues—a high chandelier with lots of light bulbs can become a real pain when it's time to change those bulbs. Having control over lighting is critical to enhance your get-together. This includes accessible, easily adjustable window shades/coverings, as well as separately switched direct and indirect artificial lighting on dimmers.

**Open floor plans** above, are conducive to entertaining.

## Informal Eating Area

A table for breakfast and a snack bar for quick dinners provides several informal eating areas. The snack bar also makes a great spot to set up a buffet.

Everyday meals mean everyday use for dinettes and snack bars. Because of its frequent use, maintenance and easy cleaning are central issues. Expect spills when you are considering flooring choices. Will you have to move chairs out of the way to sweep or vacuum? Especially at snack bars, seating suspended from the island or peninsula is a wonderful solution to ensure accessible seating that's easy to clean under. It also helps prevent damage to the flooring from chairs!

## Open Living Spaces

With the eating area, kitchen, and great room all open to each other, everyone is part of the fun. An open floor plan really pulls entertaining or family life together.

More than just eliminating walls, today's kitchens are being designed with attention to views of fireplaces and entertainment centers. Open designs have also focused new attention on views into the kitchen. This has been one reason for the rising popularity of stainless-steel appliances and glass-front cabinets.

## Outdoor Living Spaces

We are naturally drawn to the outdoors. After a hectic day at work, relaxing in the outdoors helps release tension. Research even shows that exposure to sunlight and trees has numerous health benefits.

Whether it's a barbecue or outside games, outdoor entertaining should be a natural extension of your home's flow. Covered porches are especially appreciated if inclement weather threatens your outdoor plans. For some, adding screens around the porch to control bugs means being able to truly enjoy being outside. Still others will opt for windows all around, turning their outdoor living space into a true four-seasons room.

Low maintenance, durability, price, and aesthetics all come into play when choosing the material your porch or deck will be crafted from. Wood fiber/composite decking as well as vinyl have gained in popularity as prices have come down and finish selections have increased. Wood offers unmatched beauty but requires periodic maintenance.

## Media-Related Entertaining

With today's media choices running the gamut from gaming to movies or sports to the internet, until the issue of where the

**A connection to the out-doors** is an easy way to extend entertaining areas for a large crowd.

big screen TV goes is settled, we can't seriously consider building or remodeling.

Lighting and sound are the major issues to be addressed. Glare from windows or other lighting can ruin the multimedia experience, so this must be under control. While one group wants to crank up the volume, others may want to carry on normal conversation or even get some shut-eye. Sound isolation clips for drywall walls and ceilings, insulating those cavities, or using acoustic sound mats are all reasonable approaches to controlling sound levels. Also, be sure to use a solid-core, weather-stripped door to finish sealing off a media room.

## Split Bedrooms to Control Noise

It's inevitable when friends get together that someone else in the home needs privacy—whether studying, catching up on work brought home, or needing to get some sleep. Splitting secondary bedrooms from the master suite and distancing bedrooms from entertaining areas provide much needed quiet.

Few things in life are more important than getting a good night's sleep. Inside the home, look for quiet products when selecting kitchen or bath fans and appliances. Who wants to move to another room, just because the dishwasher is running? You can also limit noise coming from outdoors through advanced insulating, caulking, and selecting quality windows and doors when your home is being built.

## Finished Basements

A finished lower level not only adds needed square footage but allows for more informal entertaining. If you are fortunate enough to be building on a basement, today's engineered floor systems make wide-open basement spaces feasible and affordable, as they can span greater distances than conventional lumber.

In many areas, builders are responding to tougher energy codes by insulating basements—a great start toward a comfortable living space. Make sure you know where you will want electrical and other wiring to be run, and meet with your electrician to go over the plans.

Moisture and humidity are key issues in tandem with temperature. A little extra spent on basement waterproofing measures could save you from expensive repairs later. And even though your air-conditioner is designed to remove excess humidity from your home in the summer, you may well find you need to run a freestanding dehumidifier in the basement as well to control humidity, mold, mildew, and possible moisture damage.

## Kids' Play Area

If there are children in your home, you will value a place where they can go and play. A place where toys and games are stored and building block creations can be left for a another day. In other words, a place where kids can be kids. Separate from their bedrooms, this flexible space may or may not have been finished space when the home was initially built.

Consider the types of activities your children will enjoy. If it is painting, for example, you will want a flooring surface that cleans up easily with a sink nearby. Also, consider how the space may be used differently as the kids age. Keep fanciful themes to more easily changed aspects, which will also keep costs down when it's time to replace stuffed animals with your boy's favorite sports theme.

**Her Plans**
at a Glance™

Storing
Entertaining
Flexible Living
De-Stressing

**M**any of the best times of our lives revolve around being with family and friends. Whether it's hosting formal get-together, holiday dinners, or your children's birthday parties, the kitchen is the hub of activity. A little extra attention spent planning flow, layout, and product selections will reward you with a kitchen that is more functional and efficient.

Due to the popularity of today's open floor plans with kitchens in full view, designing kitchens is all about zones related to the flow of activity. Kitchen design is being further refined by an emerging knowledge of how layout and product choices can actually help reduce stress, particularly while entertaining.

Storage is the initial zone, because you want items to be stored in places convenient to where they will be used. For example, you're going to want storage for your good dishes, glassware, and silverware near the serving or dining area, such as a butler pantry.

**With kitchen space at a premium,** cabinet manufacturers have introduced innovative designs with increased storage and organization, above left.

**Your back will appreciate rollout trays,** perfect for heavier small appliances and other items, above top right.

**Keep the kitchen clean** and Mom happy by including cabinets with pullout wastebaskets and recycling trays, above bottom right.

It's also essential to reduce clutter, ease accessibility, and arrange items in an organized way. Include some rollout drawers or trays. Countertop appliance garages for blenders, toasters, and coffee makers may be just what you're looking for. On the other hand, if you want to keep your counter space free, consider going underneath the counter. You can include a pull-out mixer shelf, which comes out of the cabinet and swings up—bringing your heavy mixer even with the countertop.

## Food Prep & Cooking

The food preparation zone depends on lots of counter space, plus close proximity to the refrigerator, range/oven and pantry. Ideally, this is a separate space from the serving area, allowing both areas to function simultaneously.

If you have a smaller island in your kitchen, which will be used for food preparation, keeping the countertop a uniform height will provide the maximum work space. If your island can accommodate different levels, a 36-inch work level will be appreciated by bakers, while a taller side (usually 42 inches)

shields work clutter from view and accommodates bar stools.

Your cooking zone, convenient to the food prep area, is centered around your cooktop and ovens. Two cooks in the home will require more utensils, pots, and pans, so plan storage accordingly. In addition, you may opt for separate counter spaces, cooking areas and sinks. Common ovens and waste containment may need wider corridors around a central working area.

If you are looking at an island with cooktop, make sure there is sufficient room next to the cooktop to place large items such as a big pot of boiling pasta. Also, warming drawers are great features for entertaining. They allow you to warm multiple dishes simultaneously and keep hot cooked foods at serving temperature.

## Serving & Eating Zones

Some serving zones are more formal, such as a built-in buffet in the dining area or a butler's pantry along the path from the kitchen. For casual entertaining, islands or peninsulas may be just the ticket. If your guests are usually adults, consider a 42-inch height for the serving bar.

Your eating zone may consist of a formal dining area, an informal breakfast nook, a snack bar, or some combination of all three.

Many folks find themselves most often dining at a snack bar and rarely using their dinette. If that's you, carefully consider what height best suits your family. If you have small children, they won't be able to get up on higher stools (or worse yet, they may fall off of them).

Cleanup is the final, but very important, zone when planning for entertaining. As two sinks have gained popularity, so have second dishwashers. In front of sinks, consider a small tilt-out tray to keep sponges and pot scrubbers out of view. Another item that can reduce clutter in your entertaining kitchen is a liquid soap dispenser that comes up through the countertop next to the sink.

What about trash? Typical solutions have been the unsightly tall kitchen wastebasket openly on display (or a smaller wastebasket under the kitchen sink.) Besides having to bend over to use the latter, ever notice how much stuff misses the wastebasket? Opt for a pullout wastebasket tray in your base cabinetry.

## Cleaning and Durability

Beyond how our kitchens flow, there are several other major considerations, such as ease of cleaning and durability. Think sinks, countertops, flooring, and appliances. Laminate countertops offer the greatest variety in colors, patterns and edge finishes. They don't require special cleansers nor do they need to be re-sealed every year or two.

While aesthetics and price may be the top influences for kitchen flooring choices, scratches, everyday wear, and low maintenance are major de-stressing aspects. Will spilled spaghetti sauce or grape juice stain the flooring? (Darker colors of grout for tile floors are increasingly popular for this very reason.) Will heavy or sharp items accidentally dropped damage the floor?

Appliances are one of the first items you and your guests see in the kitchen. Are the surfaces easy to clean, especially the oven/range tops and inside the microwave? How about the exterior finish? The stainless-steel look has been quite popular, but it attracts fingerprints like a giant magnet. Look for new finishes which don't show fingerprints and are easy to clean.

Quiet is an often overlooked aspect of a dream kitchen. Few things are more annoying than having to vacate the kitchen just to hear each other talk. Pay special attention when selecting your dishwasher and kitchen vent hood. Some models are actually so quiet you're not even aware they are running!

Almost universally, people describe the amount of light in their kitchens as inadequate. A light, bright and airy kitchen is de-stressing for you, your family and your guests.

As kitchens have become more open to adjacent areas of the home, they are benefiting from increased levels of natural light coming from these areas. More recently, glass block or small traditional windows are appearing between kitchen counter backsplashes and upper cabinets.

Today, recessed ceiling lighting has replaced the standard light fixture approach common years ago. Task lighting concealed under the upper kitchen cabinets offers a pleasant light level.

**Islands,** above, can serve as food prep or food service areas.

**Open plans,** below, allow you to mix activities in one area.

Whatever lighting approach you choose, make sure you're in control. From window coverings to dimmers, lighting helps establish the mood for your next get-together.

Pay extra attention to where electrical outlets are located, including connections for TV and the internet.

## Decorating

Finally, consider decorating and how you reveal who you are through what you display and how you decorate your kitchen. Most women use words such as "comfortable" or "homey" to describe their dream kitchen. Color choices throughout can have an exciting or a calming effect. Do you decorate according to the season? Is there space above the upper cabinets for display niches or plant shelves?

We cherish relationships. We take pride in a functional and orderly kitchen. With a little extra forethought and planning, our kitchens will beckon us to host a simple family dinner or an extravagant gala!

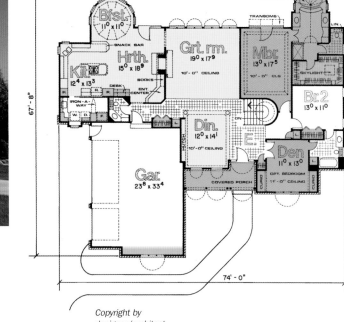

## Plan #701007

**Dimensions:** 74' W x 67'8" D

**Levels:** 1

**Square Footage:** 2,512

**Bedrooms:** 3

**Bathrooms:** 2½

**Foundation:** Basement

**Materials List Available:** Yes

**Price Category:** E

*Images provided by designer/architect.*

**CAD FILE AVAILABLE**

*Copyright by designer/architect.*

**Optional Bedroom**

## Plan #701126

**Dimensions:** 71' W x 67' D

**Levels:** 1

**Square Footage:** 2,512

**Bedrooms:** 3

**Bathrooms:** 3

**Foundation:** Slab; basement for fee

**Material List Available:** Yes

**Price Category:** E

*Images provided by designer/architect.*

**Bonus Area Floor Plan**

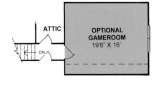

*Copyright by designer/architect.*

## Plan #701108

**Dimensions:** 77' W x 59' D

**Levels:** 1

**Square Footage:** 2,517

**Bedrooms:** 3

**Bathrooms:** 2½

**Foundation:** Slab

**Materials List Available:** Yes

**Price Category:** E

*Images provided by designer/architect.*

CAD FILE AVAILABLE

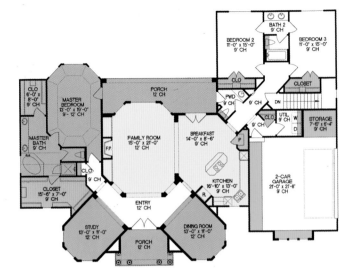

*Copyright by designer/architect.*

## Plan #701221

**Dimensions:** 50' W x 46' D

**Levels:** 2

**Square Footage:** 2,523

**Main Level Sq. Ft.:** 1,318

**Upper Level Sq. Ft.:** 1,205

**Bedrooms:** 4

**Bathrooms:** 2½

**Foundation:** Basement

**Material List Available:** Yes

**Price Category:** E

*Images provided by designer/architect.*

CAD FILE AVAILABLE

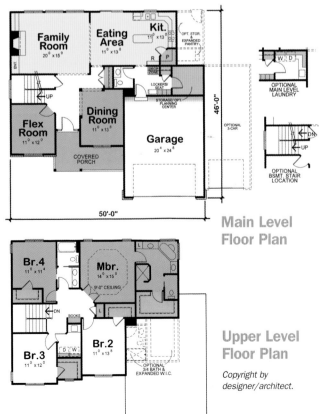

**Main Level Floor Plan**

**Upper Level Floor Plan**

*Copyright by designer/architect.*

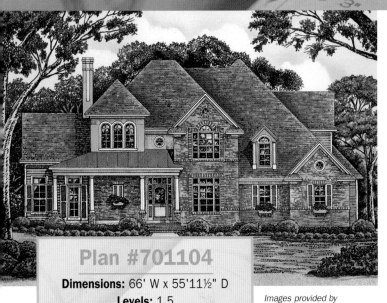

## Main Level Floor Plan

Images provided by designer/architect.

**CAD FILE AVAILABLE**

## Plan #701104

**Dimensions:** 66' W x 55'11½" D

**Levels:** 1.5

**Square Footage:** 2,537

**Main Level Sq. Ft.:** 1,794

**Upper Level Sq. Ft.:** 743

**Bedrooms:** 4

**Bathrooms:** 2½

**Foundation:** Slab; basement for fee

**Material List Available:** Yes

**Price Category:** E

## Upper Level Floor Plan

*Copyright by designer/architect.*

## Plan #701170

**Dimensions:** 68'8" W x 64'8" D

**Levels:** 1

**Square Footage:** 2,538

**Bedrooms:** 3

**Bathrooms:** 2½

**Foundation:** Basement

**Material List Available:** Yes

**Price Category:** E

Images provided by designer/architect.

**CAD FILE AVAILABLE**

*Copyright by designer/architect.*

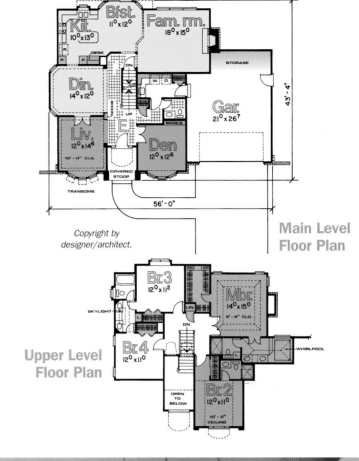

**Main Level
Floor Plan**

## Plan #701156

**Dimensions:** 56' W x 43'4" D
**Levels:** 2
**Square Footage:** 2,545
**Main Level Sq. Ft.:** 1,392
**Upper Level Sq. Ft.:** 1,153
**Bedrooms:** 4
**Bathrooms:** 3½
**Foundation:** Basement
**Material List Available:** Yes
**Price Category:** E

*Images provided by
designer/architect.*

**Upper Level
Floor Plan**

**Main Level
Floor Plan**

## Plan #701205

**Dimensions:** 77' W x 47' D
**Levels:** 1.5
**Square Footage:** 2,546
**Main Level Sq. Ft.:** 1,762
**Upper Level Sq. Ft.:** 784
**Bedrooms:** 4
**Bathrooms:** 3½
**Foundation:** Basement
**Material List Available:** Yes
**Price Category:** E

*Images provided by
designer/architect.*

**Upper Level
Floor Plan**

## Plan #701274

**Dimensions:** 56' W x 44' D
**Levels:** 2
**Square Footage:** 2,549
**Main Level Sq. Ft.:** 1,301
**Upper Level Sq. Ft.:** 1,248
**Bedrooms:** 4
**Bathrooms:** 3½
**Foundation:** Basement
**Material List Available:** Yes
**Price Category:** E

*Images provided by designer/architect.*

This inviting house has a wonderful layout and loads of charm.

**Features:**

- Family Room: Thanks to its entertainment center and fireplace, this large family room is ideal for year-round relaxation.

- Kitchen: This spacious kitchen features a walk-in pantry and open access to the dining room.

- Master Suite: You'll love this master suite that includes a beautiful bedroom with walk-in closet, his and her sinks, and private toilet.

- Secondary Bedrooms: Three additional bedrooms just down the hall from the master suite are well located for children. Two shared bathrooms handle busy mornings with ease.

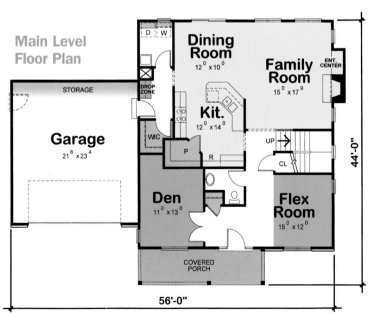

**Main Level Floor Plan**

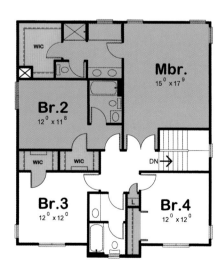

**Upper Level Floor Plan**

*Copyright by designer/architect.*

## Plan #701020

**Dimensions:** 60' W x 59'4" D
**Levels:** 2
**Square Footage:** 2,562
**Main Level Sq. Ft.:** 1,875
**Upper Level Square Footage:** 687
**Bedrooms:** 4
**Bathrooms:** 2½
**Foundation:** Basement; slab for fee
**Materials List Available:** Yes
**Price Category:** E

*Images provided by designer/architect.*

Dramatic arches are the reoccurring architectural theme in this distinctive home.

**Features:**

- Ceiling Height: 8 ft. unless otherwise noted.

- Foyer: This is a grand two-story entrance. Plants will thrive on the plant shelf thanks to light streaming through the arched window.

- Great Room: The foyer flows into the great room through dramatic 15-ft.-high arched openings.

- Kitchen: An island is the centerpiece of this highly functional kitchen that includes a separate breakfast area.

- Office: French doors open into this versatile office that features a 10-ft. ceiling and transom-topped windows.

- Master Suite: The master suite features a volume ceiling, built-in dresser, and two closets. You'll unwind in the beautiful corner whirlpool bath with its elegant window treatment.

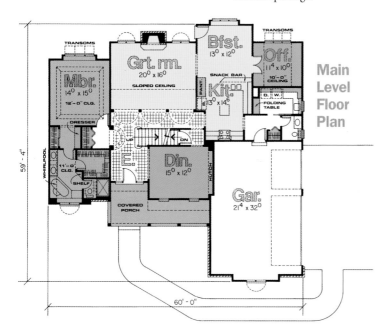

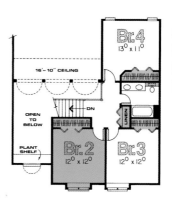

*Copyright by designer/architect.*

## Plan #701275

**Dimensions:** 56' W x 44' D

**Levels:** 2

**Square Footage:** 2,574

**Main Level Sq. Ft.:** 1,301

**Upper Level Sq. Ft.:** 1,273

**Bedrooms:** 4

**Bathrooms:** 3½

**Foundation:** Basement

**Material List Available:** Yes

**Price Category:** E

This lovely house is highlighted by lots of storage space and flexible living options.

**Features:**

- Kitchen: This kitchen is a home cook's dream, featuring plenty of room for spices and canned goods in the generous pantry, as well as abundant storage in the center island.

- Flex Room: This flexible living area can be an office, a playroom, a library, or whatever your family requires.

- Master Suite: Unwind in your spacious master suite, complete with large walk-in closet, double sinks, and private commode.

*Images provided by designer/architect.*

**Main Level Floor Plan**

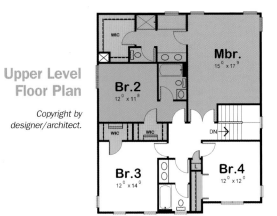

**Upper Level Floor Plan**

*Copyright by designer/architect.*

## Plan #701024

**Dimensions:** 58'8" W x 54' D
**Levels:** 1.5
**Square Footage:** 2,576
**Main Level Sq. Ft.:** 1,735
**Upper Level Sq. Ft.:** 841
**Bedrooms:** 4
**Bathrooms:** 2½
**Foundation:** Basement
**Materials List Available:** Yes
**Price Category:** E

*Images provided by designer/architect.*

This gracious home is designed with the contemporary lifestyle in mind.

**Features:**

- Ceiling Height: 8 ft. unless otherwise noted.
- Great Room: This room features a fireplace and entertainment center. It's equally suited for family gatherings and formal entertaining.
- Breakfast Area: The fireplace is two-sided so it shares its warmth with this breakfast area — the perfect spot for informal family meals.

- Master Suite: Halfway up the staircase you'll find double-doors into this truly distinctive suite featuring a barrel-vault ceiling, built-in bookcases, and his and her walk-in closets. Unwind at the end of the day by stretching out in the oval whirlpool tub.
- Computer Loft: This loft overlooks the great room. It is designed as a home office with a built-in desk for your computer.
- Garage: Two bays provide plenty of storage in addition to parking space.

**Main Level Floor Plan**

CAD FILE AVAILABLE

**Upper Level Floor Plan**

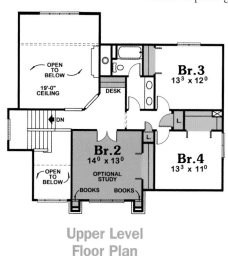

*Copyright by designer/architect.*

## Plan #701044

**Dimensions:** 70' W x 52' D
**Levels:** 1.5
**Square Footage:** 2,579
**Main Level Sq. Ft.:** 1,933
**Upper Level Sq. Ft.:** 646
**Bedrooms:** 4
**Bathrooms:** 2½
**Foundation:** Basement
**Materials List Available:** Yes
**Price Category:** E

*Images provided by designer/architect.*

Luxury will surround you in this home with contemporary styling and up-to-date amenities at every turn.

**Features:**

• Great Room: This large room shares both a see-through fireplace and a wet bar with the adjacent hearth room. Transom-topped windows add both light and architectural interest to this room.

• Den: Transom-topped windows add visual interest to this private area.

• Kitchen: A center island and corner pantry add convenience to this well-planned kitchen, and a lovely ceiling treatment adds beauty to the bayed breakfast area.

• Master Suite: A built-in bookcase adds to the ambiance of this luxury-filled area, where you're sure to find a retreat at the end of the day.

### Main Level Floor Plan

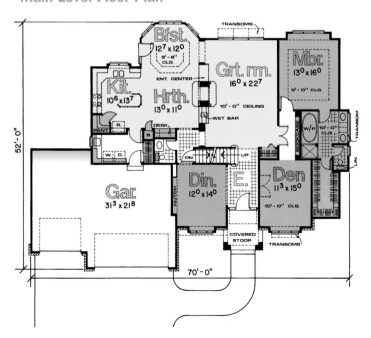

### Upper Level Floor Plan

*Copyright by designer/architect.*

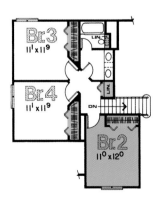

## Plan #701167

**Dimensions:** 61'4" W x 41'4" D
**Levels:** 2
**Square Footage:** 2,585
**Main Level Sq. Ft.:** 1,362
**Upper Level Sq. Ft.:** 1,223
**Bedrooms:** 4
**Bathrooms:** 2 full, 2 half
**Foundation:** Basement
**Material List Available:** Yes
**Price Category:** E

*Images provided by designer/architect.*

This beautiful brick colonial home represents gracious living at its finest.

**Features:**

- Family Room: This bright and spacious family room is perfect for play and relaxation.

- Kitchen: This roomy kitchen features a large pantry and a snack bar, perfect for sharing a quick bite. The kitchen conveniently opens to the breakfast room.

- Master Suite: Luxury is paramount in this gorgeous master suite with its 9-ft. step ceiling. The master bath features a whirlpool tub, private commode, large walk-in closet, and his and her sinks.

- Garage: This three-car garage is perfect for all of the family's cars, with plenty of extra storage room for tools and sports equipment. The garage features convenient access to the house, making it a breeze to transfer groceries from the car.

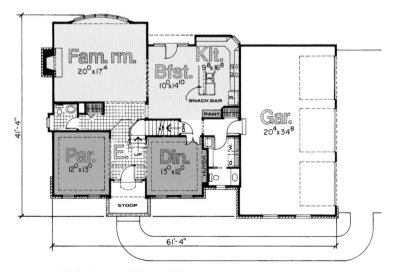

**Main Level Floor Plan**

**Upper Level Floor Plan**
*Copyright by designer/architect.*

## Plan #701116

**Dimensions:** 56' W x 71' D

**Levels:** 1.5

**Square Footage:** 2,587

**Main Level Sq. Ft.:** 2,014

**Upper Level Sq. Ft.:** 573

**Bedrooms:** 4

**Bathrooms:** 3

**Foundation:** Slab; basement for fee

**Material List Available:** Yes

**Price Category:** E

*Images provided by designer/architect.*

**Main Level Floor Plan**

**Upper Level Floor Plan**

*Copyright by designer/architect.*

## Plan #701012

**Dimensions:** 56' W x 48' D

**Levels:** 2

**Square Footage:** 2,594

**Main Level Sq. Ft.:** 1,322

**Upper Level Sq. Ft.:** 1,272

**Bedrooms:** 4

**Bathrooms:** 3

**Foundation:** Basement

**Materials List Available:** Yes

**Price Category:** E

*Images provided by designer/architect.*

**Main Level Floor Plan**

**Upper Level Floor Plan**

*Copyright by designer/architect.*

## Plan #701246

**Dimensions:** 47' W x 57'8" D

**Levels:** 1.5

**Square Footage:** 2,596

**Main Level Sq. Ft.:** 1,884

**Upper Level Sq. Ft.:** 712

**Bedrooms:** 4

**Bathrooms:** 3½

**Foundation:** Slab; crawl space for fee

**Material List Available:** Yes

**Price Category:** E

*Images provided by designer/architect.*

CAD FILE AVAILABLE

**Optional Main Level Floor Plan**

**Upper Level Floor Plan**

*Copyright by designer/architect.*

## Plan #701135

**Dimensions:** 68' W x 65' D

**Levels:** 1

**Square Footage:** 2,598

**Bedrooms:** 3

**Bathrooms:** 2½

**Foundation:** Slab; basement for fee

**Material List Available:** Yes

**Price Category:** E

*Images provided by designer/architect.*

CAD FILE AVAILABLE

**Optional Dining Room**

**Optional Stairs**

**Bonus Area Floor Plan**

**Optional Basement Level Floor Plan**

*Copyright by designer/architect.*

## Plan #701061

**Dimensions:** 62' W x 60'8" D

**Levels:** 1.5

**Square Footage:** 2,603

**Main Level Sq. Ft.:** 1,800

**Upper Level Sq. Ft.:** 803

**Bedrooms:** 4

**Bathrooms:** 3½

**Foundation:** Basement

**Materials List Available:** Yes

**Price Category:** F

If you love family life but also treasure your privacy, you'll appreciate the layout of this home.

**Features:**

• Entry: This two-story, open area features plant shelves to display your favorite plants and flowers.

• Dining Room: Open to the entry, this room features 12-ft. ceilings and corner hutches.

• Den: French doors lead to this quiet room, with its bowed window and spider-beamed ceiling.

• Gathering Room: A three-sided fireplace, shared with both the kitchen and the breakfast area, is the highlight of this room.

• Master Suite: Secluded for privacy, this suite also has a private covered deck where you can sit and recharge at any time of day. A walk-in closet is practical, and a whirlpool tub is pure comfort.

**Main Level Floor Plan**

**Upper Level Floor Plan**

## Plan #701293

**Dimensions:** 60' W x 36' D
**Levels:** 2
**Square Footage:** 2,609
**Main Level Sq. Ft.:** 1,149
**Upper Level Sq. Ft.:** 1,460
**Bedrooms:** 4
**Bathrooms:** 3½
**Foundation:** Basement
**Material List Available:** Yes
**Price Category:** F

This house is the perfect place to relax after a long day at the office.

*Images provided by designer/architect.*

**Features:**

- Family Room: Relatives and neighbors will love spending holidays at your house in the large family room, which has a fireplace and a built-in entertainment center.

- Kitchen: This corner kitchen is wonderful for the family cook. It is easy to maneuver around the cupboards and counter space, and the center island adds an extra dimension to the convenience.

- Den: Put your feet up, sit back, and relax in this den with a book or the newspaper and forget about stress.

- Master Suite: This plan's large master suite features a sitting room just off the large walk-in closet. In the nearby closet, there is space to keep organized, while keeping clutter out of sight. His and her sinks and a separate toilet area help keep stress and clutter at bay.

## Main Level Floor Plan

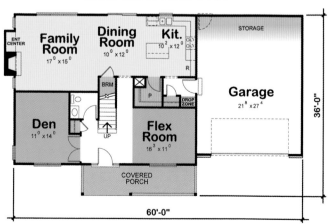

## Upper Level Floor Plan

*Copyright by designer/architect.*

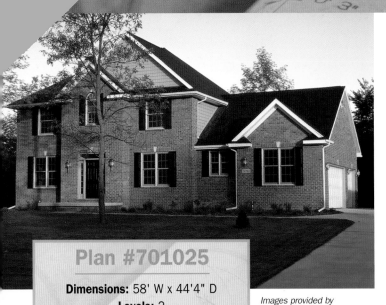

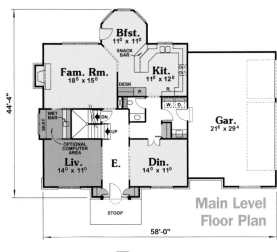

**Main Level Floor Plan**

Bfst. 11⁰ x 11⁰
SNACK BAR
Fam. Rm. 18⁰ x 15⁰
Kit. 11⁸ x 12⁰
DESK
WET BAR
SEAT
DN
UP
OPTIONAL COMPUTER AREA
Gar. 21⁸ x 29⁴
Liv. 14⁰ x 11⁰
E.
Din. 14⁰ x 11⁰
W. D.
STOOP

44'-4"
58'-0"

## Plan #701025

**Dimensions:** 58' W x 44'4" D
**Levels:** 2
**Square Footage:** 2,613
**Main Level Sq. Ft.:** 1,333
**Upper Level Sq. Ft.:** 1,280
**Bedrooms:** 4
**Bathrooms:** 2½
**Foundation:** Basement
**Materials List Available:** Yes
**Price Category:** F

*Images provided by designer/architect.*

CAD FILE AVAILABLE

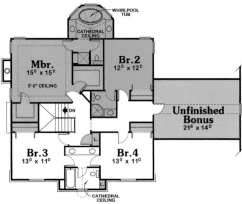

**Upper Level Floor Plan**

*Copyright by designer/architect.*

WHIRLPOOL TUB
CATHEDRAL CEILING
Mbr. 15⁰ x 15⁰
9'-0" CEILING
Br.2 12⁰ x 12⁰
DN
Unfinished Bonus 21⁸ x 14⁰
Br.3 13⁰ x 11⁰
Br.4 13⁰ x 11⁰
CATHEDRAL CEILING

---

Eating Area 14⁰ x 12⁸
Great Room 19⁰ x 21⁴ 10'-0" CEILING
SITTING AREA
CATHEDRAL CEILING
Mbr. 13⁰ x 17⁰ 10'-0" CEILING
WET BAR
Kit. 25⁸ x 16⁸
WIC
MICRO OVEN TV
HUTCH
LOCKERS
PREP PANTRY
DROP ZONE
WIC
STOR.
UP
ACTIVITY CENTER 13⁰ x 12⁰
Flex Room 11⁴ x 13⁰ 11'-0" CEILING
BROOM
W. D.
OPTIONAL DINING/ STUDY
11'-0" CEILING
WIC
Garage 23⁸ x 34⁴
COVERED PORCH
Guest Suite 12⁰ x 12⁰ OPTIONAL FLEX

68'-8"
74'-0"

*Copyright by designer/architect.*

## Plan #701250

**Dimensions:** 74' W x 68'8" D
**Levels:** 1
**Square Footage:** 2,632
**Bedrooms:** 2
**Bathrooms:** 2½
**Foundation:** Basement
**Material List Available:** Yes
**Price Category:** F

*Images provided by designer/architect.*

CAD FILE AVAILABLE

**Optional Study**

Study 12⁰ x 12⁰

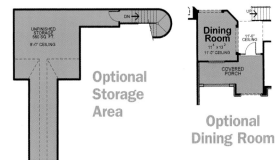

**Optional Storage Area**

UNFINISHED STORAGE 560 SQ. FT 8'-0" CEILING
DN

**Optional Dining Room**

Dining Room 11⁴ x 13⁰ 11'-0" CEILING
UP
11'-0" CEILING
COVERED PORCH

## Plan #701105

**Dimensions:** 65'6" W x 56'10" D

**Levels:** 1.5

**Square Footage:** 2,638

**Main Level Sq. Ft.:** 1,844

**Upper Level Sq. Ft.:** 794

**Bedrooms:** 4

**Bathrooms:** 3½

**Foundation:** Slab; basement for fee

**Material List Available:** Yes

**Price Category:** F

*Images provided by designer/architect.*

*This home, as shown in the photograph, may differ from the actual blueprints. For more detailed information, please check the floor plans carefully.*

**Upper Level Floor Plan**

**Main Level Floor Plan**

*Copyright by designer/architect.*

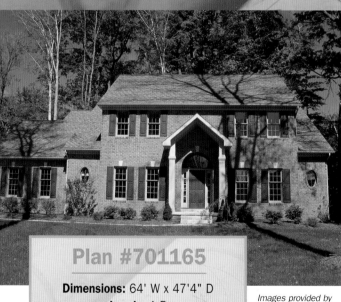

## Plan #701165

**Dimensions:** 64' W x 47'4" D

**Levels:** 1.5

**Square Footage:** 2,639

**Main Level Sq. Ft.:** 1,865

**Upper Level Sq. Ft.:** 774

**Bedrooms:** 4

**Bathrooms:** 3½

**Foundation:** Basement

**Material List Available:** Yes

**Price Category:** F

*Images provided by designer/architect.*

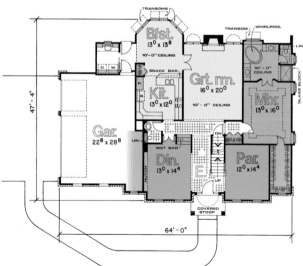

**Main Level Floor Plan**

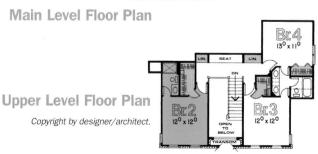

**Upper Level Floor Plan**

*Copyright by designer/architect.*

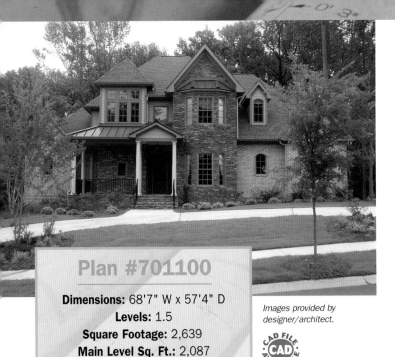

## Main Level Floor Plan

## Upper Level Floor Plan

## Plan #701100

**Dimensions:** 68'7" W x 57'4" D
**Levels:** 1.5
**Square Footage:** 2,639
**Main Level Sq. Ft.:** 2,087
**Upper Level Sq. Ft.:** 552
**Bedrooms:** 4
**Bathrooms:** 3½
**Foundation:** Slab; basement for fee
**Material List Available:** Yes
**Price Category:** F

## Plan #701197

**Dimensions:** 50' W x 70'4" D
**Levels:** 1
**Square Footage:** 2,640
**Bedrooms:** 3
**Bathrooms:** 2½
**Foundation:** Basement
**Material List Available:** Yes
**Price Category:** F

## Main Level Floor Plan

## Optional Lower Level Floor Plan

**Optional Lower Level Stairs**

## Main Level Floor Plan

## Plan #701241

**Dimensions:** 79'8" W x 57' D
**Levels:** 1
**Square Footage:** 2,641
**Bedrooms:** 3
**Bathrooms:** 3½
**Foundation:** Basement
**Material List Available:** Yes
**Price Category:** F

*Images provided by designer/architect.*

CAD FILE AVAILABLE

**Optional Bedroom**

---

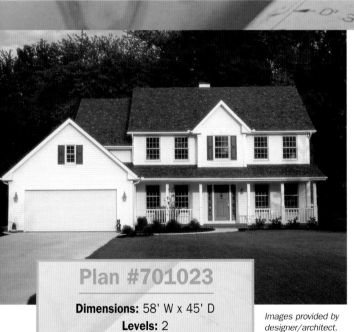

## Plan #701023

**Dimensions:** 58' W x 45' D
**Levels:** 2
**Square Footage:** 2,613
**Main Level Sq. Ft.:** 1,333
**Upper Level Sq. Ft.:** 1,280
**Bedrooms:** 4
**Bathrooms:** 2½
**Foundation:** Basement
**Materials List Available:** Yes
**Price Category:** F

*Images provided by designer/architect.*

**Main Level Floor Plan**

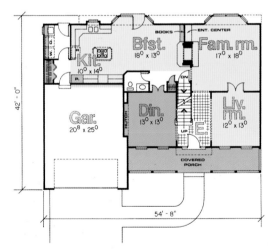

**Upper Level Floor Plan**

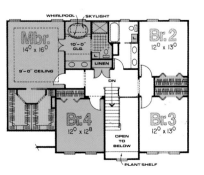

## Plan #701058

**Dimensions:** 60' W x 58' D

**Levels:** 1.5

**Square Footage:** 2,645

**Main Level Sq. Ft.:** 1,972

**Upper Level Sq. Ft.:** 673

**Bedrooms:** 4

**Bathrooms:** 2½

**Foundation:** Basement

**Materials List Available:** Yes

**Price Category:** F

*Images provided by designer/architect.*

**Main Level Floor Plan**

**Upper Level Floor Plan**

*Copyright by designer/architect.*

## Plan #701247

**Dimensions:** 69'8" W x 42'8" D

**Levels:** 2

**Square Footage:** 2,646

**Main Level Sq. Ft.:** 1,311

**Upper Level Sq. Ft.:** 1,335

**Bedrooms:** 4

**Bathrooms:** 3½

**Foundation:** Basement

**Material List Available:** Yes

**Price Category:** F

*Images provided by designer/architect.*

**CAD FILE AVAILABLE**

**Main Level Floor Plan**

**Upper Level Floor Plan**

*Copyright by designer/architect.*

## Plan #701137

**Dimensions:** 70' W x 46' D
**Levels:** 1.5
**Square Footage:** 2,651
**Main Level Sq. Ft.:** 1,904
**Upper Level Sq. Ft.:** 747
**Bedrooms:** 4
**Bathrooms:** 2½
**Foundation:** Slab; basement for fee
**Material List Available:** Yes
**Price Category:** F

*Images provided by designer/architect.*

**Main Level Floor Plan**

**Optional Main Level Floor Plan**

**Upper Level Floor Plan**

*Copyright by designer/architect.*

## Plan #701176

**Dimensions:** 66'8" W x 72'8" D
**Levels:** 1
**Square Footage:** 2,655
**Bedrooms:** 4
**Bathrooms:** 3½
**Foundation:** Basement
**Material List Available:** Yes
**Price Category:** F

*Images provided by designer/architect.*

*Copyright by designer/architect.*

## Plan #701027

**Dimensions:** 65'3" W x 57'2" D
**Levels:** 2
**Square Footage:** 2,655
**Main Level Sq. Ft.:** 1,906
**Upper Level Sq. Ft.:** 749
**Bedrooms:** 4
**Bathrooms:** 2½
**Foundation:** Slab; basement for fee
**Materials List Available:** Yes
**Price Category:** F

**CAD FILE AVAILABLE**

*Images provided by designer/architect.*

This home beautifully blends traditional architectural detail with modern amenities.

**Features:**

- Ceiling Height: 8 ft. unless otherwise noted.

- Foyer: This two-story entry enjoys views of the uniquely shaped study, a second-floor balcony, and the formal dining room.

- Formal Dining Room: With its elegant corner column, this dining room sets the stage for formal entertaining as well as family gatherings.

- Kitchen: This well-appointed kitchen features a center island for efficient food preparation. It has a butler's pantry near the dining room and another pantry in the service entry.

- Breakfast Area: Here's the spot for informal family meals or lingering over coffee.

- Rear Porch: Step out through French doors in the master bedroom and the breakfast area.

**Main Level Floor Plan**

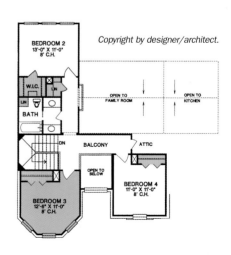

*Copyright by designer/architect.*

**Upper Level Floor Plan**

# Plan #701109

**Dimensions:** 65'10" W x 75'6" D
**Levels:** 1
**Square Footage:** 2,679
**Bedrooms:** 4
**Bathrooms:** 3
**Foundation:** Slab; basement for fee
**Material List Available:** Yes
**Price Category:** F

*Images provided by designer/architect.*

Large rooms give this home a spacious feel in a modest footprint.

## Features:

- **Family Room:** This area is the central gathering place in the home. The windows to the rear fill the area with natural light. The fireplace take the chill off on cool winter nights.

- **Kitchen:** This peninsula kitchen with raised bar is open into the family room and the breakfast area. The built-in pantry is a welcomed storage area for today's family.

- **Master Suite:** This secluded area features large windows with a view of the backyard. The master bath boasts a large walk-in closet, his and her vanities and a compartmentalized lavatory area.

- **Secondary Bedrooms:** Bedroom 2 has its own access to the main bathroom, while bedrooms 3 and 4 share a Jack-and-Jill bathroom. All bedrooms feature walk-in closets.

*Copyright by designer/architect.*

## Plan #701106

**Dimensions:** 54' W x 70' D
**Levels:** 1.5
**Square Footage:** 2,688
**Main Level Sq. Ft.:** 1,902
**Upper Level Sq. Ft.:** 786
**Bedrooms:** 4
**Bathrooms:** 3½
**Foundation:** Slab; basement for fee
**Material List Available:** Yes
**Price Category:** F

*Images provided by designer/architect.*

This gorgeous home welcomes you with its beautiful brickwork, arched entryway, and distinctive turret.

**Features:**

- Veranda: Extending around the rear of the home, this wraparound deck is ideal for outdoor dining and entertaining.

- Family Room and Living Room: Both of these two-story rooms boast 18-ft. ceilings and beautiful views of the veranda in back. A shared, two-sided fireplace invites cozy evenings with family and friends.

- Dining Room: Located in the rounded turret, this dining room's dramatic shape lends itself to unique decorating opportunities.

- Master Suite: This large master suite opens to the veranda and features a beautiful master bath with his and her sinks, private commode, tub, and spacious walk-in closet.

**Main Level Floor Plan**

**Upper Level Floor Plan**

*Copyright by designer/architect.*

## Plan #701049

**Dimensions:** 50' W x 60' D
**Levels:** 2
**Square Footage:** 2,688
**Main Level Sq. Ft.:** 1,650
**Upper Level Sq. Ft.:** 1,038
**Bedrooms:** 4
**Bathrooms:** 3½
**Foundation:** Slab
**Materials List Available:** Yes
**Price Category:** F

You'll love this open design if you're looking for a home that gives a spacious feeling while also providing private areas.

**Features:**

- Entry: The cased openings and corner columns here give an attractive view into the dining room.

- Living Room: Another cased opening defines the entry to this living room but lets traffic flow into it.

- Kitchen: This well-designed kitchen is built around a center island that gives you extra work space. A snack bar makes an easy, open transition between the sunny dining nook and the kitchen.

- Master Suite: An 11-ft. ceiling sets the tone for this private space. With a walk-in closet and adjoining full bath, it will delight you.

*Images provided by designer/architect.*

**Main Level Floor Plan**

*Copyright by designer/architect.*

**Upper Level Floor Plan**

## Plan #701059

**Dimensions:** 56' W x 50' D
**Levels:** 2
**Square Footage:** 2,689
**Main Level Sq. Ft.:** 1,415
**Upper Level Sq. Ft.:** 1,274
**Bedrooms:** 4
**Bathrooms:** 2½
**Foundation:** Basement
**Materials List Available:** Yes
**Price Category:** F

*This home, as shown in the photograph, may differ from the actual blueprints. For more detailed information, please check the floor plans carefully.*

*Images provided by designer/architect.*

You'll love the unusual details that make this home as elegant as it is comfortable.

**Features:**

• **Entry:** This two-story entry is filled with natural light that streams in through the sidelights and transom window.

• **Den:** To the right of the entry, French doors open to this room, with its 11-ft. high, spider-beamed ceiling. A triple-wide,

transom-topped window brightens this room during the daytime.

• **Family Room:** A fireplace and built-in entertainment center add comfort to this room, and the cased opening to the kitchen area makes it convenient.

• **Kitchen:** With an adjoining breakfast area, this kitchen is another natural gathering spot.

## Main Level Floor Plan

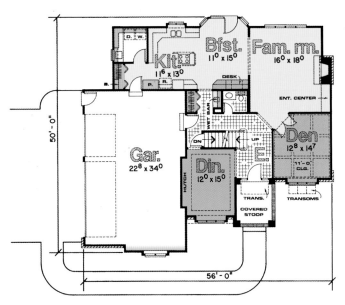

## Upper Level Floor Plan

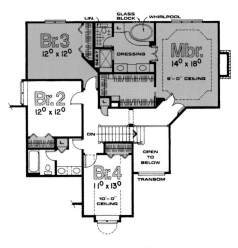

*Copyright by designer/architect.*

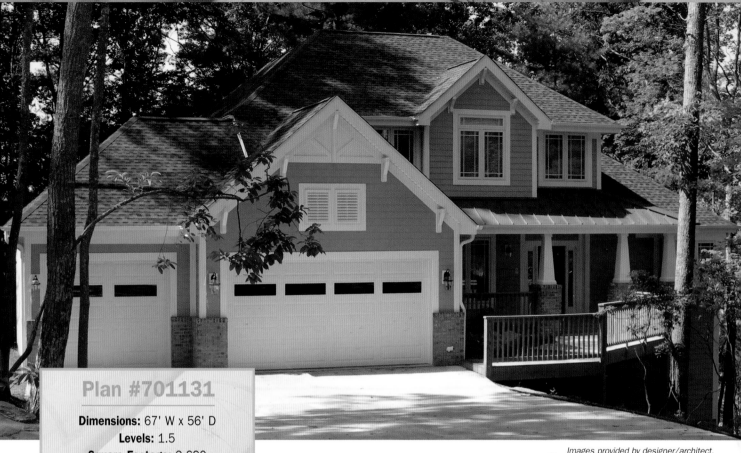

## Plan #701131

**Dimensions:** 67' W x 56' D
**Levels:** 1.5
**Square Footage:** 2,690
**Main Level Sq. Ft.:** 1,792
**Upper Level Sq. Ft.:** 898
**Bedrooms:** 4
**Bathrooms:** 2½
**Foundation:** Basement;
crawl space or slab for fee
**Materials List Available:** Yes
**Price Category:** F

This traditional Craftsman-style home has a unique design to accommodate the needs of the growing family.

**Features:**

• Porch: A long covered porch welcomes guests out of the elements or gives you outdoor living space where you can sit and greet the neighbors while listening to the sounds of the day.

• Great Room: With its cathedral ceiling and glowing fireplace, this room welcomes you home comfortably. Relax with your family or entertain your friends.

• Kitchen: Long counters, a large pantry, a stovetop island and a snack bar make this efficiently designed kitchen ideal for the family cook and expert chef alike. An attached eating area and a nearby formal dining room mean you can cater to any kind of meal.

*Images provided by designer/architect.*

• Master Bedroom: Unwind in this private space, and enjoy its conveniences. The full master bath includes a standing shower, his and her sinks, a large tub, and a spacious walk-in closet.

• Secondary Bedrooms: Each of the three bedrooms upstairs has ample living space,

large closets, and a desk, and all share access to the second full bathroom, which is compartmentalized.

• Garage: This three-car garage allows for space for both established and budding drivers, or you can use one bay for storage or a workbench.

**Upper Level Floor Plan**

**Main Level Floor Plan**
*Copyright by designer/architect.*

**Bonus Area Floor Plan**

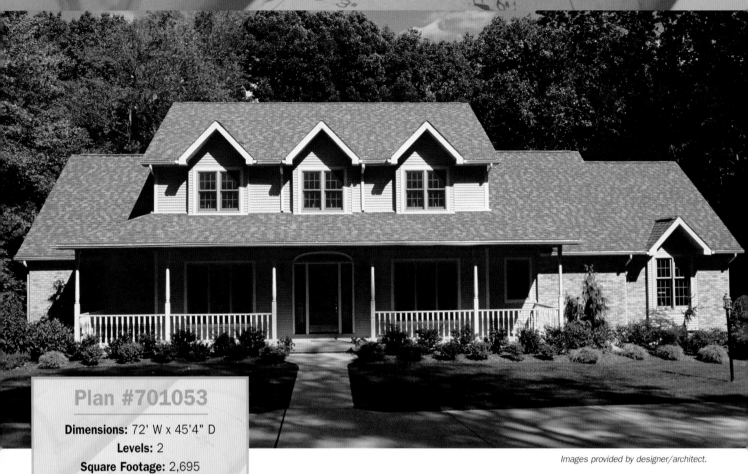

## Plan #701053

**Dimensions:** 72' W x 45'4" D

**Levels:** 2

**Square Footage:** 2,695

**Main Level Sq. Ft.:** 1,881

**Upper Level Sq. Ft.:** 814

**Bedrooms:** 4

**Bathrooms:** 3½

**Foundation:** Basement

**Materials List Available:** Yes

**Price Category:** F

*Images provided by designer/architect.*

You'll love this home for its soaring entryway ceiling and well-designed layout.

**Features:**

• Entry: A balcony from the upper level looks down into this two-story entry, which features a decorative plant shelf.

• Great Room: Comfort is guaranteed in this large room, with its built-in bookcases framing a lovely fireplace and trio of transom-topped windows along one wall.

• Living Room: Save both this formal room and the formal dining room, both of which flank the entry, for guests and special occasions.

• Kitchen: This convenient work space includes a gazebo-shaped breakfast area where friends and family will gather at any time of day.

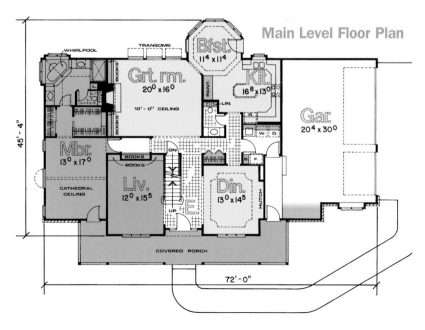

**Main Level Floor Plan**

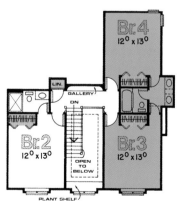

**Upper Level Floor Plan**

*Copyright by designer/architect.*

## Plan #701133

**Dimensions:** 69'4" W x 55'8" D
**Levels:** 1.5
**Square Footage:** 2,704
**Main Level Sq. Ft.:** 1,849
**Upper Level Sq. Ft.:** 855
**Bedrooms:** 4
**Bathrooms:** 3½
**Foundation:** Basement;
crawl space for fee
**Material List Available:** Yes
**Price Category:** F

This stunning and expansive home is ideal for family living and entertaining.

*Images provided by designer/architect.*

**Features:**

• Great Room: This breathtaking, two-story great room features an 18-ft. ceiling and corner fireplace, making it a luxurious place to entertain guests.

• Kitchen: The family chef can cook and bake in style in this roomy kitchen connected to the dining area.

• Master Suite: You'll want to nestle forever in this spacious suite with its 10-ft. ceiling, two-sided walk-in closet, and bath area with private commode and his and her sinks.

• Secondary Bedrooms: On the upper level, three secondary bedrooms share two bathrooms, making them perfect for siblings or houseguests.

**Upper Level Floor Plan**

**Main Level Floor Plan**

*Copyright by designer/architect.*

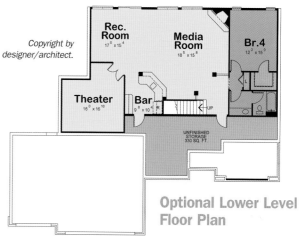

**Optional Lower Level Floor Plan**

## Plan #701042

**Dimensions:** 56' W x 59'4" D
**Levels:** 1.5
**Square Footage:** 2,708
**Main Level Sq. Ft.:** 1,860
**Upper Level Sq. Ft.:** 848
**Bedrooms:** 4
**Bathrooms:** 3½
**Foundation:** Basement
**Materials List Available:** Yes
**Price Category:** F

*Images provided by designer/architect.*

You'll love this home because it is such a perfect setting for a family and still has room for guests.

**Features:**

- Family Room: Expect everyone to gather in this room, near the built-in entertainment centers that flank the lovely fireplace.

- Living Room: The other side of the see-through fireplace looks out into this living room, making it an equally welcoming spot in chilly weather.

- Kitchen: This room has a large center island, a corner pantry, and a built-in desk. It also features a breakfast area where friends and family will congregate all day long.

- Master Suite: Enjoy the oversized walk-in closet and bath with a bayed whirlpool tub, double vanity, and separate shower.

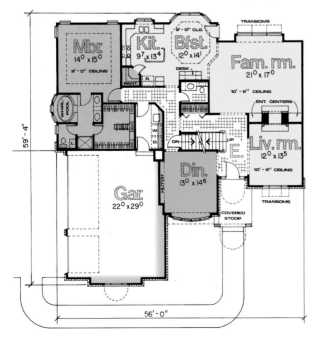

**Main Level Floor Plan**

**Upper Level Floor Plan**

*Copyright by designer/architect.*

## Plan #701099

**Dimensions:** 75'1 1/2" W x 38' D
**Levels:** 2
**Square Footage:** 2,715
**Main Level Sq. Ft.:** 1,400
**Upper Level Sq. Ft.:** 1,315
**Bedrooms:** 4
**Bathrooms:** 3½
**Foundation:** Slab; basement for fee
**Material List Available:** Yes
**Price Category:** F

This would be the perfect house for raising your family.

**Features:**

- Living Room: This formal gathering area is open to the entry and features a view of the front yard. The open stair railing adds a distinctive design element to the room.

- Family Room: This family room provides a place for relatives and friends to gather in a casual environment. The large fireplace adds a cozy feel to the area.

- Master Suite: A tray ceiling and a bay window accent this private retreat. The master bath is filled with elegance and includes a tub and two walk-in closets.

- Secondary Bedrooms: Three bedrooms accompany the master suite on the upper level. Bedroom 2 boasts a private bathroom, while the remaining bedrooms share a Jack-and-Jill bathroom.

*Images provided by designer/architect.*

**Main Level Floor Plan**

*Copyright by designer/architect.*

**Upper Level Floor Plan**

**Main Level Floor Plan**

Optional Basement Stairs

## Plan #701136

**Dimensions:** 62' W x 47' D
**Levels:** 2
**Square Footage:** 2,736
**Main Level Sq. Ft.:** 1,436
**Upper Level Sq. Ft.:** 1,300
**Bedrooms:** 4
**Bathrooms:** 2½
**Foundation:** Slab; basement for fee
**Material List Available:** Yes
**Price Category:** F

*Images provided by designer/architect.*

CAD FILE CAD AVAILABLE

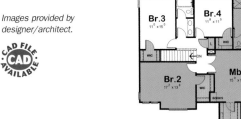

**Upper Level Floor Plan**

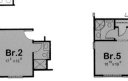
Optional Bedroom Floor Plan

Optional Bedroom Floor Plan

*Copyright by designer/architect.*

---

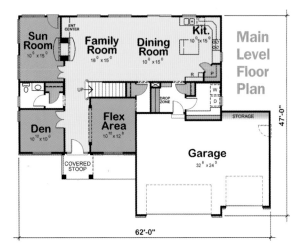

**Main Level Floor Plan**

## Plan #701261

**Dimensions:** 62' W x 47' D
**Levels:** 2
**Square Footage:** 2,736
**Main Level Sq. Ft.:** 1,436
**Upper Level Sq. Ft.:** 1,300
**Bedrooms:** 4
**Bathrooms:** 2½
**Foundation:** Basement
**Material List Available:** Yes
**Price Category:** F

*Images provided by designer/architect.*

CAD FILE CAD AVAILABLE

**Upper Level Floor Plan**

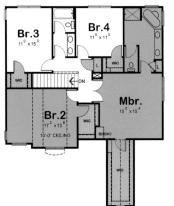

*Copyright by designer/architect.*

Images provided by designer/architect.

*Copyright by designer/architect.*

## Plan #701184

**Dimensions:** 66'8" W x 72'8" D

**Levels:** 1

**Square Footage:** 2,750

**Bedrooms:** 4

**Bathrooms:** 3½

**Foundation:** Basement

**Material List Available:** Yes

**Price Category:** F

---

## Main Level Floor Plan

## Upper Level Floor Plan

Images provided by designer/architect.

*Copyright by designer/architect.*

## Plan #701210

**Dimensions:** 84' W x 66' D

**Levels:** 1.5

**Square Footage:** 2,758

**Main Level Sq. Ft.:** 2,148

**Upper Level Sq. Ft.:** 610

**Bedrooms:** 3

**Bathrooms:** 3½

**Foundation:** Basement

**Material List Available:** Yes

**Price Category:** F

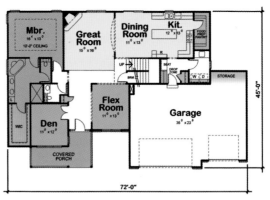

**Main Level Floor Plan**

Mbr. 16⁴ x13⁰ 10'-0" CEILING · Great Room 15⁰ x 16⁸ · Dining Room 11⁰ x13⁰ · Kit. 12⁰ x13⁰ · FOOD PREP PANTRY · Den 11⁰ x12⁰ · Flex Room 11⁸ x13⁰ · Garage 35⁰ x23⁰ · STORAGE · COVERED PORCH · WIC

72'-0" · 45'-0"

**Optional Basement Stair Location**  **Optional Laundry Room**

*Images provided by designer/architect.*

CAD FILE AVAILABLE

## Plan #701284

**Dimensions:** 72' W x 45' D
**Levels:** 1.5
**Square Footage:** 2,765
**Main Level Sq. Ft.:** 1,855
**Upper Level Sq. Ft.:** 910
**Bedrooms:** 4
**Bathrooms:** 3½
**Foundation:** Basement
**Material List Available:** Yes
**Price Category:** F

**Upper Level Floor Plan**

*Copyright by designer/architect.*

DESK · Br.4 11³ x11⁵ · WIC · SLOPED CEILING · OPEN TO BELOW · Br.3 11⁰ x13⁰ · Br.2 11⁰ x15⁰ · WIC · DN

**Optional Bathroom**

Br.3 11⁰ x13⁰ · WIC · DN

---

**Main Level Floor Plan**

W H D · LOCKERS · Dining Room 14⁰ x 11⁰ · COVERED PORCH · Kit. 14⁰ x14⁰ · Great Room 20⁰ x 14² · Garage 21⁴ x 31⁸ · Study 14⁰ x12⁰

57'-4" · 45'-4"

## Plan #701200

**Dimensions:** 57'4" W x 45'4" D
**Levels:** 2
**Square Footage:** 2,766
**Main Level Sq. Ft.:** 1,305
**Upper Level Sq. Ft.:** 1,461
**Bedrooms:** 4
**Bathrooms:** 2½
**Foundation:** Basement
**Material List Available:** Yes
**Price Category:** F

*Images provided by designer/architect.*

CAD FILE AVAILABLE

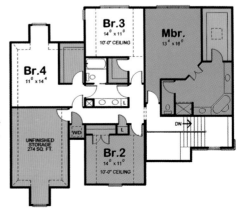

**Upper Level Floor Plan**

*Copyright by designer/architect.*

Br.3 14⁰ x 11⁰ 10'-0" CEILING · Mbr. 13⁴ x 16⁰ · Br.4 11⁰ x 14⁰ · UNFINISHED STORAGE 274 SQ. FT · W/D · Br.2 14⁰ x 11⁰ 10'-0" CEILING · DN

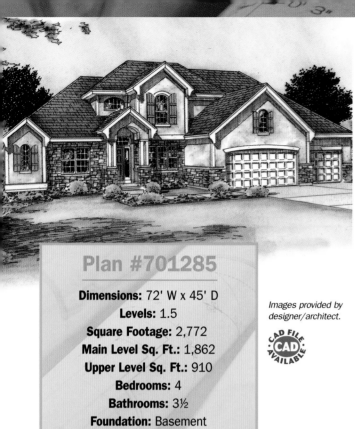

**Optional Laundry Room**

**Upper Level Floor Plan**

# Plan #701285

**Dimensions:** 72' W x 45' D

**Levels:** 1.5

**Square Footage:** 2,772

**Main Level Sq. Ft.:** 1,862

**Upper Level Sq. Ft.:** 910

**Bedrooms:** 4

**Bathrooms:** 3½

**Foundation:** Basement

**Material List Available:** Yes

**Price Category:** F

*Images provided by designer/architect.*

CAD FILE AVAILABLE

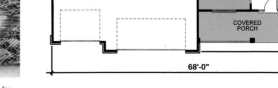

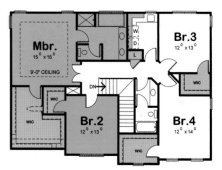

# Plan #701262

**Dimensions:** 68' W x 41' D

**Levels:** 2

**Square Footage:** 2,797

**Main Level Sq. Ft.:** 1,337

**Upper Level Sq. Ft.:** 1,460

**Bedrooms:** 4

**Bathrooms:** 2½

**Foundation:** Basement

**Material List Available:** Yes

**Price Category:** F

*Images provided by designer/architect.*

CAD FILE AVAILABLE

**Upper Level Floor Plan**

*Copyright by designer/architect.*

**Main Level Floor Plan**

PANTRY
DROP ZONE
**Kit.** 13'0 x 14'0
**Dining Room** 15'0 x 14'3
**Family Room** 17'6 x 16'0
EXIT CENTER
O/M
R
BRM
**Garage** 33'4 x 24'0
**Flex Room** 12'0 x 13'0
UP
**Den** 12'0 x 13'0
41'-0"
68'-0"

**Upper Level Floor Plan**

*Copyright by designer/architect.*

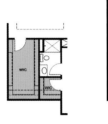

**Optional Bathroom**

WIC

**Mbr.** 15'0 x 16'0
9'-0" CEILING
**Br.3** 12'0 x 13'0
W
D
L
WIC
WIC
DN
**Br.2** 12'0 x 15'0
10'-0" CEILING
**Br.4** 12'0 x 13'0
DESK
WIC

## Plan #701263

**Dimensions:** 68' W x 41' D
**Levels:** 2
**Square Footage:** 2,850
**Main Level Sq. Ft.:** 1,329
**Upper Level Sq. Ft.:** 1,521
**Bedrooms:** 4
**Bathrooms:** 2½
**Foundation:** Basement
**Material List Available:** Yes
**Price Category:** F

*Images provided by designer/architect.*

CAD FILE AVAILABLE

---

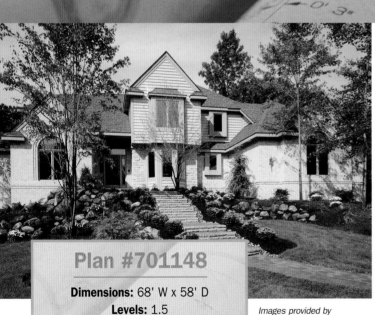

**Main Level Floor Plan**

**Mbr.** 15'3 x 15'3
9'-0" CEILING
**Grt.rm** 16'0 x 22'0
VALLEY CATHEDRAL
**Bfst** 15'4 x 11'0
DESK
SNACK BAR
W/P
SKYLIGHT
UP
DN
**Kit.** 15'3 x 14'0
BOOKS
**Liv** 12'0 x 16'0
10'-0" CEILING
**Din** 13'0 x 15'0
CVRD STOOP
F
**Gar.** 20'0 x 31'4
58'-0"
68'-0"

**Upper Level Floor Plan**

OPEN TO BELOW
VALLEY CATHEDRAL
**Br.** 11'0 x 13'0
BALCONY
LIN
LIN
**Br.** 12'4 x 13'0
DN
OPEN TO BELOW
**Br.** 12'0 x 13'0
TRANS.
10'-0" CEILING

*Copyright by designer/architect.*

## Plan #701148

**Dimensions:** 68' W x 58' D
**Levels:** 1.5
**Square Footage:** 2,865
**Main Level Sq. Ft.:** 1,972
**Upper Level Sq. Ft.:** 893
**Bedrooms:** 4
**Bathrooms:** 3½
**Foundation:** Basement
**Material List Available:** Yes
**Price Category:** F

*Images provided by designer/architect.*

CAD FILE AVAILABLE

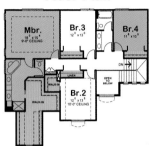

**Main Level Floor Plan**

Hearth Room 14⁰ x 11⁰

Kit. 14⁰ x 11⁰

Eating Area 14⁰ x 11⁰

Family Room 19⁸ x 15⁴

Garage 31⁴ x 27⁴

Dining Room 13⁴ x 13⁵

Covered Stoop

53'-0"

62'-0"

*Copyright by designer/architect.*

## Plan #701249

**Dimensions:** 62' W x 53' D
**Levels:** 2
**Square Footage:** 2,879
**Main Level Sq. Ft.:** 1,400
**Upper Level Sq. Ft.:** 1,479
**Bedrooms:** 4
**Bathrooms:** 2½
**Foundation:** Basement
**Material List Available:** Yes
**Price Category:** F

*Images provided by designer/architect.*

**CAD FILE AVAILABLE**

**Upper Level Floor Plan**

**Optional Upper Level Floor Plan**

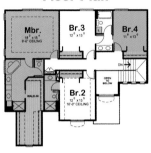

Mbr. 16⁵ x 15⁴ 9'-0" CEILING · Br.3 12⁰ x 13⁰ · Br.4 11⁵ x 13⁰

Br.2 12⁰ x 13⁵ 10'-0" CEILING

---

**Main Level Floor Plan**

Family Room 19³ x 15⁰

Dining Room 11⁰ x 15⁰

Kit. 11⁰ x 12⁰

Den 12⁰ x 12⁰

Flex Room 12⁰ x 13⁰

Garage 33⁰ x 24⁴

Storage

Drop Zone

Covered Porch

44'-0"

66'-0"

## Plan #701291

**Dimensions:** 66' W x 44' D
**Levels:** 2
**Square Footage:** 2,892
**Main Level Sq. Ft.:** 1,410
**Upper Level Sq. Ft.:** 1,482
**Bedrooms:** 4
**Bathrooms:** 3½
**Foundation:** Basement
**Material List Available:** Yes
**Price Category:** F

*Images provided by designer/architect.*

**CAD FILE AVAILABLE**

Br.4 11⁰ x 11³

Mbr. 19⁷ x 15⁰ 9'-0" CEILING

Sitting Area

His WIC

Her WIC

Br.3 12⁰ x 12⁰

Br.2 12⁰ x 13⁸

**Upper Level Floor Plan**

*Copyright by designer/architect.*

## Plan #701244

**Dimensions:** 65' W x 65'8" D
**Levels:** 1.5
**Square Footage:** 2,894
**Main Level Sq. Ft.:** 2,394
**Upper Level Sq. Ft.:** 500
**Bedrooms:** 3
**Bathrooms:** 3½
**Foundation:** Basement
**Material List Available:** Yes
**Price Category:** F

Attractive and inviting, this plan is perfect for an active family.

*Images provided by designer/architect.*

**Features:**

- Great Room: Gather in front of the fireplace in this spacious great room for reading or board games.

- Kitchen: This kitchen and adjacent eating area make meals a delight to prepare and serve. The open plan allows plenty of room for the whole family.

- Master Suite: Relax in airy comfort under the 10-ft. ceiling in this master suite. The connecting bath features a private commode, large walk-in closet with seat, tub, and double sinks.

- Secondary Bedrooms: A secondary bedroom on the main floor and another one upstairs are ideally situated to give siblings or guests an extra bit of privacy. Each bedroom features its own bathroom and ample closet space.

**Main Level Floor Plan**

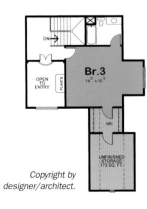

**Upper Level Floor Plan**

*Copyright by designer/architect.*

# Plan #701043

**Dimensions:** 58' W x 59'4" D
**Levels:** 2
**Square Footage:** 2,914
**Main Level Sq. Ft.:** 1,583
**Upper Level Sq. Ft.:** 1,331
**Bedrooms:** 4
**Bathrooms:** 3½
**Foundation:** Basement
**Materials List Available:** Yes
**Price Category:** F

*Images provided by designer/architect.*

You'll love this design if you're looking for a home to complement a site with a lovely rear view.

**Features:**

- **Family Room:** A trio of lovely windows looks out to the rear of this home. The French doors in this room open to the breakfast area for everyone's convenience.

- **Kitchen:** Designed to suit a gourmet cook, this kitchen includes a roomy pantry and an island with a snack bar.

- **Breakfast Area:** The boxed window here is perfect for houseplants or a collection of culinary herbs. A door leads to the rear porch, where you'll love to dine in good weather.

- **Master Suite:** On the upper level, the bedroom features a cathedral ceiling and two walk-in closets. The bath also has a cathedral ceiling and includes dual lavatories, a large dressing area, and a sunlit whirlpool tub.

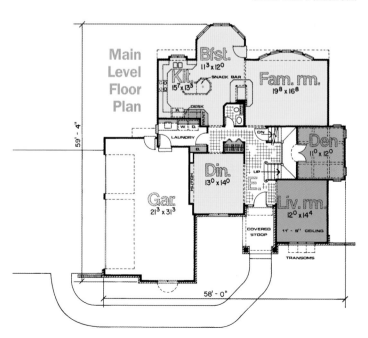

*Copyright by designer/architect.*

## Plan #701292

**Dimensions:** 66' W x 44' D
**Levels:** 2
**Square Footage:** 2,917
**Main Level Sq. Ft.:** 1,410
**Upper Level Sq. Ft.:** 1,507
**Bedrooms:** 4
**Bathrooms:** 3½
**Foundation:** Basement
**Material List Available:** Yes
**Price Category:** F

*Images provided by designer/architect.*

If you are planning to build on a site with great views, this home is designed to make the most of them.

**Features:**

• Family Room: Nestle in front of the fireplace and enjoy the spectacular views from the large windows in this family room.

• Kitchen: Generous work and storage space are the hallmarks of this kitchen, conveniently open to the dining room.

• Master Suite: This master suite features such dream details as a 9-ft. ceiling, sitting area, his and hers walk-in closet, private commode, and double sinks.

• Secondary Bedrooms: Three secondary bedrooms boast walk-in closets and share two bathrooms located in a central hallway.

### Main Level Floor Plan

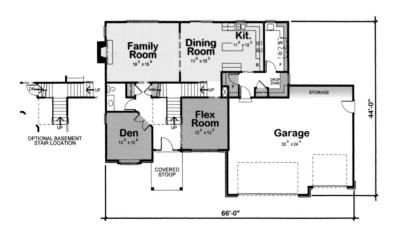

### Upper Level Floor Plan

*Copyright by designer/architect.*

# Plan #701052

**Dimensions:** 68'8" W x 60' D

**Levels:** 2

**Square Footage:** 2,932

**Main Level Sq. Ft.:** 2,084

**Upper Level Sq. Ft.:** 848

**Bedrooms:** 4

**Bathrooms:** 3½

**Foundation:** Basement

**Materials List Available:** Yes

**Price Category:** F

*Images provided by designer/architect.*

Enjoy the spacious covered veranda that gives this house so much added charm.

**Features:**

- **Great Room:** A volume ceiling enhances the spacious feeling in this room, making it a natural gathering spot for friends and family. Transom-topped windows look onto the veranda, and French doors open to it.

- **Den:** French doors from the entry lead to this room, with its unusual ceiling detail, gracious fireplace, and transom-topped windows.

- **Hearth Room:** Three skylights punctuate the cathedral ceiling in this room, giving it an extra measure of light and warmth.

- **Kitchen:** This kitchen is a delight, thanks to its generous working and storage space.

**Main Level Floor Plan**

## Upper Level Floor Plan

*Copyright by designer/architect.*

# Choosing Curtains and Draperies

ong ago, but not so far in the past, curtains were just a way to keep out the cold or extreme light. Today, these fabric-based coverings can still be used to control the amount of natural light in a room and limit heat gain in the summer and heat loss during the winter. But technology and the modern insulating qualities of glass allow curtains and draperies to be more, or even less, than practical. With limitless combinations of fabric, color, and trim, these window treatments can be simply decorative.

Throughout this article, the terms "draperies" and "curtains" are used interchangeably. But to some people, they

the smart approach to
window
DECOR
CREATIVE HOMEOWNER®
THIRD EDITION
revised and expanded

Lynn Elliott and Lisa Lent

The following article was reprinted from *The Smart Approach to Window Decor* (Creative Homeowner 2007).

**Below-sill-length curtains,** trimmed in a colorful print, are arranged to hightlight the graceful curve of the arched window, above.

**Hanging from a rod** high above the window frame, these puddling drapery panels create an illusion of height, above.

have slightly different meanings. Draperies are usually pleated, lined, and floor length, with a tailored, formal style. They are attached via hooks to a traverse rod; a cord mechanism is used to close them. Curtains are normally suspended from rods by rings, tabs, ties, or a rod-pocket casing; they look less formal.

**This formal living area** is enhanced by the drapery treatment accentuating the architectural beauty of the windows, opposite.

When choosing curtains or draperies for your windows, make note of how far you will be able to retract the panels. Stack-back refers to how compactly curtains or draperies can be drawn back on a rod. When there is minimal wall space around a window or when you want to maximize a view, the depth of the stack-back is a concern.

## Curtain Basics

Curtains encompass three basic styles: panels, cafés, and tiers. Heading variations, including pocket casings, tabs, loops, ties, grommets, and pleats, can change the personality of each style. In addition, curtains can be lined, unlined, or—for extra body and insulation—interlined. All of these elements work together to influence the ultimate appearance of your window treatment.

### Types of Curtains

The basic panel is the most versatile and straightforward type of window dressing. It can be any length and have any type of heading. It can be hung straight, without any adornment, or tied back in one of the various positions. It looks wonderful with all sorts of hardware, including traverse rods, decorative poles with finials, curtain rings, café clips, tiebacks, and holdbacks. This multipurpose treatment can be made in a variety of fabrics with trimmings— from fringe to gimp—to reflect any decor.

A café curtain covers the lower half of a window. A longer version goes approximately three-quarters up the window, leaving a small section at the top of the window exposed. Café curtains are usually hung from a pole by rings, clips, tabs, ties, or a rod-pocket heading. This type of casual treatment suits cottage-style interiors. Similar to café curtains, tiered curtains are a team of two half curtains covering the upper and lower sections of a window. They, too, have a homey, comfortable ambiance and are hung on curtain rods.

### Curtain Lengths

The curtain length influences the style of the treatment. A sill-length curtain has a casual air; drapery that falls to the floor connotes elegance. Curtain lengths also affect activity in the area near a window. Are the windows close to a breakfast table? If so, shorter curtains are less intrusive and leave clearance around the table. Is there a heat source underneath the window? Curtains should never touch or block a radiator, heat vent, or heating unit. Is the treatment hung on or around

**An extra allowance of fabric** at the bottom edge of these draperies looks pretty, but be careful: puddled panels near the door opening may cause someone to trip.

a glazed door? Make sure that it doesn't block the opening and that you can open and close the door—and the curtain, if desired—easily.

Curtain lengths can camouflage problems, too. Is the window awkwardly shaped? Or is there an architectural flaw that you would like to conceal? A floor-length treatment, hung above the window frame, can help disguise the problem. In some rooms, windows may be different widths and lengths. If this is the case, plan the largest window treatment first. Dress the remaining windows in a scaled-down version of this treatment. For visual unity, install all the upper hardware at the same height.

In general, a window treatment looks best when it falls in line with the sill or floor. The most common lengths for drapery are sill, below sill, floor, and puddled. As the description implies, a *sill-length* curtain skims the windowsill. Favored for horizontal windows, it can start from the top of the window to the sill or, when café style, from the middle of the window to the sill. A curtain at this length is typically easy to operate, so it is a good choice for a window that will be opened and closed often.

The *below-sill length* falls at least 4 inches beneath the window frame so that it covers the apron, the horizontal board that runs under the sill. If the curtain is too far

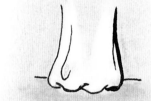

**Too Short**

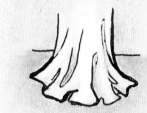

**Too Long**

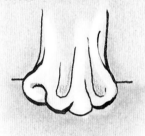

**Correct**

**When puddling curtains,** increase the length of the fabric by at least 6 to 8 inches for the best results, above.

**Fan pleats** add a decorative touch to these colorful sill-length panels; curtain rings allow the panels to glide easily across the pole when the homeowner wants to block harsh late-afternoon sunlight, left.

below the sill, however, it looks awkward and unfinished. A sill-length panel, too, can be used for café or three-quarter curtains, and it can cover up an unattractive window frame. It generally looks best on picture windows and above window seats.

A *floor-length* curtain makes a strong visual statement. Make sure that the curtain is only ½ inch above the floor because, like a hem that's too high on pants, floor-length treatments that fall short can suffer the "floods." (In humid areas, however, the curtain can be an inch off the floor to allow for the rise and fall of the fabric.) If you install layered drapery, the inner curtain can be ¼ to ½ inch shorter than the outer curtain.

To avoid seeing the back of the heading from the outside, add 4 inches to the curtain's length so that it hangs above the window frame. This length works well with double-hung windows, bay windows, sliding glass doors, and tall, narrow openings, such as French doors.

*Puddling* is the term used for a floor-length curtain with an extra allowance of fabric that is arranged into a soft pouf (the puddle) on the floor. This is a dramatic length that falls 6 to 8 inches onto the floor. (For the correct length, see the illustrations on above.) Particularly appropriate for floor-to-ceiling windows, puddling has some drawbacks. A puddled curtain often needs adjustment, as it can be easily disarranged. Also, it isn't the right choice for high-traffic aisles or doorways, because the extra fabric can block the function of a door or cause someone to trip.

## Tieback Positions

How a curtain frames an opening is an important part of a window dressing's overall design. You can leave a curtain hanging unadorned, but by using a tieback, you can create a sculpted silhouette of fabric against a window. You can also

**Loosely gathered fabric** creates a ruffle effect above the valance's rod pocket, enhancing the feminine ambiance of this homey bedroom.

control the amount of light that comes into the room and create a dramatic frame that enhances a view or covers an unsightly one.

Where you position the tieback affects the way a curtain hangs. The curtain can be caught back in a dramatic swoop of fabric, or it can be gently held open, revealing a colorful contrasting lining. The traditional tieback positions—high, midway, and low—are some of the most effective placements. Looping a tieback around or just below a pole, angled *high*, creates a short curve of fabric; don't use this arrangement where the curtain is moved often. A tieback positioned *midway* shouldn't fall exactly in the center; the best placement is slightly above or below the middle of the curtain. Two-thirds of the way down the curtain is the proper place for a *low* tieback. When using this position, check that a tasseled tieback doesn't brush the floor, however.

A *center tie*—when one or two curtains are gathered at the middle so that they curve on both sides—can look impressive if it's on a bay or bow window. Use a rope tieback or, if the material is light-

SMARTtip

## Curtain Weights

A breeze can stir up a floor-length curtain, leaving it in disarray. A curtain weight can minimize the problem, plus it helps drapery to hang more smoothly. You will find two types of curtain weights: disk weights and fabric-covered weights. A disk weight is a small, round piece of lead that is inserted into the hem at each corner and each seam. To prevent it from rubbing and wearing out the fabric, insert it into a pocket made of lining fabric or muslin. A fabric-covered weight consists of links of metal encased in a fabric tube. This type, which comes in different sizes to correspond to the weight of the fabric, is attached along the hem.

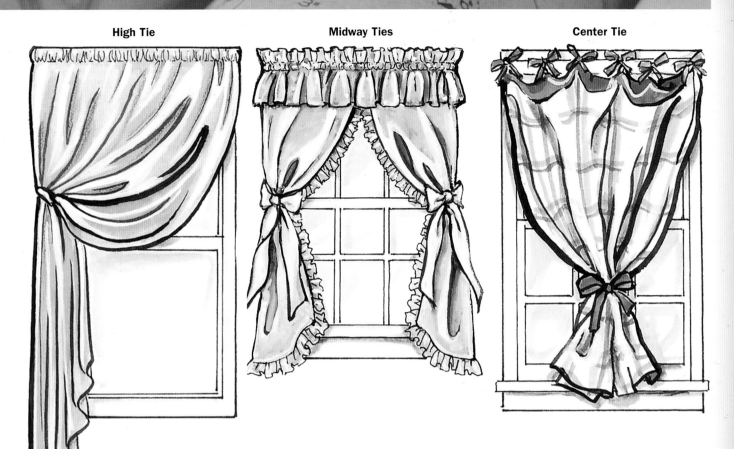

**High Tie**  **Midway Ties**  **Center Tie**

weight, literally knot the fabric. A crisscross arrangement requires two curtain rods and looks best with lightweight or sheer fabrics. When each panel is caught midway, the top halves overlap.

To create a *bishop's sleeve*, arrange two center ties at different points on a curtain (one high, one midway). Pull out the fabric above each tie to create a double tier of soft poufs. Try an *angled double tie* with a sheer undertreatment because the sinuous outline stands out against a gauzy backdrop. Slightly different from the bishop's sleeve, the two ties are arranged at the high and midway points on the panel so that the curtain swoops into graceful curves on only one side of the window.

## What's Your Style?

Whether you are choosing curtains for an entire house or just one room, the process is the same. You need to make three basic decisions about your treatment. Will it be formal or informal? Lined or unlined? What type of heading? Once these decisions are made, you can finalize a design.

### Formal Verses Informal Style

A room's window treatments are influenced by a number of elements, including the function of the space, the architectural style of the house, and the decorating preferences of the homeowner. The result is that the same windows can be treated quite differently. For example, picture a dining room with a bay window. That type of window is often given a multilayered, floor-length window dressing—in other words, a formal window treatment. But if you

prefer a more casual style, you can choose the informal look of café curtains with sill-length, tied-back side panels.

**A Full Formal Treatment.** Formal treatments often involve two or three layers. One layer, called the casement curtain, is installed inside the window's trim area. Typically it's a sheer, solid, or lace panel that lays straight or is gathered at the top. Overdraperies, often referred to simply as draperies, make up the second layer. Generally, they cover the window and the trim and, space permitting, extend beyond to the sides or the area above the window. The third, and optional, layer of a full formal window treatment is a valance, sometimes called a pelmet, which runs horizontally across the top of the window and covers the drapery or curtain heading. A hard valance, also called a cornice or a lambrequin, is usually made of wood and covered with fabric or upholstery. To some eyes, the window treatment is unfinished without this last element, but this is strictly a matter of taste. Luxurious, heavyweight fabrics, such as damasks, brocades, silks, tapestries, and velvets, enhance the sophistication of formal treatments. However, remember that these fabrics require professional cleaning every couple of years.

**An Informal Treatment.** Informal treatments may consist of one or two layers or nothing at all. If location and privacy considerations permit, a beautiful window looks attractive without a dressing—especially when there's also something pleasant to see outside. Sometimes simple casement curtains look attractive in casual rooms. If only the lower half of the window needs covering, café curtains offer privacy without blocking light. Fabrics that lend

**Low Ties**

**Angled Double Ties**

**Crisscrossed Ties**

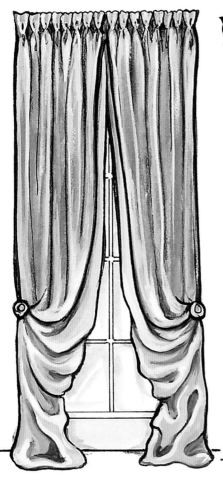

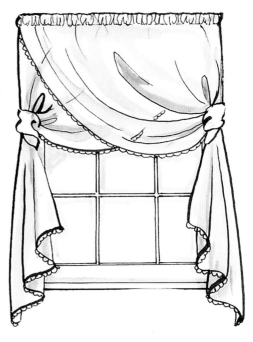

**Unlined Curtains.** An *unlined curtain* diffuses daylight, but it does not exclude it. It is the simplest form of window dressing, and it is effective on its own or as an undertreatment. Because an unlined treatment lacks the extra thickness of a lining, it stacks back tightly. Choose a fabric with no right or wrong side so that it looks equally attractive from both the outside and inside of the window. Voile, lace, muslin, and sheers made of cotton or silk organza are the classic fabric choices for unlined treatments. Textured fabrics with open weaves are also suitable.

An unlined curtain filters light beautifully and provides a hazy screen from prying eyes. However, because it offers little privacy in the evening when lamps are turned on, consider pairing sheers with shades or blinds to maintain privacy where necessary. Sunlight damage is another drawback to

themselves to an informal look include all cottons, such as chintz, ticking, toile de Jouy, linen, gingham, and muslin. Unlike the fabric that is typical of formal draperies, most of these are washable.

## Lining

The style of curtains—formal or informal—often dictates whether the treatment will be lined. Other considerations include how much natural light you want in a room and how long you expect the arrangement to last.

## How to Dress a Curtain

To make the folds fall evenly, train the curtains by tying them back for 48 hours or more. This is a process known as dressing the curtain and results in drapery that holds its shape and hangs well. To start, draw the drapery into the stack-back position. Fix the pleats and gaps in the heading until you are pleased with the arrangement. If the treatment is hanging below a curtain rod, position the gaps to fold toward the back; if the curtain hangs in front of the rod or pole, the gaps will fold forward. Smooth each pleat from the heading downward as far as

possible. Then work from the bottom upward, gathering the pleats together. With a strip of fabric, make a loose tie just below the heading to hold the pleats in place. Tie another fabric strip midway down the curtain, smoothing the pleats as you go. Follow with a tie near the hemline. The ties should be tight enough to hold the fabric without marking it. Next, steam the curtains with a hand steamer. You may need a friend to hold the curtain while you fasten the ties. Leave the curtains undisturbed for a couple of days before removing the ties.

unlined curtains. Without a protective lining, the fabric deteriorates quickly.

**Lined Curtains.** A *lined* curtain has body, improving its appearance by creating softer, deeper folds. A lining blocks sunlight, protecting the curtain fabric and other elements in the room from fading, particularly where there is western or southern exposure. Sunlight also adds a yellow tint to unlined fabric that may throw off your room's color scheme. A lining preserves the true color of the face fabric. Linings increase privacy, reduce outside noise, and block drafts and dust. Check for linings treated to resist rot and sun damage. Once a lining has deteriorated, the curtain can be relined or hung without the lining. To achieve the best protection possible, buy the best quality lining fabric that you can afford.

If you line one curtain in a room, do the same to the rest so that the color and drape of the curtains match. Typically, lining fabric comes in white or off-white. Although colored linings are available, be aware that light shining through a lining affects the hue of a lightweight curtain fabric. Get samples of your intended lining and curtain fabric, and then test them together at the window for color change.

**Interlinings.** If you are set on having a colored lining, consider adding an *interlining*, which is a soft, blanket-like layer of material that is sandwiched between the lining and the curtain fabric. Like a lining, it increases the insulation and light-blocking qualities of the drapery, as well as extending the life of the curtains. It also gives a professional finish to pleats by improving the drape of the fabric. A lining is usually sewn on, but it can also be attached with special double tape or pinned on with buttonholes that slip over drapery hooks. The latter allows the lining and face fabric to be cleaned separately. If you need a dark bedroom during the daytime because you work nights, try a *blackout lining*, which almost completely blocks sunlight. Other specialty linings include *insulating* and *reflective* types. These types of linings can be sewn on, but they can also be hung on a separate rod and drawn closed only when needed.

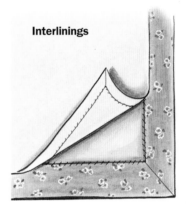

Interlinings

**A sheer curtain** allows light to filter in during the day while the drapery panels provide pattern, color and privacy when needed, above left.

**Fashionable yet functional** sheer-linen shades highlight these oversize windows, above right, while reducing sun glare.

**Tiebacks on full-length, lined draperies,** below, emphasize the swooping effect at the bottom edge, softening the sliding glass patio doors.

## Plan #701228

**Dimensions:** 108'9" W x 78'4" D

**Levels:** 1

**Square Footage:** 2,956

**Bedrooms:** 4

**Bathrooms:** 1 full, 2 half

**Foundation:** Basement

**Material List Available:** Yes

**Price Category:** F

*Images provided by designer/architect.*

**Main Level Floor Plan**

*Copyright by designer/architect.*

**Optional Lower Level Floor Plan**

## Plan #701215

**Dimensions:** 88'8" W x 61'8" D

**Levels:** 1

**Square Footage:** 2,962

**Bedrooms:** 3

**Bathrooms:** 2 full, 2 half

**Foundation:** Basement

**Material List Available:** Yes

**Price Category:** F

*Images provided by designer/architect.*

**Main Level Floor Plan**

**Optional Lower Level Floor Plan**

*Copyright by designer/architect.*

## Upper Level Floor Plan

*Copyright by designer/architect.*

BEDROOM 3
11'4" X 12'6"

OPEN TO BELOW

STUDY
12'6" X 10'10"

WALKWAY

RAIL

DN

RAIL

PLAY ROOM
13'8" X 11'6"

OPEN TO BELOW

BEDROOM 4
11'4" X 12'8"

### Plan #701112

**Dimensions:** 66' W x 51' D
**Levels:** 1.5
**Square Footage:** 2,978
**Main Level Sq. Ft.:** 2,101
**Upper Level Sq. Ft.:** 877
**Bedrooms:** 4
**Bathrooms:** 3
**Foundation:** Slab; basement for fee
**Material List Available:** Yes
**Price Category:** F

*Images provided by designer/architect.*

## Main Level Floor Plan

66'

NOOK
10'6" X 10'8"

PORCH

3 CAR GARAGE
21'4" X 28'6"

EATING BAR

FAMILY ROOM
17' X 17'6"

2-STORY CLG.

LINEN

KITCHEN
12'6" X 14'10"

51'

MASTER SUITE
13'6" X 16'8"

12' CLG.

WALK-IN PANTRY

OPEN TO ABOVE

TRAY CLG

MASTER RETREAT
6'8" X 7'

BUTLER'S PANTRY

OPTIONAL BASEMENT STAIRS

UP

W D

AC WH

STORAGE

DINING ROOM
13'8" X 11'6"

OPEN TO ABOVE

LIVING ROOM
11'4" X 12'8"

BEDROOM 2
13'4" X 11'

VAULT

VAULT

---

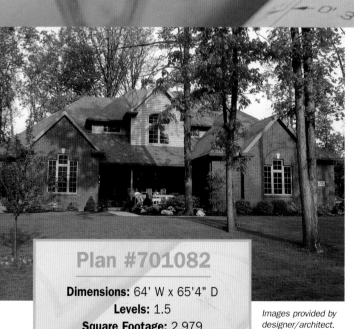

## Main Level Floor Plan

WHIRLPOOL LIN.

TRANS.

TRAPS

TRANS.

Bfst.
14'0 x 12'0

TRANS.

TRAPS

TRANS.

Grt. rm.
18'0 x 16'0
17'-0" CEILING

Kit.
14'8 x 14'8

SNACK BAR

Gath. rm.
17'0 x 16'0

CATHEDRAL CEILING

BOOKS

Mbr.
13'0 x 16'0
10'-0" CEILING

Din.
12'0 x 15'0

HUTCH

Den
12'0 x 13'0
10'-0" CLG.

COVERED PORCH

Gar.
22'0 x 31'4

TRANSOM

64'-0"

TRANSOM

65'-4"

### Plan #701082

**Dimensions:** 64' W x 65'4" D
**Levels:** 1.5
**Square Footage:** 2,979
**Main Level Sq. Ft.:** 2,158
**Upper Level Sq. Ft.:** 821
**Bedrooms:** 4
**Bathrooms:** 3½
**Foundation:** Basement; crawl space for fee
**Material List Available:** Yes
**Price Category:** F

*Images provided by designer/architect.*

## Upper Level Floor Plan

*Copyright by designer/architect.*

TRAPS

TRANS.

TRANS.

OPEN TO GREAT ROOM
17'-10" CEILING

Br. 2
14'0 x 11'

DN

OPEN TO BELOW

PLANT SHELF

Br. 4
11'0 x 13'0
11'-0" CEILING

Br. 3
12'0 x 13'0

## Plan #701225

**Dimensions:** 60' W x 60' D
**Levels:** 1.5
**Square Footage:** 2,999
**Main Level Sq. Ft.:** 1,872
**Upper Level Sq. Ft.:** 1,127
**Bedrooms:** 4
**Bathrooms:** 3½
**Foundation:** Basement
**Material List Available:** Yes
**Price Category:** F

*Images provided by designer/architect.*

This spectacular home features stunning architectural details both inside and out.

### Features:

- **Family Room:** This uniquely shaped, two-story family room features large windows on both levels to maximize views.

- **Kitchen:** This beautiful kitchen is a home cook's dream. Features include plentiful work and storage space and a center island that overlooks the dining room.

- **Master Suite:** Step into this luxurious master suite and you may never want to leave. An 11-ft. tray ceiling graces the expansive bedroom area. There is also a walk-in closet with sloped ceiling, private commode, a tub, and his and her sinks.

- **Secondary Bedrooms:** These three extra bedrooms are perfect for siblings or houseguests.

**Main Level Floor Plan**

**Upper Level Floor Plan**

*Copyright by designer/architect.*

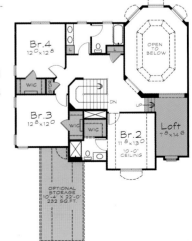

## Plan #701307

**Dimensions:** 56' W x 52' D

**Levels:** 2

**Square Footage:** 3,025

**Main Level Sq. Ft.:** 1,583

**Upper Level Sq. Ft.:** 1,442

**Bedrooms:** 4

**Bathrooms:** 3½

**Foundation:** Basement

**Materials List Available:** Yes

**Price Category:** G

*Images provided by designer/architect.*

This large home with a contemporary feeling is ideal for the family looking for comfort and amenities.

**Features:**

- Entry: Stacked windows bring sunlight into this two-story entry, with its stylish curved staircase.

- Library: French doors off the entry lead to this room, with its built-in bookcases flanking a large, picturesque window.

- Family Room: Located in the rear of the home, this family room is sunken to set it apart. A spider-beamed ceiling gives it a contemporary feeling, and a bay window, wet bar, and pass-through fireplace add to this impression.

- Kitchen: The island in this kitchen makes working here a pleasure. The corner pantry joins a breakfast area and hearth room to this space.

### Main Level Floor Plan

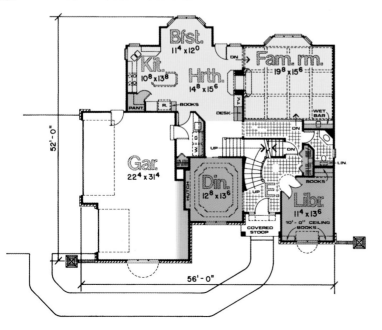

### Upper Level Floor Plan

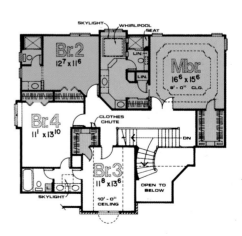

*Copyright by designer/architect.*

## Plan #701090

**Dimensions:** 66' W x 66' D
**Levels:** 1.5
**Square Footage:** 3,040
**Main Level Sq. Ft.:** 2,215
**Upper Level Sq. Ft.:** 825
**Bedrooms:** 4
**Bathrooms:** 3½
**Foundation:** Basement; crawl space for fee
**Material List Available:** Yes
**Price Category:** G

Classic and gracious outside, elegantly functional inside, this expansive home will be the highlight of the neighborhood.

**CAD FILE AVAILABLE**

**Features:**

- Great Room: This spectacular great room is open to the second floor and features an 18-ft. ceiling. It shares a two-sided fireplace with the hearth area off the kitchen.

- Kitchen: This corner kitchen is wonderful for the family chef. A center island, pantry, and snack bar are just some of the amenities offered in this generous plan.

- Breakfast Room: This breakfast room is a welcoming place to begin your day. Multiple windows capture the outdoor view so you can enjoy the sunrise with your morning coffee.

- Master Suite: Step into this master suite and be transported to your private oasis. An 11-ft. ceiling graces the bedroom, while the spacious bath features his-and-hers sinks, private commode, and a whirlpool tub for extra pampering.

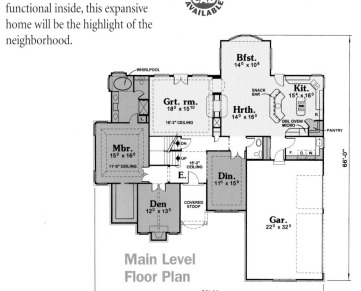

**Main Level Floor Plan**

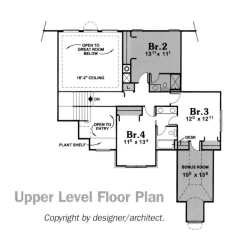

**Upper Level Floor Plan**

## Plan #701019

**Dimensions:** 60' W x 58' D
**Levels:** 2
**Square Footage:** 3,057
**Main Level Sq. Ft.:** 1,631
**Second Level Sq. Ft.:** 1,426
**Bedrooms:** 4
**Bathrooms:** 2½
**Foundation:** Basement;
crawl space for fee
**Materials List Available:** Yes
**Price Category:** G

*Images provided by designer/architect.*

This distinctive home offers plenty of space and is designed for gracious and convenient living.

**Features:**

- Ceiling Height: 8 ft. unless otherwise noted.

- Foyer: A curved staircase in this elegant entry will greet your guests.

- Living Room: This room invites you with a volume ceiling flanked by transom-topped windows that flood the room with sunlight.

- Screened Veranda: On warm summer nights, throw open the French doors in the living room and enjoy a breeze on the huge screened veranda.

- Dining Room: This distinctive room is overlooked by the veranda.

- Family Room: At the back of the home is this comfortable family retreat with its soaring cathedral ceiling and handsome fireplace flanked by bookcases.

- Master Suite: This bayed bedroom features a 10-ft. vaulted ceiling.

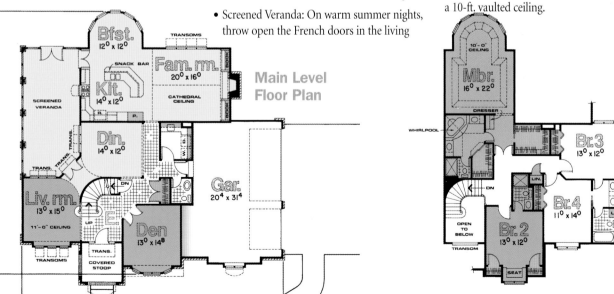

**Main Level
Floor Plan**

**Upper Level Floor Plan**

## Plan #701047

**Dimensions:** 64' W x 60'8" D
**Levels:** 2
**Square Footage:** 3,067
**Main Level Sq. Ft.:** 2,169
**Upper Level Sq. Ft.:** 898
**Bedrooms:** 4
**Bathrooms:** 3½
**Foundation:** Basement
**Materials List Available:** Yes
**Price Category:** G

You'll love the combination of formal features and casual, family-friendly areas in this spacious home with an elegant exterior.

**Features:**

• Entry: The elegant windows in this two-story area are complemented by the unusual staircase.

• Family Room: This family room features an 11-ft. ceiling, wet bar, fireplace, and trio of windows that look out to the covered porch.

• Living Room: Columns set off both this room and the dining room. Decorate to accentuate their formality, or make them blend into a more casual atmosphere.

• Master Suite: Columns in this suite highlight a bayed sitting room where you'll be happy to relax at the end of the day or on weekend mornings.

• Bedrooms: Bedroom 2 has a private bath, making it an ideal guest room, and you'll find private vanities in bedrooms 3 and 4.

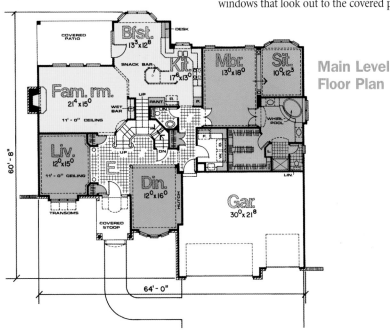

**Main Level Floor Plan**

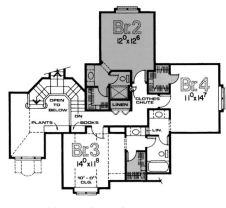

**Upper Level Floor Plan**

*Copyright by designer/architect.*

## Plan #701028

**Dimensions:** 67'8" W x 57' D
**Levels:** 1.5
**Square Footage:** 3,072
**Main Level Sq. Ft.:** 2,116
**Upper Level Sq. Ft.:** 956
**Bedrooms:** 4
**Bathrooms:** 3½
**Foundation:** Slab; basement for fee
**Materials List Available:** Yes
**Price Category:** G

A long porch and a trio of roof dormers give this gracious home a sophisticated country look.

### Features:

- **Ceiling Height:** 8 ft. unless otherwise noted.

- **Balcony:** This balcony overlooks the entry and the staircase hall.

- **Dining Room:** Columns and a cased opening lend elegance, making this the perfect venue for stylish dinner parties.

- **Family Room:** A cathedral ceiling gives this room a light and airy feel. The handsome fireplace framed by windows is sure to become a favorite family gathering place.

- **Master Suite:** This architecturally distinctive bedroom features a bayed sitting area and a tray ceiling.

- **Bedrooms:** One of the bedrooms enjoys a private bath, making it a perfect guest room. Other bedrooms feature walk-in closets.

**CAD FILE AVAILABLE**

## Main Level Floor Plan

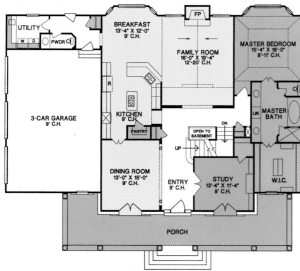

## Upper Level Floor Plan

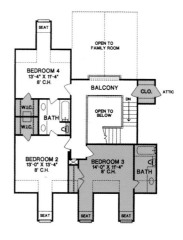

*Copyright by designer/architect.*

# Plan #701240

**Dimensions:** 67' W x 69' D
**Levels:** 1.5
**Square Footage:** 3,080
**Main Level Sq. Ft.:** 2,059
**Upper Level Sq. Ft.:** 1,021
**Bedrooms:** 4
**Bathrooms:** 3½
**Foundation:** Basement
**Material List Available:** Yes
**Price Category:** G

*Images provided by designer/architect.*

Step through the arched entryway of this impressive home and enjoy family living to its fullest.

**Features:**

- **Great Room:** Sit back and relax in this spacious great room, featuring two entertainment centers, a wall of windows, and a beautiful fireplace.

- **Kitchen:** You can chat with guests while whipping up a gourmet meal in this open kitchen area. A center island that separates the

kitchen from the great room and dining area is both stylish and functional. All three rooms open to the second floor, creating a bright and open space for entertaining and socializing.

- **Porch:** With direct access from the dining area, this covered porch is a wonderful spot for alfresco dining and parties.

- **Master Suite:** The ceiling height throughout this master suite is almost 12 feet. Luxurious amenities include a walk-in closet, private commode, and double sinks.

## Main Level Floor Plan

## Upper Level Floor Plan

*Copyright by designer/architect.*

## Plan #701102

**Dimensions:** 67'1" W x 65'10⅛" D
**Levels:** 1.5
**Square Footage:** 3,094
**Main Level Sq. Ft.:** 2,112
**Upper Level Sq. Ft.:** 982
**Bedrooms:** 4
**Bathrooms:** 3½
**Foundation:** Slab; basement for fee
**Material List Available:** Yes
**Price Category:** G

*This home, as shown in the photograph, may differ from the actual blueprints. For more detailed information, please check the floor plans carefully.*

*Images provided by designer/architect.*

This beautiful brick home has unique architecture, which is sure to make it stand out.

**Features:**

• Living Room: This spectacular octagonal two-story living room is a wonderful place to entertain family and friends.

• Family Room: Entertain two or twenty in this two-story family room, which has an 18-ft.-ceiling and direct access to the rear porch.

• Kitchen: This corner kitchen with island is conveniently located next to the breakfast room and family room for easy food transportation.

• Master Suite: You'll love this master suite, with its large bedroom, direct access to the rear porch, his and her sinks, his and her walk-in closets, separate toilet area, and tub.

**Main Level Floor Plan**

**Upper Level Floor Plan**

*Copyright by designer/architect.*

# Plan #701259

**Dimensions:** 58' W x 66' D
**Levels:** 1.5
**Square Footage:** 2,774
**Main Level Sq. Ft.:** 1,832
**Upper Level Sq. Ft.:** 942
**Bedrooms:** 4
**Bathrooms:** 2½
**Foundation:** Basement
**Material List Available:** Yes
**Price Category:** F

*Images provided by designer/architect.*

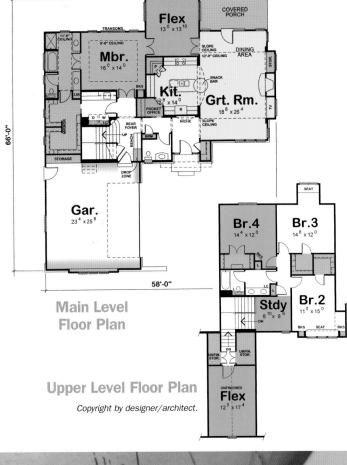

**Main Level Floor Plan**

**Upper Level Floor Plan**

*Copyright by designer/architect.*

# Plan #701217

**Dimensions:** 62' W x 68'8" D
**Levels:** 1.5
**Square Footage:** 3,124
**Main Level Sq. Ft.:** 1,988
**Upper Level Sq. Ft.:** 1,136
**Bedrooms:** 4
**Bathrooms:** 3 full, 2 half
**Foundation:** Basement
**Material List Available:** Yes
**Price Category:** G

*Images provided by designer/architect.*

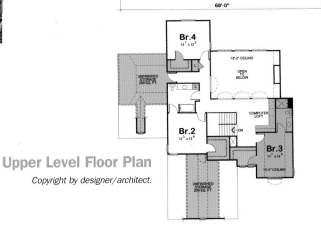

**Main Level Floor Plan**

**Upper Level Floor Plan**

*Copyright by designer/architect.*

## Plan #701304

**Dimensions:** 66'8" W x 75' D
**Levels:** 1.5
**Square Footage:** 3,161
**Main Level Sq. Ft.:** 2,407
**Upper Level Sq. Ft.:** 754
**Bedrooms:** 3
**Bathrooms:** 3½
**Foundation:** Slab
**Material List Available:** Yes
**Price Category:** G

*Images provided by designer/architect.*

**Main Level Floor Plan**

**Upper Level Floor Plan**

*Copyright by designer/architect.*

---

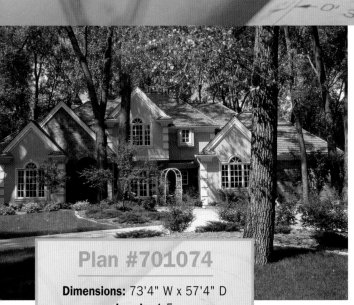

## Plan #701074

**Dimensions:** 73'4" W x 57'4" D
**Levels:** 1.5
**Square Footage:** 3,172
**Main Level Sq. Ft.:** 2,252
**Upper Level Sq. Ft.:** 920
**Bedrooms:** 4
**Bathrooms:** 3½
**Foundation:** Basement; crawl space for fee
**Material List Available:** Yes
**Price Category:** G

*Images provided by designer/architect.*

**Front View**

**Main Level Floor Plan**

**Upper Level Floor Plan**

*Copyright by designer/architect.*

## Plan #701060

**Dimensions:** 65'4" W x 52'8" D
**Levels:** 1
**Square Footage:** 3,225
**Main Level Sq. Ft.:** 1,887
**Basement Level Sq. Ft.:** 1,338
**Bedrooms:** 3
**Bathrooms:** 2½
**Foundation:** Basement
**Materials List Available:** Yes
**Price Category:** G

*Images provided by designer/architect.*

This is the design if you want a home that will be easy to expand as your family grows.

**Features:**

- Entry: Both the dining room and great room are immediately accessible from this lovely entry.

- Great Room: The transom-topped bowed windows highlight the spacious feeling here.

- Gathering Room: Also with an angled ceiling, this room has a fireplace as well as a built-in

entertainment center and bookcases.

- Dining Room: This elegant room features a 13-ft. boxed ceiling and majestic window around which you'll love to decorate.

- Kitchen: Designed for convenience, this kitchen includes a lovely angled ceiling and gazebo-shaped breakfast area.

- Basement: Use the plans for finishing a family room and two bedrooms when the time is right.

### Main Level Floor Plan

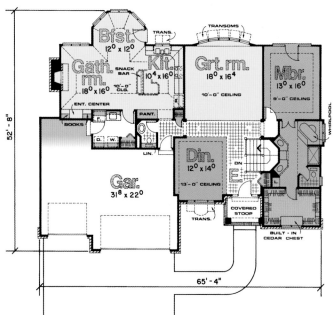

### Basement Level Floor Plan

*Copyright by designer/architect.*

## Plan #701258

**Dimensions:** 64' W x 74' D
**Levels:** 1.5
**Square Footage:** 3,261
**Main Level Sq. Ft.:** 2,300
**Upper Level Sq. Ft.:** 961
**Bedrooms:** 4
**Bathrooms:** 4
**Foundation:** Basement
**Material List Available:** Yes
**Price Category:** G

Practicality and luxury come in one beautiful package in the form of this traditional-style home.

**Features:**

- Patio: Wonderful for parties or relaxing after dinner, this covered patio has a 14-ft.-high ceiling for a touch of luxury and some protection from the sun.

- Family Room: Open to the second floor, this two-story family room is great for entertaining guests or family.

- Kitchen: The open design of this kitchen is great for working on multiple projects at once. The center island provides more work space, or an extra surface for the adjoining dining room.

- Master Suite: This master suite is filled with luxuries that you'll adore, such as its his and her sinks, separate toilet area, walk-in closet, and high ceiling.

*Images provided by designer/architect.*

**Main Level Floor Plan**

*Copyright by designer/architect.*

**Upper Level Floor Plan**

## Plan #701086

**Dimensions:** 54'8" W x 68' D
**Levels:** 2
**Square Footage:** 3,273
**Main Level Sq. Ft.:** 1,598
**Upper Level Sq. Ft.:** 1,675
**Bedrooms:** 4
**Bathrooms:** 3½
**Foundation:** Basement;
crawl space for fee
**Material List Available:** Yes
**Price Category:** G

*Images provided by designer/architect.*

This home's eye-catching columns and beautiful two-story front porch make it as attractive as it is comfortable.

**Features:**

- Porches: The two-story front porch is a great place to relax, get some sun, and read a book. At the back of the house, a screened-in porch is wonderful for entertaining friends and family, rain or shine.

- Kitchen: This spacious kitchen is open to both the breakfast room and a covered porch on the side of the house. A snack bar and a walk-in pantry simplify working and storing ingredients.

- Master Suite: Step into luxury in this master suite with its two walk-in closets, 9-ft.-high step ceiling, his and her sinks, and whirlpool bath.

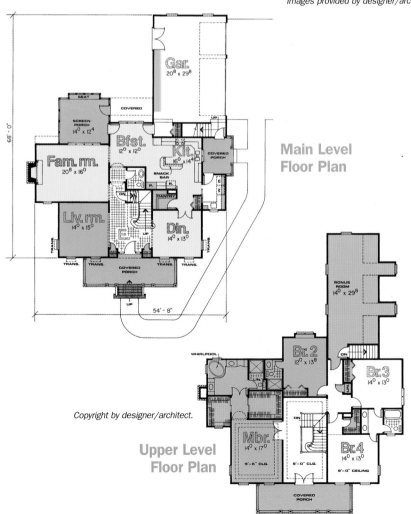

**Main Level Floor Plan**

*Copyright by designer/architect.*

**Upper Level Floor Plan**

## Plan #701064

**Dimensions:** 62' W x 55'4" D
**Levels:** 2
**Square Footage:** 3,306
**Main Level Sq. Ft.:** 1,709
**Upper Level Sq. Ft.:** 1,597
**Bedrooms:** 4
**Bathrooms:** 3½
**Foundation:** Basement;
slab or crawl space for fee
**Material List Available:** Yes
**Price Category:** G

*Images provided by designer/architect.*

**Features:**

- Family Room: The entire family can fit comfortably in this large family room, complete with a fireplace and wet bar.

- Kitchen: You won't run out of space in this roomy kitchen equipped with snack bar, salad sink, desk, and open access to the breakfast room, which is a wonderful place to start your day.

- Library: Need a little peace and quiet? Retreat to the library, where a large built-in bookshelf will hold everything from Aesop to Shakespeare.

- Master Suite: This spacious and luxurious master suite will easily be your favorite room in the house, where you can enjoy the 9-ft.-high step ceiling, windowed sitting area, two walk-in closets, dressing area, skylight, separate toilet area, and his and her sinks.

With its dramatic roof detailing, this European-style house is a beautiful addition to any neighborhood.

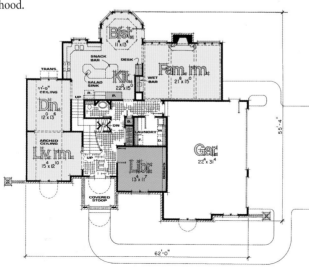

**Main Level Floor Plan**

**Upper Level Floor Plan**

*Copyright by designer/architect.*

## Plan #701192

**Dimensions:** 90'11" W x 81'3" D
**Levels:** 1
**Square Footage:** 3,312
**Bedrooms:** 3
**Bathrooms:** 3
**Foundation:** Basement
**Material List Available:** Yes
**Price Category:** G

*Images provided by designer/architect.*

*This home, as shown in the photograph, may differ from the actual blueprints. For more detailed information, please check the floor plans carefully.*

CAD FILE AVAILABLE

This expansive one-story home has beautiful architecture and details that everyone in your family will appreciate.

**Features:**

- **Family Room:** This family room's spacious area and close proximity to the kitchen makes it a wonderful place to entertain friends and neighbors.

- **Kitchen:** Work with ease in this large kitchen, which has plenty of counter space and storage room. The attached breakfast area is a lovely nook that catches the sunlight for a picturesque start to your day.

- **Master Suite:** Enjoy the seclusion in the wing of this home dedicated to the master suite. A private hallway connects the bedroom and bathroom, so your oasis will not become heavily trafficked by guests. The master bathroom features his and her sinks, a separate toilet area, and a whirlpool bath.

- **Secondary Bedrooms:** Siblings will enjoy these two bedrooms, each with its own toilet, sink, and walk-in closet for privacy. The shared bath connects the two rooms.

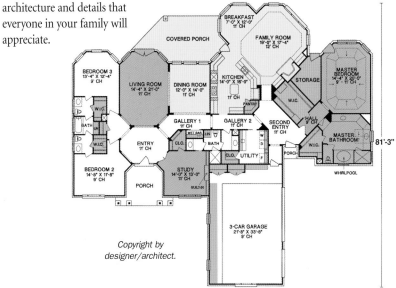

*Copyright by designer/architect.*

Living Room/Dining Room

## Plan #701029

**Dimensions:** 82' W x 60'8" D
**Levels:** 2
**Square Footage:** 3,335
**Main Level Sq. Ft.:** 2,054
**Upper Level Sq. Ft.:** 1,281
**Bedrooms:** 4
**Bathrooms:** 3½
**Foundation:** Slab; basement for fee
**Materials List Available:** Yes
**Price Category:** G

This charming European-style home creates a welcoming environment with its covered porch, two-story foyer, and attractive accommodations.

**Features:**

• Great Room: Bask in the quiet glow of abundant natural light; cozy up to the smoldering fireplace; or gather with the family in this large, relaxing area.

• Kitchen: This design creates a great balance between workspace and play space. The kitchen surrounds the household with workspace without feeling closed-in. A breakfast bar opens into the large breakfast area, making life a little simpler in the mornings.

• Master Suite: This spacious room is yours for the styling, a private space that features a walk-in closet and full bath, which includes his and her sinks, a standing shower, and a large tub.

• Second Floor: "Go to your room" sounds much better when that room is separated by a story. Identically sized bedrooms with ample closet space save you from family squabbles. The second floor has everything you need, with a compartmentalized full bathroom and computer loft.

*Images provided by designer/architect.*

### Upper Level Floor Plan

### Third Floor Bedroom Floor Plan

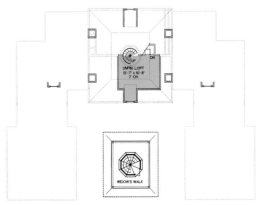

*Copyright by designer/ architect.*

### Main Level Floor Plan

## Plan #701194

**Dimensions:** 64'11" W x 76'7" D
**Levels:** 1.5
**Square Footage:** 3,397
**Main Level Sq. Ft.:** 2,144
**Upper Level Sq. Ft.:** 1,253
**Bedrooms:** 3
**Bathrooms:** 3½
**Foundation:** Basement
**Material List Available:** Yes
**Price Category:** G

*Images provided by designer/architect.*

### Features:

- **Living Room:** This two-story living room shares the two-way fireplace with the family room and is a gorgeous place to entertain friends and family.

- **Family Room:** A two-way fireplace shared with the living room is the focal point of this room. It is framed by two built-in cabinets that can be used for a variety of purposes.

- **Kitchen:** This kitchen will be a favorite of the family chef, with plenty of counter space, a center island, pantry, and open access to the breakfast and family rooms.

- **Master Suite:** Every bit of this master suite is spacious and detailed for your enjoyment. The large bedroom has a 10-ft.-high ceiling opens up to a dressing area, two walk-in closets, a tub, his and her sinks, and a separate toilet area.

Stunning architectural details complete both the interior and exterior of this home.

**Main Level Floor Plan**

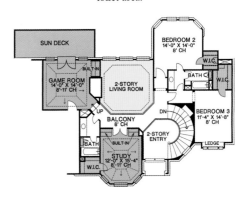

**Upper Level Floor Plan**

*Copyright by designer/architect.*

## Plan #701329

**Dimensions:** 62' W x 55'4" D
**Levels:** 2
**Square Footage:** 3,407
**Main Level Sq. Ft.:** 1,719
**Upper Level Sq. Ft.:** 1,688
**Bedrooms:** 4
**Bathrooms:** 2½
**Foundation:** Basement;
crawl space for fee
**Materials List Available:** Yes
**Price Category:** G

*This home, as shown in the photograph, may differ from the actual blueprints. For more detailed information, please check the floor plans carefully.*

If you love contemporary design, the unusual shapes of the rooms in this home will delight you.

**Features:**

• Entry: You'll see a balcony from the upper level that overlooks this entryway, as well as the lovely curved staircase to this floor.

• Great Room: This room is sunken to set it apart. A fireplace, wet bar, spider-beamed ceiling, and row of arched windows give it character.

• Dining Room: Columns define this lovely octagon room, where you'll love to entertain guests or create lavish family dinners.

• Master Suite: A multi-tiered ceiling adds a note of grace, while the fireplace and private library create a real retreat. The gracious bath features a gazebo ceiling and a skylight.

**Upper Level
Floor Plan**

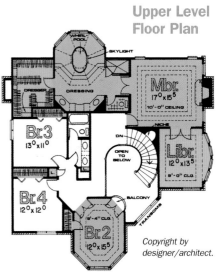

*Copyright by designer/architect.*

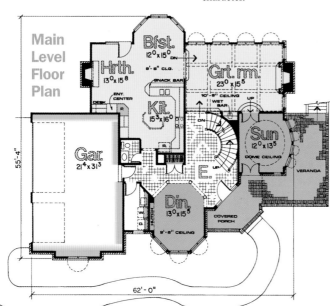

## Plan #701328

**Dimensions:** 70' W x 62' D
**Levels:** 1.5
**Square Footage:** 3,448
**Main Level Sq. Ft.:** 2,375
**Upper Level Sq. Ft.:** 1,073
**Bedrooms:** 4
**Bathrooms:** 3½
**Foundation:** Basement
**Materials List Available:** Yes
**Price Category:** G

You'll love this design if you're looking for a comfortable home with dimensions and details that create a sense of grandeur.

**Features:**

• Entry: A soaring ceiling, curved staircase, and balcony that overlooks a tall plant shelf combine to create your first impression of grandeur in this home.

• Great Room: A transom-topped bowed window highlights this room, with its 11-ft., beamed ceiling, built-in wet bar, and see-through fireplace.

• Kitchen: Designed for the gourmet cook, this kitchen has every amenity you could desire.

• Breakfast Room: Adjacent to the great room and the kitchen, this gazebo-shaped breakfast area lights both the kitchen and hearth room.

## Upper Level Floor Plan

**Main Level Floor Plan**

## Plan #701039

**Dimensions:** 84' W x 52' D
**Levels:** 2
**Square Footage:** 3,473
**Main Level Sq. Ft.:** 2,500
**Upper Level Sq. Ft.:** 973
**Bedrooms:** 4
**Bathrooms:** 3½
**Foundation:** Basement;
crawl space or slab for fee
**Materials List Available:** Yes
**Price Category:** G

*Images provided by designer/architect.*

Enjoy the many amenities in this well-designed and gracious home.

**Features:**

• Entry: A large sparkling window and a tapering split staircase distinguish this lovely entryway.

• Great Room: This spacious great room will be the heart of your new home. It has a 14-ft. spider-beamed ceiling that serves to highlight its built-in bookcase, built-in entertainment center, raised hearth fireplace,

wet bar, and lovely arched windows topped with transoms.

• Kitchen: Anyone who walks into this kitchen will realize that it's designed for both convenience and efficiency.

• Master Suite: The tiered ceiling in the bedroom gives an elegant touch, and the bay window adds to it. The two large walk-in closets and the spacious bath, with columns setting off the whirlpool tub and two vanities, complete this dream of a suite.

### Main Level Floor Plan

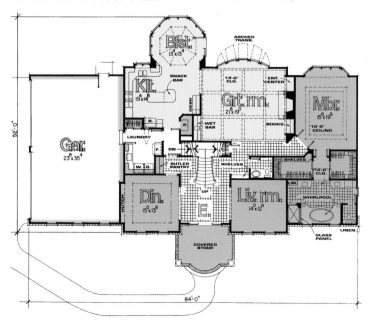

### Upper Level Floor Plan

*Copyright by designer/architect.*

## Plan #701017

**Dimensions:** 76' W x 58'8" D
**Levels:** 2
**Square Footage:** 3,556
**Main Level Sq. Ft.:** 2,555
**Upper Level Sq. Ft.:** 1,001
**Bedrooms:** 4
**Bathrooms:** 3 full, 2 half
**Foundation:** Basement
**Materials List Available:** Yes
**Price Category:** H

Dramatic soaring ceilings are the hallmark of this large and luxurious home.

**Features:**

- Ceiling Height: 8 ft. except as noted.
- Gathering Room: Guests and family will be drawn to this room with its cathedral ceiling and its fireplace flanked by built-ins.
- Den: To the right of the entry, French doors lead to a handsome den with a tall, spider-beamed ceiling.
- Great Room: This room will be flooded with sunlight thanks to stacked windows that take advantage of its 18-ft. ceiling.
- Formal Dining Room: Upon entering the 13-ft. entry, your guests will see this elegant room with its arched windows and decorative ceiling.
- Master Suite: Unwind at day's end in this luxurious suite featuring two walk-in closets, a sky-lit whirlpool and his and her vanities.

## Main Level Floor Plan

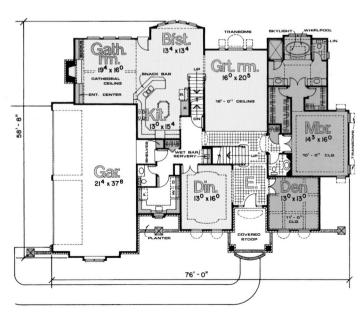

## Upper Level Floor Plan

*Copyright by designer/architect.*

## Plan #701051

**Dimensions:** 76'8" W x 68' D

**Levels:** 1.5

**Square Footage:** 3,623

**Main Level Sq. Ft.:** 2,603

**Upper Level Sq. Ft.:** 1,020

**Bedrooms:** 4

**Bathrooms:** 4½

**Foundation:** Basement

**Materials List Available:** Yes

**Price Category:** G

*This home, as shown in the photograph, may differ from the actual blueprints. For more detailed information, please check the floor plans carefully.*

You'll love this impressive home if you're looking for a perfect spot for entertaining as well as a home for comfortable family living.

**Features:**

• Entry: Walk into this grand two-story entryway through double doors, and be greeted by the sight of a graceful curved staircase.

• Great Room: This two-story room features stacked windows, a fireplace flanked by an entertainment center, a bookcase, and a wet bar.

• Dining Room: A corner column adds formality to this room, which is just off the entryway for the convenience of your guests.

• Hearth Room: Connected to the great room by a lovely set of French doors, this room features another fireplace as well as a convenient pantry.

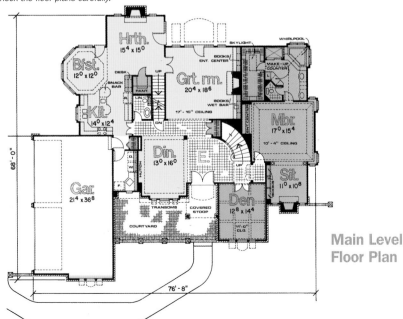

**Main Level Floor Plan**

**Upper Level Floor Plan**

*Copyright by designer/architect.*

## Plan #701065

**Dimensions:** 83'5" W x 73'4" D
**Levels:** 1.5
**Square Footage:** 3,689
**Main Level Sq. Ft.:** 2,617
**Upper Level Sq. Ft.:** 1,072
**Bedrooms:** 4
**Bathrooms:** 4½
**Foundation:** Basement; slab or crawl space for fee
**Material List Available:** Yes
**Price Category:** H

*Images provided by designer/architect.*

*This home, as shown in the photograph, may differ from the actual blueprints. For more detailed information, please check the floor plans carefully.*

Gorgeous details make this home unique and luxurious.

**Features:**

- **Living Room:** You and your guests will love to spend time in this living room, with its 10-ft.-high ceiling, wet bar, and transom windows for beautiful views.

- **Kitchen:** This beautiful kitchen is great for cooking, in addition to grabbing quick meals or hanging out at the snack bar. The adjoining breakfast nook is a wonderful place to relax in the morning before a busy day.

- **Master Suite:** An 11-ft.-high ceiling, whirlpool tub, his and her sinks, separate toilet area, and spacious walk-in closet make this suite a place you will never want to leave.

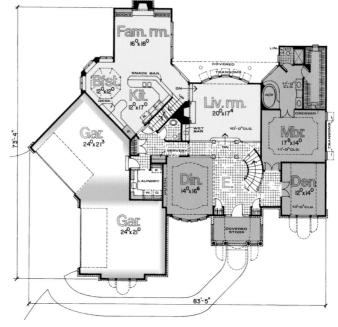

**Main Level Floor Plan**

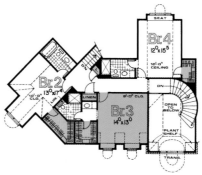

**Upper Level Floor Plan**

*Copyright by designer/architect.*

## Plan #701312

**Dimensions:** 100'10" W x 80'5" D
**Levels:** 2
**Square Footage:** 3,750
**Main Level Sq. Ft.:** 2,274
**Upper Level Sq. Ft.:** 1,476
**Bedrooms:** 4
**Bathrooms:** 3½
**Foundation:** Slab; basement for fee
**Material List Available:** Yes
**Price Category:** H

*Images provided by designer/architect.*

If you love uniquely shaped homes and sunlight-filled rooms, this plan is for you.

**Features:**

- Great Room: This uniquely shaped great room is a wonderful place to entertain guests or relax with your family in front of the fireplace.

- Kitchen: This beautiful kitchen is surrounded by workspace and counter space, and is conveniently located near the garage for quick grocery trips in and out of the house.

- Game Room: Upstairs, the octagonal game room will be a favorite room of the children and the children-at-heart.

- Master Suite: Relax in this large master suite, with its 10-ft.-high ceiling, spacious walk-in closet, tub, separate toilet area, and his and her sinks.

### Main Level Floor Plan

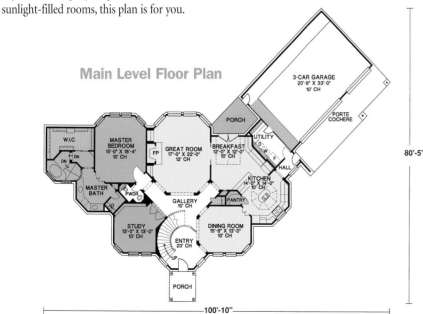

### Upper Level Floor Plan

*Copyright by designer/architect.*

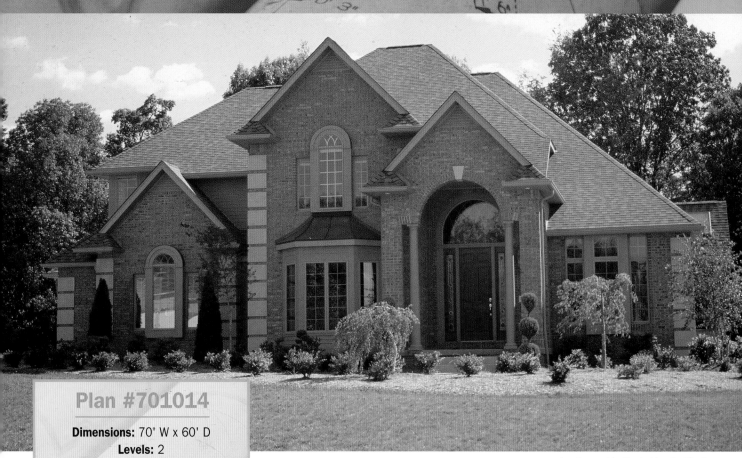

## Plan #701014

**Dimensions:** 70' W x 60' D
**Levels:** 2
**Square Footage:** 3,775
**Main Level Sq. Ft.:** 1,923
**Upper Level Sq. Ft.:** 1,852
**Bedrooms:** 4
**Bathrooms:** 3½
**Foundation:** Basement;
crawl space or slab for fee
**Materials List Available:** Yes
**Price Category:** H

*Images provided by designer/architect.*

The grand exterior presence is carried inside, beginning with the dramatic curved staircase.

**Features:**

- Ceiling Height: 8 ft.

- Den: French doors lead to this sophisticated den, with its bayed windows and wall of bookcases.

- Living Room: A curved wall and a series of arched windows highlight this large space.

- Formal Dining Room: This room shares the curved wall and arched windows found in the living room.

- Screened Porch: This huge space features skylights and is accessible by another French door from the dining room.

- Family Room: Family and guests alike will be drawn to this room, with its trio of arched windows and fireplace flanked by bookcases.

- Kitchen: An island adds convenience and distinction to this large, functional kitchen.

- Garage: This spacious three-bay garage provides plenty of space for cars and storage.

**Main Level Floor Plan**

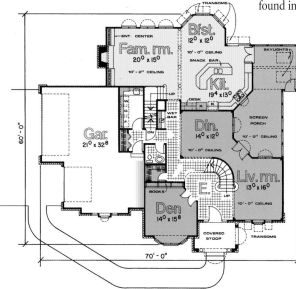

**Upper Level Floor Plan**

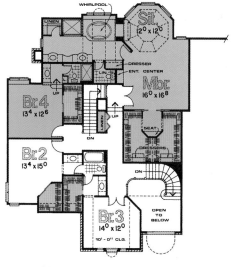

*Copyright by designer/architect*

# Plan #701070

**Dimensions:** 67'4" W x 66' D
**Levels:** 2
**Square Footage:** 3,806
**Main Level Sq. Ft.:** 2,126
**Upper Level Sq. Ft.:** 1,680
**Bedrooms:** 4
**Bathrooms:** 4½
**Foundation:** Basement;
crawl space for fee
**Material List Available:** Yes
**Price Category:** H

*Images provided by designer/architect.*

*This home, as shown in the photograph, may differ from the actual blueprints. For more detailed information, please check the floor plans carefully.*

Elegant architecture and stylish details define this home.

**Features:**

- **Hearth Room:** This spacious hearth room features an entertainment center, open access to the kitchen, and a two-way fireplace shared with the great room.

- **Kitchen:** You'll love the elegant details in this kitchen, which includes a walk-in pantry and snack bar. The brightly lit connecting breakfast area is a perfect place for your morning cup of coffee.

- **Master Suite:** This master suite will become your oasis with its large bedroom, beautiful ceiling details, spacious walk-in closet, his and her sinks, a separate toilet room, and a large whirlpool bath surrounded by windows for a truly relaxing experience.

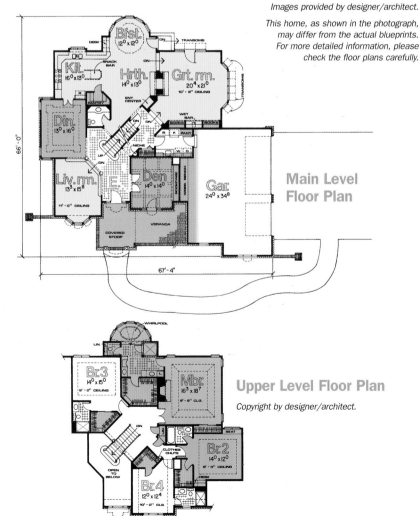

**Main Level Floor Plan**

**Upper Level Floor Plan**

*Copyright by designer/architect.*

## Plan #701018

**Dimensions:** 85'5" W x 74'8" D

**Levels:** 2

**Square Footage:** 3,904

**Main Level Sq. Ft.:** 2,813

**Upper Level Sq. Ft.:** 1,091

**Bedrooms:** 4

**Bathrooms:** 3½

**Foundation:** Basement

**Materials List Available:** Yes

**Price Category:** H

*Images provided by designer/architect.*

Spacious and gracious, here are all the amenities you expect in a fine home.

**Features:**

- Ceiling Height: 8 ft. except as noted.
- Foyer: This magnificent entry features a graceful curved staircase with balcony above.
- Sunken Living Room: This sunken room is filled with light from a row of bowed windows. It's the perfect place for social gatherings both large and small.

- Den: French doors open into this truly distinctive den with its 11-ft. ceiling and built-in bookcases.
- Formal Dining Room: Entertain guests with style and grace in this dining room with corner column.
- Master Suite: Another set of French doors leads to this suite that features two walk-in closets, a whirlpool flanked by vanities, and a private sitting room with built-in bookcases.

**Main Level Floor Plan**

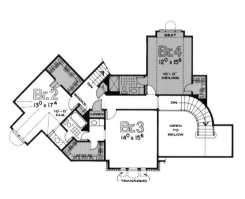

**Upper Level Floor Plan**

*Copyright by designer/architect.*

## Plan #701021

**Dimensions:** 66'8" W x 76' D

**Levels:** 2

**Square Footage:** 3,926

**Main Level Sq. Ft.:** 2,351

**Upper Level Sq. Ft.:** 1,575

**Bedrooms:** 4

**Bathrooms:** 3 full, 2 half

**Foundation:** Basement

**Materials List Available:** Yes

**Price Category:** H

*Images provided by designer/architect.*

Plenty of space and architectural detail make this a comfortable and gracious home.

**Features:**

• Ceiling Height: 8 ft. unless otherwise noted.

• Family Room: A soaring cathedral ceiling makes this great room seem even more spacious than it is, while the fireplace framed by windows lends warmth and comfort.

• Eating Area: There's a dining room for more formal entertaining, but this informal eating area to the left of the great room will get plenty

of daily use. It features a built-in desk for compiling shopping lists and recipes and access to the backyard.

• Kitchen: Next door to the eating area, this kitchen is designed to make food preparation a pleasure. It features a center cooktop, a recycling area, and a corner pantry.

### Main Level Floor Plan

*Copyright by designer/architect.*

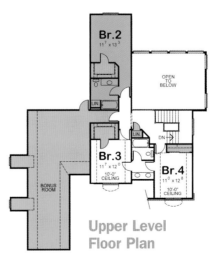

**Upper Level Floor Plan**

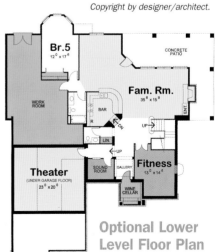

**Optional Lower Level Floor Plan**

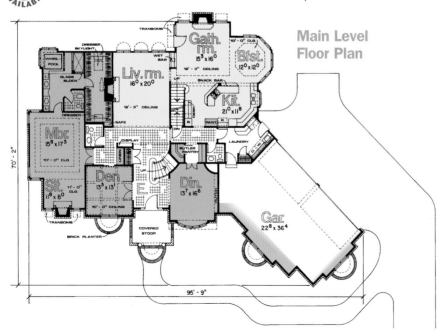

## Plan #701326

**Dimensions:** 95'9" W x 70'2" D

**Levels:** 2

**Square Footage:** 3,950

**Main Level Sq. Ft.:** 2,839

**Upper Level Sq. Ft.:** 1,111

**Bedrooms:** 4

**Bathrooms:** 4 full, 2 half

**Foundation:** Basement

**Materials List Available:** Yes

**Price Category:** H

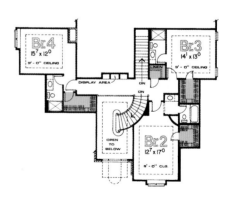

*Images provided by designer/architect.*

A spectacular two-story entry with a floating curved staircase welcomes you home.

**Features:**

- Ceiling Height: 8 ft. except as noted.
- Den: To the left of the entry, French doors lead to a spacious and stylish den featuring a spider-beamed ceiling.
- Living Room: The volume ceiling, transom windows, and large fireplace evoke a gracious traditional style.

- Gathering Rooms: There is plenty of space for large-group entertaining in the gathering rooms that also feature fireplaces and transom windows.
- Master Suite: Here is the height of luxurious living. The suite features an oversized walk-in closet, tiered ceilings, and a sitting room with fireplace. The pampering bath has a corner whirlpool and shower.
- Garage: An angle minimizes the appearance of the four-car garage.

**Main Level Floor Plan**

**Upper Level Floor Plan**

*Copyright by designer/architect.*

## Plan #701144

**Dimensions:** 72'8" W x 77' D
**Levels:** 1.5
**Square Footage:** 4,139
**Main Level Sq. Ft.:** 2,489
**Upper Level Sq. Ft.:** 1,650
**Bedrooms:** 4
**Bathrooms:** 3½
**Foundation:** Slab
**Material List Available:** Yes
**Price Category:** I

This breathtaking home, with its gorgeous architectural details, will be the envy of the neighborhood.

*Images provided by designer/architect.*

### Features:

- **Living Room:** This two-story living room is the perfect place to gather with friends and family in front of the fireplace.

- **Kitchen:** This large kitchen is wonderful for the family cook, with its expansive counter space and center island. The breakfast nook, which is surrounded by windows, is a beautiful and sunny place to start your day.

- **Game Room:** Upstairs, a game room lined with windows is fun for everyone. This room looks out onto the sun deck, the perfect place to read a book or chat while catching some rays.

- **Master Suite:** You'll love waking up every morning in this master suite, with its 11-ft.-high ceiling, whirlpool bath, separate toilet area, his and her sinks, and enormous walk-in closet.

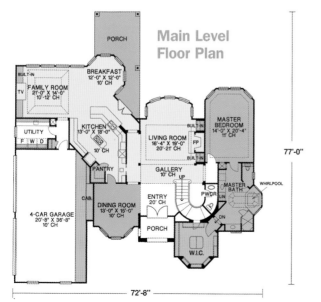

*Copyright by designer/architect.*

# Plan #701111

**Dimensions:** 84'10" W x 102'3" D

**Levels:** 1.5

**Square Footage:** 4,629

**Main Level Sq. Ft.:** 3,337

**Upper Level Sq. Ft.:** 1,292

**Bedrooms:** 4

**Bathrooms:** 4½

**Foundation:** Slab; basement for fee

**Material List Available:** No

**Price Category:** I

*Images provided by designer/architect.*

The exquisite exterior of this stunning design offers hints of the stylish features waiting inside.

**Features:**

- Family Room: This large entertaining area features a coffered ceiling and a beautiful fireplace. French doors allow access to the rear yard.

- Kitchen: This island workspace has everything the chef in the family could want. The breakfast room merges with the main kitchen, allowing conversation during cleanup.

- Master Suite: This ground-level suite features a cathedral ceiling and access to the rear yard. The master bath has a marvelous whirlpool tub, dual vanities, and a separate toilet room.

- Upper Level: A large game room, with an overhead view of the family room, and bedrooms 3 and 4 occupy this level. Each bedroom has a private bathroom.

Front View

**Main Level Floor Plan**

**Upper Level Floor Plan**

*Copyright by designer/architect.*

# Let Us Help You Plan Your Dream Home

**Whether you've always dreamed of building your own home** or you can't find the right house from among the dozens you've toured, our collection of affordable plans can help you achieve the home of your dreams. You could have an architect create a one-of-a-kind home for you, but the design services alone could end up costing up to 15 percent of the cost of construction—a hefty premium for any building project. Isn't it a better idea to select from among the hundreds of unique designs shown in our collection for a fraction of the cost?

## What does Creative Homeowner Offer?

In this book, Creative Homeowner provides hundreds of home plans with extra focus on aspects of the home that are important to women. Whether your taste runs from traditional to contemporary, Victorian to early American, you are sure to find the best house design for you and your family. Our plans packages include detailed drawings to help you or your builder construct your dream house. **(See page 278.)**

## Can I Make Changes to the Plans?

Creative Homeowner offers three ways to help you achieve a truly unique home design. Our customizing service allows for extensive changes to our designs. **(See page 279.)** We also provide reverse images of our plans, or we can give you and your builder the tools for making minor changes on your own. **(See page 282.)**

## Can You Help Me Manage My Costs?

To help you stay within your budget, Creative Homeowner has teamed up with the leading estimating company to provide one of the most accurate, complete, and reliable building material take-offs in the industry. **(See page 280.)** If that is too much detail for you, we can provide you with general construction costs based on your zip code. **(See page 282.)** Also, many of our plans come with the option of buying detailed materials lists to help you price out construction costs.

## How Can I Begin the Building Process?

To get started building your dream home, fill out the order form on page 283, call our order department at 1-800-523-6789, or visit ultimateplans.com. If you plan on doing all or part of the work yourself, or want to keep tabs on your builder, we offer best-selling building and design books available at www.creativehomeowner.com.

# Our Plans Packages Offer:

"Square footage" refers to the total "heated square feet" of this plan. This number does not include the garage, porches, or unfinished areas. All of our home plans are the result of many hours of work by leading architects and professional designers. Most of our home plans include each of the following:

## Frontal Sheet

This artist's rendering of the front of the house gives you an idea of how the house will look once it is completed and the property landscaped.

## Detailed Floor Plans

These plans show the size and layout of the rooms. They also provide the locations of doors, windows, fireplaces, closets, stairs, and electrical outlets and switches.

## Foundation Plan

A foundation plan gives the dimensions of basements, walk-out basements, crawl spaces, pier foundations, and slab construction. Each house design lists the type of foundation included. If the plan you choose does not have the foundation type you require, our customer service department can help you customize the plan to meet your needs.

## Roof Plan

In addition to providing the pitch of the roof, these plans also show the locations of dormers, skylights, and other elements.

## Exterior Elevations

These drawings show the front, rear, and sides of the house as if you were looking at it head on. Elevations also provide information about architectural features and finish materials.

## Interior Elevations and Details

Interior elevations show specific details of such elements as fireplaces, kitchen and bathroom cabinets, built-ins, and other unique features of the design.

## Cross Sections

These show the structure as if it were sliced to reveal construction requirements, such as insulation, flooring, and roofing details.

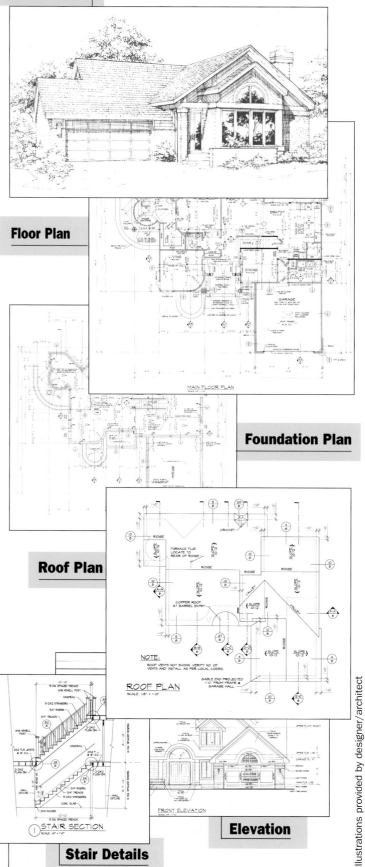

**Frontal Sheet**

**Floor Plan**

**Foundation Plan**

**Roof Plan**

**Cross Sections**

**Stair Details**

**Elevation**

Illustrations provided by designer/architect

# Customize Your Plans in 4 Easy Steps

**1** **Select the home plan** that most closely meets your needs. Purchase of a reproducible master is necessary in order to make changes to a plan.

**2** **Call 1-800-523-6789 to place your order.** Tell our sales representative you are interested in customizing your plan. To receive your customization cost estimate, our modification company will contact you (via fax or email) requesting a list or sketch of the changes requested to one of our plans. There is a $50 nonrefundable consultation fee for this service. If you decide to continue with the custom changes, the $50 fee is credited to the total amount charged.

**3** **Fax or email your request** to our modification company. Within three business days of receipt of your request, a detailed cost estimate will be provided to you.

**4** **Once you approve the estimate,** a 75% retainer fee is collected and customization work begins. Preliminary drawings typically take 10 to 15 business days. After approval of the design, the balance of your customization fee is due before modified plans can be shipped. You will receive five sets of blueprints, a reproducible master, or CAD files, depending on which package was purchase.

## Modification Pricing Guide

| Categories | Average Cost For Modification |
|---|---|
| Add or remove living space | Quote required |
| Bathroom layout redesign | Starting at $150 |
| Kitchen layout redesign | Starting at $120 |
| Garage: add or remove | Starting at $600 |
| Garage: front entry to side load or vice versa | Starting at $300 |
| Foundation changes | Starting at $220 |
| Exterior building materials change | Starting at $200 |
| Exterior openings: add, move, or remove | $75 per opening |
| Roof line changes | Starting at $600 |
| Ceiling height adjustments | Starting at $280 |
| Fireplace: add or remove | Starting at $90 |
| Screened porch: add | Starting at $300 |
| Wall framing change from 2x4 to 2x6 | Starting at $250 |
| Bearing and/or exterior walls changes | Quote required |
| Non-bearing wall or room changes | $65 per room |
| Metric conversion of home plan | Starting at $495 |
| Adjust plan for handicapped accessibility | Quote required |
| Adapt plans for local building code requirements | Quote required |
| Engineering stamping only | Quote required |
| Any other engineering services | Quote required |
| Interactive illustrations (choices of exterior materials) | Quote required |

*Note:* Any home plan can be customized to accommodate your desired changes. The average prices above are provided only as examples of the most commonly requested changes, and are subject to change without notice. Prices for changes will vary according to the number of modifications requested, plan size, style, and method of design used by the original designer. To obtain a detailed cost estimate, please contact us.

**Before Customization**

**After**

# Turn your dream home into reality with

# UltimateEstimate

When purchasing a home plan with Creative Homeowner, we recommend you order one of the most complete materials lists in the industry.

## 1 What comes with an Ultimate Estimate?

### Quote

- Basis of the entire estimate.

- Detailed list of all the framing materials needed to build your project, listed from the bottom up, in the order that each one will actually be used.

### Comments

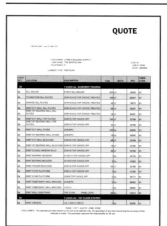

- Details pertinent information beyond the cost of materials.

- Includes any notes from our estimator.

### Express List

- A version of the Quote with space for SKU numbers listed for purchasing the items at your local lumberyard.

- Your local lumberyard can then price out the materials list.

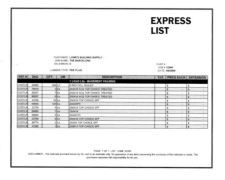

### Construction-Ready Framing Diagrams

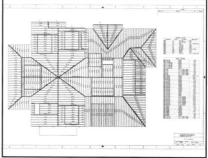

- Your "map" to exact roof and floor framing.

### Millwork Report

- A complete count of the windows, doors, molding, and trim.

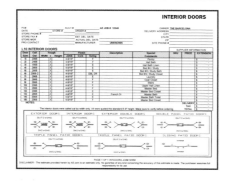

### Man-Hour Report

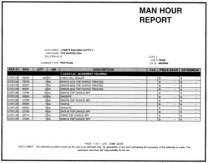

- Calculates labor on a line-by-line basis for all items quoted and presented in man-hours.

## Why an Ultimate Estimate?

**Accurate.** Professional estimators break down each individual item from the blueprints using advanced software, techniques, and equipment.

**Timely.** You will be able to start your home-building project quickly—knowing the exact framing materials you need to order from your local lumberyard.

**Detailed.** Work with your local lumberyard associate to complete your quote with the remaining products needed for your new home.

**3**

## So how much does it cost?

Pricing is determined by the total square feet of the home plan—including living area, garages, decks, porches, finished basements, and finished attics.

| Square Feet Range | UE Tier* | Price |
|---|---|---|
| Up to 5,000 total square feet | XB | $299.00 |
| 5,001 to 10,000 total square feet | XC | $499.00 |

*Please see the Plan Index to determine your plan's Ultimate Estimate Tier (UE Tier).
Note: All prices subject to change.

Call our toll-free number (800-523-6789), or visit ultimateplans.com to order your Ultimate Estimate.

**4**

## What else do I need to know?

Call our toll-free number (800-523-6789), or visit **ultimateplans.com** to order your Ultimate Estimate.

# Turn your dream home into reality.

CRE▲TIVE
HOMEOWNER®

# Decide What Type of Plan Package You Need

## How many Plans Should You Order?

**Standard 8-Set Package.** We've found that our 8-set package is the best value for someone who is ready to start building. The 8-set package provides plans for you, your builder, the subcontractors, mortgage lender, and the building department.

**Minimum 5-Set Package.** If you are in the bidding process, you may want to order only five sets for the bidding round and reorder additional sets as needed.

**1-Set Study Package.** The 1-set package allows you to review your home plan in detail. The plan will be marked as a study print, and it is illegal to build a house from a study print alone. It is a violation of copyright law to reproduce a blueprint without permission.

## Buying Additional Sets

If you require additional copies of blueprints for your home construction, you can order additional sets within 60 days of the original order date at a reduced price. The cost is $45.00 for each additional set. For more information, contact customer service.

## Reproducible Masters

If you plan to make minor changes to one of our home plans, you can purchase reproducible masters. These plans are printed on bond or vellum paper that is easy to alter. They clearly indicate your right to modify, copy, or reproduce the plans. Reproducible masters allow an architect, designer, or builder to alter our plans to give you a customized home design. This package also allows you to print as many copies of the modified plans as you need for the construction of one home.

## CAD (Computer Aided Design) Files

CAD files are the complete set of home plans in an electronic file format. Choose this option if there are multiple changes you wish made to the home plans and you have a local design professional able to make the changes. Not available for all plans. Please contact our order department or visit our Web site to check the availability of CAD files for your plan.

## Mirror-Reverse Sets/Right-Reading Reverse

Plans can be printed in mirror-reverse—we can "flip" plans to create a mirror image of the design. This is useful when the house would fit your site or personal preferences if all the rooms were on the opposite side than shown. As the image is reversed, the letter-ing and dimensions will also be reversed, meaning they will read backwards. Therefore, when ordering mirror-reverse drawings, you must order at least one set of the original plan unreversed. A $50.00 fee per plan order will be charged for mirror-reverse (regardless of the number of mirror-reverse sets ordered). Some plans are available in right-reading reverse, this feature will show the plan in reverse, but the writing on the plan will be readable. A $150.00 fee per plan order will be charged for right-reading reverse (regardless of the number of right-reading reverse sets ordered). Please contact our order department or visit our website to check the availibility of this feature for your chosen plan.

## EZ Quote: Home Cost Estimator

EZ Quote is our response to one of the most frequently asked questions we hear from customers: "How much will the house cost me to build?" EZ Quote: Home Cost Estimator will enable you to obtain a calculated building cost to construct your home, based on labor rates and building material costs within your zip code area. This summary is useful for those who want to get an idea of the total construction costs before purchasing sets of home plans. It will also provide a level of comfort when you begin soliciting bids. The cost is $29.95 for the first EZ Quote and $19.95 for each additional one. Available only in the U.S. and Canada.

## Materials List

Available for most of our plans, the Materials List provides you an invaluable resource in planning and estimating the cost of your home. Each Materials List outlines the quantity, dimensions, and type of materials needed to build your home (with the exception of mechanical systems). You will get faster, more-accurate bids from your contractors and building suppliers. A Materials List may only be ordered with the purchase of at least five sets of home plans.

## CompleteCost Estimator

CompleteCost Estimator is a valuable tool for use in planning and constructing your new home. It provides more detail than a materials list and will act as a checklist for all items you will need to select or coordinate during your building process. CompleteCost Estimator is only available for certain plans (please see Plan Index) and may only be ordered with the purchase of at least five sets of home plans. The cost is $125.00 for CompleteCost Estimator.

## Ultimate Estimate (See page 280.)

# Before You Order

## Our Exchange Policy

Blueprints are nonrefundable. However, should you find that the plan you have purchased does not fit your needs, you may exchange that plan for another plan in our collection within 60 days from the date of your original order. The entire content of your original order must be returned before an exchange will be processed. You will be charged a processing fee of 20% of the amount of the original order, the cost difference between the new plan set and the original plan set (if applicable), and all related shipping costs for the new plans. Contact our order department for more information. Please note: reproducible masters may only be exchanged if the package is unopened and CAD files cannot be exchanged and are nonrefundable.

## Building Codes and Requirements

All plans offered for sale in this book and on our website (www.ultimateplans.com) are continually updated to meet the latest International Residential Code (IRC). Because building codes vary from area to area, some drawing modifications and/or the assistance of a professional designer or architect may be necessary to comply with your local codes or to accommodate specific building site conditions. We strongly advise you to consult with your local building official for information regarding codes governing your area.

## Multiple Plan Discount

Purchase **3** different home plans in the **same order** and receive **5% off** the plan price.

Purchase **5** or more different home plans in the **same order** and receive **10% off** the plan price. (Please Note: Study sets do not apply.)

## Blueprint Price Schedule

| Price Code | 1 Set | 5 Sets | 8 Sets | Reproducible Masters | CAD | Materials List |
|---|---|---|---|---|---|---|
| A | $400 | $440 | $475 | $575 | $1,025 | $85 |
| B | $440 | $525 | $555 | $685 | $1,195 | $85 |
| C | $510 | $575 | $635 | $740 | $1,265 | $85 |
| D | $560 | $605 | $665 | $800 | $1,300 | $95 |
| E | $600 | $675 | $705 | $845 | $1,400 | $95 |
| F | $650 | $725 | $775 | $890 | $1,500 | $95 |
| G | $720 | $790 | $840 | $950 | $1,600 | $95 |
| H | $820 | $860 | $945 | $1,095 | $1,700 | $95 |
| I | $945 | $975 | $1,075 | $1,195 | $1,890 | $105 |
| J | $1,010 | $1,080 | $1,125 | $1,250 | $1,900 | $105 |
| K | $1,125 | $1,210 | $1,250 | $1,380 | $2,030 | $105 |
| L | $1,240 | $1,335 | $1,375 | $1,535 | $2,270 | $105 |

Note: All prices subject to change

## Ultimate Estimate Tier (UE Tier)

| UE Tier* | Price | |
|---|---|---|
| XB | $299 | * Please see the Plan Index to determine |
| XC | $499 | your plan's Ultimate Estimate Tier (UE Tier). |

## Shipping & Handling

| | 1-4 Sets | 5-7 Sets | 8+ Sets or Reproducibles | CAD |
|---|---|---|---|---|
| **US Regular** (7–10 business days) | $18 | $20 | $25 | $25 |
| **US Priority** (3–5 business days) | $25 | $30 | $35 | $35 |
| **US Express** (1–2 business days) | $40 | $45 | $50 | $50 |
| **Canada Express** (1–2 business days) | $80 | $80 | $80 | $80 |
| **Worldwide Express** (3–5 business days) | $100 | $100 | $100 | $100 |

Note: All delivery times are from date the blueprint package is shipped (typically within 1-2 days of placing order).

# Order Form
Please send me the following:

**Plan Number:** _____ **Price Code:** _____ (See Plan Index.)

Indicate Foundation Type: (Select ONE. See plan page for availability.)

❏ Slab    ❏ Crawl space    ❏ Basement    ❏ Walk-out basement

❏ Optional Foundation for Fee _____ $_____
*(Please enter foundation here)*

*Please call all our order department or visit our website for optional foundation fee*

**Basic Blueprint Package**                                    **Cost**

❏ CAD Files                                                   $_____
❏ Reproducible Masters                                        $_____
❏ 8-Set Plan Package                                          $_____
❏ 5-Set Plan Package                                          $_____
❏ 1-Set Study Package                                         $_____
❏ Additional plan sets:
   __ sets at $45.00 per set                    $_____
❏ Print in mirror-reverse: $50.00 per order                   $_____
   *Please call all our order department
   or visit our website for availibility*
❏ Print in right-reading reverse: $150.00 per order           $_____
   *Please call all our order department
   or visit our website for availibility*

**Important Extras**

❏ Ultimate Estimate (See Price Tier above.)                   $_____
❏ Materials List                                              $_____
❏ CompleteCost Materials Report at $125.00                    $_____
   Zip Code of Home/Building Site _____
❏ EZ Quote for Plan #_____ at $29.95                   $_____
❏ Additional EZ Quotes for Plan #s_____                $_____
   at $19.95 each
**Shipping** (see chart above)                                $_____
**SUBTOTAL**                                                  $_____
**Sales Tax** (NJ residents only, add 7%)                     $_____
**TOTAL**                                                     $_____

Order Toll Free: 1-800-523-6789   By Fax: 201-760-2431
Creative Homeowner (Home Plans Order Dept.)
24 Park Way
Upper Saddle River, NJ 07458

Name _____
*(Please print or type)*

Street _____
*(Please do not use a P.O. Box)*

City _____ State _____

Country _____ Zip _____

Daytime telephone (     ) _____

Fax (     ) _____
*(Required for reproducible orders)*

E-Mail _____

**Payment** ❏ Bank check/money order. No personal checks.
*Make checks payable to Creative Homeowner*

❏ VISA    ❏ MasterCard    ❏ American Express    ❏ Discover

Credit card number _____

Expiration date (mm/yy) _____

Signature _____

*Please check the appropriate box:*
❏ Building Home for Myself    ❏ Building Home for Someone Else

| SOURCE CODE | CA850 |
|---|---|

# Copyright Notice

All home plans sold through this publication are protected by copyright. Reproduction of these home plans, either in whole or in part, including any form and/or preparation of derivative works thereof, for any reason without prior written permission is strictly prohibited. The purchase of a set of home plans in no way transfers any copyright or other ownership interest in it to the buyer except for a limited license to use that set of home plans for the construction of one, and only one, dwelling unit. The purchase of additional sets of the home plans at a reduced price from the original set or as a part of a multiple-set package does not convey to the buyer a license to construct more than one dwelling.

Similarly, the purchase of reproducible home plans (sepias, mylars) carries the same copyright protection as mentioned above. It is generally allowed to make up to a maximum of 10 copies for the construction of a single dwelling only. To use any plans more than once, and to avoid any copyright license infringement, it is necessary to contact the plan designer to receive a release and license for any extended use. Whereas a purchaser of reproducible plans is granted a license to make copies, it should be noted that because blueprints are copyrighted, making photocopies from them is illegal.

Copyright and licensing of home plans for construction exist to protect all parties. Copyright respects and supports the intellectual property of the original architect or designer. Copyright law has been reinforced over the past few years. Willful infringement could cause settlements for statutory damages to $150,000.00 plus attorney fees, damages, and loss of profits.

# Index *For pricing, see page 283.*

| Plan # | Price Code | Page | Total Finished Area Square Feet | Materials List Available | Complete Cost | UE Tier |
|---|---|---|---|---|---|---|
| 701001 | D | 99 | 3583 | Y | N | XB |
| 701002 | B | 19 | 1347 | Y | N | XB |
| 701003 | E | 185 | 5706 | Y | N | XC |
| 701004 | C | 53 | 2162 | Y | N | XB |
| 701005 | B | 29 | 1945 | Y | N | XB |
| 701006 | C | 65 | 2161 | Y | N | XB |
| 701007 | E | 196 | 5807 | Y | N | XC |
| 701008 | C | 50 | 3879 | Y | N | XB |
| 701009 | B | 23 | 3410 | Y | N | XB |
| 701010 | D | 96 | 3770 | Y | N | XB |
| 701011 | D | 111 | 3900 | Y | N | XB |
| 701012 | E | 206 | 2594 | Y | N | XB |
| 701013 | E | 167 | 2353 | Y | N | XB |
| 701014 | H | 270 | 6424 | Y | N | XC |
| 701015 | E | 180 | 5722 | Y | N | XC |
| 701016 | E | 153 | 3877 | Y | N | XB |
| 701017 | H | 266 | 3556 | Y | N | XB |
| 701018 | H | 272 | 7745 | Y | N | XC |
| 701019 | G | 249 | 3738 | Y | N | XB |
| 701020 | E | 201 | 5120 | Y | N | XB |
| 701021 | H | 273 | 3926 | Y | N | XB |
| 701022 | C | 51 | 1660 | Y | N | XB |
| 701023 | F | 213 | 4533 | Y | N | XB |
| 701024 | E | 203 | 4846 | Y | N | XB |
| 701025 | F | 210 | 3623 | Y | N | XB |
| 701026 | C | 70 | 3540 | Y | N | XB |
| 701027 | F | 216 | 3337 | Y | N | XB |
| 701028 | G | 251 | 5863 | Y | N | XC |
| 701029 | G | 261 | 4580 | Y | N | XB |
| 701030 | D | 108 | 6721 | Y | N | XC |
| 701031 | D | 84 | 4211 | Y | N | XB |
| 701032 | E | 178 | 3553 | Y | N | XB |
| 701033 | C | 46 | 3765 | Y | N | XB |
| 701034 | B | 27 | 3457 | Y | N | XB |
| 701035 | E | 160 | 5336 | Y | N | XC |
| 701036 | C | 33 | 3624 | Y | N | XB |
| 701037 | C | 72 | 4089 | Y | N | XB |
| 701038 | B | 18 | 1339 | Y | N | XB |
| 701039 | G | 265 | 10352 | Y | N | XC |
| 701040 | D | 89 | 3321 | Y | N | XB |
| 701041 | D | 120 | 5796 | Y | N | XC |
| 701042 | F | 224 | 7694 | Y | N | XC |
| 701043 | F | 233 | 6563 | Y | N | XC |
| 701044 | E | 204 | 7839 | Y | N | XC |
| 701045 | E | 182 | 5677 | Y | N | XC |
| 701046 | E | 165 | 5288 | Y | N | XC |
| 701047 | G | 250 | 6893 | Y | N | XC |
| 701048 | E | 149 | 2712 | Y | N | XB |
| 701049 | F | 219 | 3565 | Y | N | XB |
| 701050 | E | 171 | 3258 | Y | N | XB |
| 701051 | H | 267 | 7027 | Y | N | XC |
| 701052 | F | 235 | 6606 | Y | N | XC |
| 701053 | F | 222 | 3407 | Y | N | XB |
| 701054 | D | 110 | 5653 | Y | N | XC |
| 701055 | D | 124 | 2704 | Y | N | XB |
| 701056 | E | 164 | 5245 | Y | N | XC |
| 701058 | F | 214 | 5349 | Y | N | XC |
| 701059 | F | 220 | 4925 | Y | N | XB |
| 701060 | G | 256 | 6399 | Y | N | XC |
| 701061 | F | 208 | 7939 | Y | N | XC |
| 701062 | C | 68 | 3631 | Y | N | XB |
| 701063 | E | 158 | 5279 | Y | N | XC |
| 701064 | G | 259 | 5736 | Y | N | XC |
| 701065 | H | 268 | 7341 | Y | N | XC |
| 701066 | C | 41 | 3416 | Y | N | XB |
| 701067 | B | 10 | 1583 | Y | N | XB |
| 701068 | D | 128 | 2789 | Y | N | XB |
| 701069 | C | 42 | 2070 | Y | N | XB |
| 701070 | H | 271 | 4650 | Y | N | XB |
| 701071 | C | 62 | 2223 | Y | N | XB |
| 701072 | D | 92 | 2462 | Y | N | XB |
| 701073 | C | 49 | 2134 | Y | N | XB |
| 701074 | G | 255 | 3818 | Y | N | XB |
| 701075 | D | 125 | 2960 | Y | N | XB |
| 701076 | D | 107 | 2527 | Y | N | XB |
| 701077 | E | 156 | 3013 | Y | N | XB |
| 701078 | D | 130 | 2852 | Y | N | XB |
| 701079 | C | 47 | 2084 | Y | N | XB |
| 701080 | D | 90 | 2337 | Y | N | XB |
| 701081 | D | 127 | 2658 | Y | N | XB |
| 701082 | F | 245 | 3671 | Y | N | XB |
| 701083 | E | 157 | 3640 | Y | N | XB |
| 701084 | D | 82 | 2354 | Y | N | XB |
| 701086 | G | 258 | 4420 | Y | N | XB |
| 701087 | E | 184 | 3141 | Y | N | XB |
| 701088 | C | 69 | 2312 | Y | N | XB |
| 701089 | D | 133 | 2788 | Y | N | XB |
| 701090 | G | 248 | 3954 | Y | N | XB |
| 701092 | B | 17 | 2308 | Y | N | XB |
| 701093 | B | 16 | 1907 | Y | N | XB |
| 701094 | B | 21 | 1864 | Y | N | XB |
| 701095 | C | 55 | 2164 | Y | N | XB |
| 701096 | D | 113 | 2683 | Y | N | XB |
| 701097 | D | 93 | 2648 | Y | N | XB |
| 701098 | D | 94 | 2677 | Y | N | XB |
| 701099 | F | 225 | 3346 | Y | N | XB |
| 701100 | F | 212 | 3459 | Y | N | XB |
| 701101 | E | 169 | 3036 | Y | N | XB |
| 701102 | G | 253 | 3744 | Y | N | XB |
| 701103 | D | 105 | 2313 | Y | N | XB |
| 701104 | E | 198 | 3050 | Y | N | XB |
| 701105 | F | 211 | 3221 | Y | N | XB |
| 701106 | F | 218 | 3737 | Y | N | XB |
| 701107 | E | 146 | 3009 | Y | N | XB |
| 701108 | E | 197 | 3235 | Y | N | XB |
| 701109 | F | 217 | 3627 | Y | N | XB |
| 701110 | E | 161 | 3188 | Y | N | XB |

# Index *For pricing, see page 283.*

| Plan # | Price Code | Page | Total Finished Area Square Feet | Materials List Available | Complete Cost | UE Tier | Plan # | Price Code | Page | Total Finished Area Square Feet | Materials List Available | Complete Cost | UE Tier |
|--------|-----------|------|-------------------------------|-------------------------|---------------|---------|--------|-----------|------|-------------------------------|-------------------------|---------------|---------|
| 701111 | I | 276 | 5554 | Y | N | XC | 701166 | E | 160 | 3056 | Y | N | XB |
| 701112 | F | 245 | 3752 | Y | N | XB | 701167 | E | 205 | 3319 | Y | N | XB |
| 701113 | D | 97 | 2337 | Y | N | XB | 701168 | D | 101 | 2413 | Y | N | XB |
| 701114 | C | 31 | 2307 | Y | N | XB | 701169 | D | 131 | 2906 | Y | N | XB |
| 701115 | D | 126 | 3082 | Y | N | XB | 701170 | E | 198 | 3293 | Y | N | XB |
| 701116 | E | 206 | 3793 | Y | N | XB | 701172 | D | 116 | 2522 | Y | N | XB |
| 701117 | C | 47 | 2766 | Y | N | XB | 701173 | C | 59 | 2209 | Y | N | XB |
| 701118 | C | 31 | 2270 | Y | N | XB | 701175 | C | 73 | 2242 | Y | N | XB |
| 701120 | E | 150 | 2524 | Y | N | XB | 701176 | F | 215 | 3350 | Y | N | XB |
| 701121 | D | 88 | 3523 | Y | N | XB | 701177 | E | 186 | 3691 | Y | N | XB |
| 701122 | C | 43 | 3167 | Y | N | XB | 701178 | C | 30 | 1977 | Y | N | XB |
| 701123 | E | 177 | 4328 | Y | N | XB | 701179 | C | 40 | 2071 | Y | N | XB |
| 701124 | D | 95 | 3228 | Y | N | XB | 701180 | E | 166 | 3089 | Y | N | XB |
| 701125 | C | 54 | 3832 | Y | N | XB | 701181 | D | 116 | 2571 | Y | N | XB |
| 701126 | E | 196 | 4492 | Y | N | XB | 701182 | D | 91 | 2409 | Y | N | XB |
| 701127 | D | 104 | 3891 | Y | N | XB | 701183 | C | 64 | 2252 | Y | N | XB |
| 701128 | C | 40 | 2426 | Y | N | XB | 701184 | F | 227 | 3606 | Y | N | XB |
| 701129 | B | 22 | 2106 | Y | N | XB | 701185 | D | 87 | 2723 | Y | N | XB |
| 701130 | E | 183 | 3267 | Y | N | XC | 701186 | D | 129 | 2706 | Y | N | XB |
| 701131 | F | 221 | 3475 | Y | N | XB | 701187 | D | 109 | 2456 | Y | N | XB |
| 701132 | D | 86 | 2856 | Y | N | XB | 701188 | D | 162 | 2949 | Y | N | XB |
| 701133 | F | 223 | 3704 | Y | N | XB | 701189 | B | 25 | 1937 | Y | N | XB |
| 701134 | E | 154 | 3181 | Y | N | XB | 701190 | B | 21 | 1904 | Y | N | XB |
| 701135 | E | 207 | 4380 | Y | N | XB | 701191 | C | 56 | 2207 | Y | N | XB |
| 701136 | F | 226 | 3610 | Y | N | XB | 701192 | G | 260 | 4070 | Y | N | XB |
| 701137 | F | 215 | 3758 | Y | N | XB | 701194 | G | 262 | 4094 | Y | N | XB |
| 701138 | C | 32 | 2061 | Y | N | XB | 701195 | D | 114 | 3204 | Y | N | XB |
| 701139 | E | 144 | 2758 | Y | N | XB | 701196 | E | 142 | 2838 | Y | N | XB |
| 701140 | D | 98 | 3915 | N | N | XB | 701197 | F | 212 | 3297 | Y | N | XB |
| 701141 | B | 14 | 1271 | Y | N | XB | 701199 | E | 176 | 3355 | Y | N | XB |
| 701142 | B | 12 | 1205 | Y | N | XB | 701200 | F | 228 | 3945 | Y | N | XB |
| 701143 | B | 13 | 1212 | Y | N | XB | 701202 | D | 123 | 3206 | Y | N | XB |
| 701144 | I | 275 | 5233 | Y | N | XC | 701203 | B | 20 | 1998 | Y | N | XB |
| 701146 | C | 57 | 2167 | Y | N | XB | 701204 | B | 14 | 1782 | Y | N | XB |
| 701147 | B | 24 | 2084 | Y | N | XB | 701205 | E | 199 | 4195 | Y | N | XB |
| 701148 | F | 230 | 3523 | Y | N | XB | 701206 | E | 147 | 3510 | Y | N | XB |
| 701149 | E | 172 | 3016 | Y | N | XB | 701207 | D | 107 | 3727 | Y | N | XB |
| 701150 | E | 155 | 2680 | Y | N | XB | 701208 | E | 170 | 4174 | Y | N | XB |
| 701152 | C | 34 | 2007 | Y | N | XB | 701209 | D | 87 | 3736 | Y | N | XB |
| 701153 | D | 128 | 2850 | Y | N | XB | 701210 | F | 227 | 5145 | Y | N | XC |
| 701154 | D | 122 | 2525 | Y | N | XB | 701211 | D | 100 | 3433 | Y | N | XB |
| 701155 | D | 117 | 2632 | Y | N | XB | 701212 | E | 143 | 3225 | Y | N | XB |
| 701156 | E | 199 | 3153 | Y | N | XB | 701213 | C | 55 | 2237 | Y | N | XB |
| 701157 | E | 175 | 3018 | Y | N | XB | 701214 | D | 117 | 3312 | Y | N | XB |
| 701158 | C | 71 | 2281 | Y | N | XB | 701215 | F | 244 | 4470 | Y | N | XB |
| 701159 | C | 60 | 2190 | Y | N | XB | 701216 | E | 151 | 3180 | Y | N | XB |
| 701160 | D | 102 | 2465 | Y | N | XB | 701217 | G | 254 | 4402 | Y | N | XB |
| 701161 | C | 44 | 2059 | Y | N | XB | 701219 | C | 48 | 2413 | N | N | XB |
| 701162 | C | 37 | 2036 | Y | N | XB | 701220 | D | 106 | 2896 | Y | N | XB |
| 701163 | B | 30 | 1992 | Y | N | XB | 701221 | E | 197 | 3174 | Y | N | XB |
| 701164 | C | 39 | 2003 | Y | N | XB | 701222 | D | 86 | 3044 | Y | N | XB |
| 701165 | F | 211 | 3277 | Y | N | XB | 701223 | D | 122 | 3306 | Y | N | XB |

# Index For pricing, see page 283.

# Ultimate Estimate

## The fastest way to get started building your dream home

One of the most complete materials lists in the industry

Work with our order department to get you started today

To learn more go to page 280
or visit

CRE**A**TIVE
HOMEOWNER®

online at ultimateplans.com